A Game of Two Halves

ARCHIE MACPHERSON

THE AUTOBIOGRAPHY

A Game of Two Halves

BLACK & WHITE PUBLISHING

First published 2009
by Black & White Publishing Ltd
29 Ocean Drive, Edinburgh EH6 6JL

1 3 5 7 9 10 8 6 4 2   09 10 11 12

ISBN: 978 1 84502 279 2

Typeset by Ellipsis Books Limited, Glasgow
Printed and bound by MPG Books Ltd, Bodmin, Cornwall

CONTENTS

ACKNOWLEDGEMENTS

I am principally in debt to the scores of editors, producers, directors, cameramen, sound supervisors, and studio-lighting experts, all of whom propped me up through the years. They were the true invigilators of longevity. I am, of course, thankful to the late Peter Thomson of the BBC, for having started it all in the early sixties, and to my friendships with different generations of journalists, without whom many of the anecdotes within the narrative I would never have been able to recount.

My two grandchildren have also inspired me to offer them something more than the verbal reminiscences they have had, so far, to endure. And, about my indispensable researcher Pat Woods, I can only reiterate what was once said of him by the late Bob Crampsey, 'He is a scholar and gentleman.'

For Jess

INTRODUCTION

As a boy I spent a lot of my time in the cinema. Mostly I would sit through the full A and B films twice, until search parties were sent out to look for me. The dazzling light of a torch would shine along the rows of seats until they found me, hunkered down, like we were asked to do when in the air-raid shelters, and a relative would be there with the usherette of the Palaceum Cinema in Edrom Street, Shettleston to make it clear that I had overstayed my welcome. They weren't all that hard on me, since they realised I was incurable. I was especially hooked on Coming Attractions, which were the previews which simply aggravated the lust for more films. In my cinema projectionist mode, I have strung together my own preview, edited randomly by the quirks of memory with no regard for time or space. The box office appeal hangs decidedly in the balance.

June 1945. 2pm approx. Near a railway bridge at Sandyhills Road between Shettleston and Baillieston. I am standing with my mother. She is holding my hand because the little knot of people at the kerbside is beginning to push forward a little, as an open-top limousine moves slowly towards us. 'There he is,' she says simply. And indeed there he is, Winston Churchill. 'I think he's wearing make-up,' mother says.

1977. Rio de Janeiro. 7.30pm local time. Half an hour before kick-off. Ally MacLeod has been saved from drowning on Leblon Beach under rollers from an agitated sea, the day before. I then watch the Scottish team being 'drowned' by Zico & Co in the near dereliction called the Maracana Stadium.

1988. London. 4am. The doorbell rings. It is dark outside. The London taxi driver is a wit. 'Right, guv?' he says. 'Had your jog yet?' Very funny. He is like that every morning. Just as he approaches the gates of BBC Television Centre he asks me bluntly, 'Tell me, what's it like working with Jeremy Paxman?' And bluntly I tell him.

1949. Shettleston, East End of Glasgow, back row of the State Cinema. I have cramp. I have been playing football in Tollcross Park and the leg is seizing some hours later. It is a problem, for I have designs on the rather tentative girl I have taken there. Although any time I try to explore my girl the leg seems as if caught in a gin-trap and I have to stand and straighten it. It is the only lasting erection of the evening.

1989. Buckingham Palace. The Princess Royal's suite. She is sitting very composed, looking more delicately featured than any photograph of her reveals. The bright lights of my television camera do not affect her composure. Prince Andrew pops his head in and tells her to behave properly in front of us. She waves a royal wave at him to piss off. 'Now what questions are you going to ask me?' she says daintily to me.

1984. Blackhill, Glasgow. Midnight. We sit neatly and correctly in Arthur Thompson's house aware that we are being befriended by a man who, it is said, used to work for the Krays and that parking a car outside can occasionally lead to it being blown up. 'I'm going to do you a favour,' he says. 'What's that?' I ask politely.

1965. County Buildings, Hamilton. 3pm. Councillors are in session. The chairman speaks, 'Mr Macpherson, I am pleased to tell you that you are now the headmaster of Swinton School.'

1990. 1pm. Paris. The Left Bank. Lunch by the Seine. I am surrounded by a motley, multilingual crew of European broadcasters. French, Germans, Dutch, English and me, the Scot. Eurosport is the name of the new channel. It is called other names by its detractors.

1945. 8pm. Wellshot Road, close to Shettleston Public Library and the Co-op Halls. Labour have won the General Election. We are out on the streets celebrating. The pleasure in the defeat of the hated Tories, and Winston Churchill, is akin to that experienced at a rare Scotland victory at Wembley.

1977. Wembley. The crossbar on the pitch is creaking under the weight of Scottish humanity. In my commentary box I am surrounded by English indignation. Inwardly, I wish I was sitting there on that crossbar with them.

2006. 9am. Deepest Lanarkshire. A phone call from a journalist whose opinions I respect. 'What a load of crap,' he says. 'Who thought that one up?' He is talking about the programme the night before which goes by the name of *Scotsport*, but it is not the feisty original model of the days of presenter Arthur Montford. It is the pantomime version.

Time now, as they say, for the main feature which commences in the year the *Queen Mary* slipped into the waters of the Clyde for the first time, Adolf Hitler became Führer, the SNP was born, Italy won the first European-based World Cup, and 90,000 at Wembley witnessed England beating Scotland 3–0, thus inducing in my father a pain which far exceeded the birth pangs of my mother.

1

A CLOSE THING

It was an uncle of mine who first spread the story that shortly after I was born, high up in a tenement bedroom, my father took me to an open window and inclined my head towards the street, so that I could hear the occasional sounds of an Old Firm game gushing down the brown canyon which was Shettleston Road. You could, indeed, hear the rumbles from Parkhead competing with the clangings of the tramcars, as the vitriol spilled out into the East End. I believe the uncle, who was possessed of a romantic imagination, peddled that fictional image much later in life, almost as if to show people that I had been through some secular baptism that was to infect me for the rest of life. Football, as it were, went in one ear, and never came out again. That was his neat explanation. Life, influences and events made the endurance test of broadcasting much more complicated.

That uncle was a Black, my mother's brother. And although the Blacks and Macphersons were hardly the Montagues and Capulets there was a distinct cultural difference between them, which the Blacks in particular showed little reluctance to conceal. My mother looked upon the Macpherson family very frequently with the disdain of a working-class Lady Bracknell. That both sides of the family were bound together by the basic necessity of struggling to make ends meet did not affect the view of the Blacks that they were, somehow, of a different breed.

So there I was, very early on, conscious of the presence of a supposed hierarchy amongst folk who, in fact, had so much in common, and from it emerged the understanding of the truer complexity of the simple over-arching phrase, 'working-class'. The Macphersons gambled, drank, went to football, never went to church. The Blacks were abstemious, largely church-going, politically conscious, never went to football and above all were readers of books – this in that thriving Glasgow stratum of self-learning which existed outside formal schooling, made them seem worldly-wise. They were great quoters, particularly of political and religious writings. It was not until later in life that I began to appreciate that two of the most influential forces in development towards adulthood were the two uncles on the Black side. They had both left school early on to become brick-layers. One bludgeoned his way through life from a single-end flat in the East End to become a millionaire. The other was a vernacular Glasgow poet whose sense of attaining civilised values was through reading books until the eyelids protested, and who ended up writing for STV and broadcast in various ways for the BBC. I soaked in their contrasting styles. One ruth-less, the other a romancer. So between the families I was brought up within this polarisation, bouncing pleasantly between these opposing influences.

The Macphersons took me to football, lifted me over turn-stiles and instilled in me the belief that life would be infinitely the poorer without the Saturday 'gemme' and an occasional dram. They enjoyed life in an uncomplicated way and I was the beneficiary of that. I loved their company. The Blacks showed me the route to the public library and talked to me of the life led by others, in the world beyond the stretch of the Glasgow tramcar. Perhaps not the bedding-ground for the rise of Renaissance Man, but it filled the formative years with a variety of experience that might have astonished those who would have looked at the Glasgow tenement and imagined its occupants were simply passive captives of their environment. There must have been hardship all around, but the world never seemed hostile to me, surrounded, as many children like me were, by the caresses of the extended family.

The outsider would not have perceived Shettleston as the village it actually was. For although it formed part of the huge metropolis of the Second City of the Empire, the boundaries always seemed close by. You could define it by saying that you felt nobody was a stranger, however densely populated it was. It attained notoriety in later years, during a parliamentary by-election in 2008, as one of the most under-developed, under-privileged areas in the entire UK, with a health record that Bangladesh would have been ashamed of, or so media reports had it. That image does not block out the richness of its past, and the sense of how many look back on it, not just with naive nostalgia, but as a positive springboard for those with ambition. To the outsider it could appear rough and untamed. We certainly did not enjoy the neatness of privet-hedges, but much better than that, we had dykes: long ones seeming to stretch into infinity; deformed ones which hinted at imminent collapse, but never did. And with them their sidekicks, their inevitable props the dustbins, the creative use of which could turn a backcourt into Hampden Park or the Siegfried Line depending on the mood of the day.

Our special dyke ran parallel with Shettleston Road, separating two rows of tenements. You didn't really belong to our backcourt until you could successfully negotiate this 80-yard stretch of narrow, high wall with disaster on either side. I still see in that dyke the origin of the word 'feartie'. It was that slur that would be thrown against you if you refused to try and walk along its length. Health and Safety ordinances did not exist in those days, except perhaps in the shape of an old invalided woman, who sat constantly at her window and waved an admonitory finger at us, as we risked life and limb in this initiation test. We came of age on that dyke, by denying the slur of 'feartie'. Sort of.

But we did have the benefit of a respite on it. Halfway along this wall we would come to the broad-decked, flat roof of Coleman's bakery. In winter this was our heat therapy. You could lie back on its clingy, tarry surface and feel the warmth from the ovens below seeping into your bones. In the summer it became very sticky and it could burn the feet off you. Below there, my father worked as a baker, at least for part of his career, and if we chose our time right he would slip me and my mates some dough-nuts, straight from the fryer. I never did tell them the technique my father admitted the bakers used with the doughnuts, as even then in the early forties and still in primary school, I had enough nous to know they might not appreciate the delicacy of the tech-nique. He had told me that to test the readiness of the dough-nuts, they would spit into the fat. If the spittle bounced back off the surface of the fat, the doughnuts were ready. If it disappeared below the surface, you left them a little longer.

There used to be a shop selling nothing but doughnuts on the east side of Fifth Avenue in New York. One day, as I was being presented with one of their flamboyant productions, I described the Glasgow process to the girl behind the counter and asked her if this was how they made theirs. 'This is America,' she said with a straight face, like one of those insufferable, self-assured Young Republicans defending the flag.

I was very proud of his abilities, and thought what a wonderful place a bakery would be to pass your time in, working and eating when you like, and spitting with glee into vats of fat. But my parents had other ideas for me. They wanted me to pick up the tools at the age of fifteen and become a bricklayer, which was an honourable tradition on my mother's side of the family. Her brother Willie was skilled enough with the trowel to eventually run his own Europe-wide company, possess a vast baronial-type spread in Renfrewshire and flats in Monaco and London's Mayfair. Where there was cement there was money. The men on the Black side had the thick, roughened hands of toilers but this certainly did not hinder their maturing sophistication. In London once, having lunch in Langham's Brasserie in Mayfair, I saw that same roughened Shettleston hand of my uncle reaching out for a glass to sample the Château Pétrus offered by the waiter, with the remark, 'I think we'll have that decanted.' He who used to swear by 'mince and totties'.

The point is that Shettleston's ways of getting on in the world were conventional and traditional, but underneath it all creative minds were thrumming, just waiting to change rhythm. It was all around us and we didn't really appreciate it at the time. Willie, our family millionaire, as we might call him, started his career at the age of twelve by pinching orange boxes from shops, breaking them up into sticks and selling them round the tenements as firewood. Indeed, the entrepreneurial spirit, claimed as an invention of the right wing during the Thatcher years, abounded in Shettleston just after the war. Through the years I was to bump into East End of Glasgow men who had carved out successful careers for themselves. None of them was short of self-confidence, all of them suggested in their body language they could pick you up and put you through the nearest 'windae', in pursuit of career, but above all else they were intelligent; not the anaemic intelligence revealed by verbal reasoning tests, but that which astutely assessed the ways of men, what mattered and what didn't, and especially what an invaluable asset it is in life to be underestimated. They had emerged from an environment of thrift, hard work, and respect for skill and apprenticeship, and despite not a chance in hell of any outward expressions of capitalist beliefs ever leaving their lips, knew full well that there had to be more out there in life than simply being able to afford a fish supper at the 'Tallies'.

Our family millionaire, for example, used to command the captain of his ocean-going yacht *Minty*, which was berthed mainly at Inverkip on the Clyde, to make sure he was always back home in time to vote Labour. Old habits die hard even if you are, oft times, floating out at sea like the Great Gatsby, although it was unlikely that he would be 'borne back ceaselessly into the past' to his Shettleston mode of life.

Voting Labour in the East End was simply respectable. And respectability, indeed, seemed to be the principal ideology of my formative years, based as it was on honest endeavour, fidelity to a pair of dungarees, and a nod occasionally in the direction of the church. Whatever you did, you had never to bring discredit to your ain folk, or perhaps even worse, to encourage tittle-tattle and gossip about yourself and others.

An aunt of mine, for example, broke through the conventions by marrying a Catholic Irishman from Donegal and converting. She was not thereafter considered leprous, as others in similar circumstances certainly were by the bigots, because she was not endowed with Hellenic beauty, and had incredible bowlegs through which you could have passed a Corporation tramcar, and the family thought that dying as a Catholic was marginally better than dying as an old maid, which they had previously thought was inevitable. So she was taken to our bosom affectionately as a kind of harmless eccentric who took to putting up statuettes and portraits of strange-looking men in gowns in her ground-floor single-end, at the tail end of Shettleston Road. Mark you, nobody actually boasted publicly about it, in a spirit of ecumenism, a concept which was as foreign then as Zen Buddhism.

The overall feeling in the area was that some families would rather have had a women caught lying flat on her back in adultery than bent on her knees in new-found supplication. So indeed I recall a lot of whispering about women whose men had been off to the war and who had been seen in huddles in dark closes with their more than adequate replacements. But it was never with acrimony. It was merely comedic disapproval. No name, no shame. Certainly, with gaslight still in existence in the 1940s at the front of the close, the light did not penetrate all that much to the rear at 771 Shettleston Road, which would have reminded members of the Raj of the gloom of the Black Hole of Calcutta. When you were being taken upstairs to our level, you sometimes became aware of shuffling and giggling coming from there, and you were whisked away briskly by the hand. That act in itself only increased your own speculation and heightened the intrigue. What were these huddles? What human activity could possibly go on in the dark?

The close was brighter at the front, and like many, the walls were decorated there with tiny graffiti or scrawlings of one kind or another. And an East End John Betjeman had scraped high up on one wall, probably the first rhyme I had ever read, and which certainly influenced me in all kinds of ways, suggesting perhaps a connection with the dark huddles:

'No matter how much you shake your peg,
The last little drop always runs down your leg.'

It remained there for years. I am not at all sure if the introduction of electric lights replacing the gas lamps reduced the incidence of alfresco sex in Shettleston but they did introduce a new luminosity to some closes which seemed now, by comparison, to be brighter than a thousand suns. Johnny, the lamplighter, who went up and down the stairs with his long pole and his wee ladder, barely saying a word, setting gas alight, simply stopped coming, and was missed, most desperately by those who felt his subdued use of lighting contributed much to the eroticism of a Glasgow close. He spent most of his time thereafter, I was told, sitting downing his 'hauf and hauf-pints' in Deans's Pub but a hundred yards away from the close. He was now lighting himself up, along with many others, in one of the busiest drinking establishments this side of the Pecos. For some women, to hear that their man was in Deans's was as bad as hearing that he was stuffing the wage-packet down the lavvy pan. Much damage to relationships came out of that place, although, it has to be said, much pleasure as well.

Now, I never saw my father drunk, because he looked after himself for the sake of his athletic pursuits. He was a trained sprinter and played football professionally, with King's Park (later to become Stirling Albion), and signed for them the year I was born. But he gave himself little chance of making it, by taking on the necessary lifestyle of coming off night-shift at the bakery and travelling by train to Stirling or elsewhere, already jaded before a ball was kicked.

Nevertheless he would occasionally drop into Deans's for a dram and I would sit outside on the pavement, amusing myself by occasionally racing the tramcars to the Wellshot Road tram-stop about a hundred yards away. Deans's being considered a den of iniquity, by the Blacks in particular, I was never allowed to even poke my head in there. So, paradoxically, a pub so close to where I was largely brought up I walked into for the first time only decades later, to extol the virtues of Kenny Dalglish, who although then at Liverpool, had bought a pub next door to Deans's, to be run by his father-in-law, Pat. At the official opening I was invited to say a few words, then took a dram. Not like my father, who inside the pub for a short time, with me outside, would throw it back, shake any minute droplet remaining into the 'hauf-pint' and then sluice it down. Mine were the tiny sips of gentrification. I had eventually made it to a Shettleston pub, though, after all that time.

The war meant that eventually my father went off to serve his country. His first posting was as a baker on a merchant ship, which was torpedoed off the coast of South Africa. He was a strong swimmer and survived. Then he joined the RAF. During that period my mother took my sister and me off to Argyll, to Ardrishaig, to get away from it all, for almost a year, and I discovered beaches, palm trees (the Gulf Stream, you know), kids with a funny accent and a teacher who was a mix of Cruella de Vil and Freddy from Elm Street. She would hit me with a ruler over the knuckles, and simply thought I was different because of my accent, and her apparent judgement that I was lazy. So she screamed at me, in between assaulting me. I wish I could say I believe in redemption but, honestly, I hope she is still rotting in hell. What should have been a paradisal period for me, in a beautiful part of the world, was scarred by her presence. Shettleston seemed like a place of asylum after that and a haven of security. As if to underline that, all the men around me then, who left for the war in different capacities, survived. There was only one casualty who registers with me. The man who gave us a banana.

His name was Bertie Hooper, a relative of the Blacks. He had been born in Shettleston but his family had emigrated to the States when he was about twelve. He turned up on our doorstep one day, during the war, in an American uniform, in transit to London, then Europe, and was desperate to see his ain folk again. Being a cinema addict already, it was fascinating for me to hear the American accent in a living, human being, rather than on the silver screen. We asked him to sing at a party we held for him, almost as if anybody coming from the States ought to be a budding Bing Crosby. He wasn't. His voice was a modest drone, but the family helped out by joining in with him for a rousing 'White Cliffs of Dover'. But the service he paid the family was in the presenting of the banana.

He had taken it from the troopship, and aware of the conditions of wartime Britain, had, with amazing foresight, produced this object I had never seen before, nor had others for years. I was allowed to hold this yellow curve with the black splodges of over-ripeness, but only with the care of someone clutching a Ming vase. So this was a banana! After Bertie left, my grannie cut it up into what seemed to be about two dozen tiny slices to share out. We all sat around with the glazed expressions of a Shanghai opium den, me holding the tiny fragment in my mouth for as long as I could, so that this taste would linger. It did, along with the image of this modest young man in the neat American uniform. He was killed in the Battle of the Bulge in January 1945. We learned that about a year later. It is the only time during the entire war period I saw tears being shed so copiously around me. The Shettleston boy, in a foreign uniform, dying in the mud of the Ardennes for what was said to be a noble cause, would be remembered, not for his defence of democracy, but for his act of kinship, in delivering us a touch of the tropics.

By then the bombs had stopped falling. That did not obliterate the memory, earlier in the war, of lying flat in an incomplete air-raid shelter just off Sandyhills Road looking through a space above us to see the searchlights criss-crossing the sky, with tiny beads of light, which I was told were German planes sneaking their way towards Clydebank, the night they clobbered it. I can still visualise that. Death was not near, to be frank, but it was more than a rumour. During the days, after raids, we took to searching for shrapnel as plenty of ammunition was fired off from so many different parts. There the little pieces lay, like fossils from another age, and the more we found, and the more Shettleston and the area around seemed largely untouched, so the war increasingly appeared to be a game played by adults with nothing much else to do in their lives. But there was no underestimating the joy of VE day and the crushing of bodies together in George Square, as the entire city seemed to assemble there to rejoice.

My mother became one of the first casualties of the hard-fought peace by having her ribs crushed in the squeeze. The following day we went up to Shettleston Hill, high up on a plateau covered with football pitches, from where you could see the dreaming spires of the industrial East End, to watch a victory tournament played by pub teams from around the area. There, on the ash pitches, with the wind blowing eddies of dust into our eyes, we saw ferocious games being played by men of the hostelries. The tackles brutal, the ball booted about like it ought to be punished for its existence, the rampaging from one end of the pitch to the other with all the finesse of the Calgary Stampede, effing and blinding rending the air in repeated explosions. It was all such a beautiful sight. Hitler beaten, peace in our time, the new future beckoning, and this. I didn't of course know it then, but the feeling I had about what I was watching was really the beginning of a very long love affair.

2

MIND GAMES

We played football everywhere. We played round the back-court, in the streets, in the lobby, in the park until it was too dark to see, and in the closes where we had 'wee headies' championships against the walls. We played with friends, with strangers, with adults, with the talented and the untalented. Everybody could play tolerably well. There were no passengers, no fakers. They all could trap, or feint, or dribble, some markedly better than others, but all with an unregistered quality of acceptable, basic ability. There were geniuses on the ball, as well, who simply were never heard of again; boys who could play like Best, or Jinky, or Slim Jim, but simply disappeared. Social conditions did for them? The bevvy? Women? Who knows? I feel now the phrase 'lost generation' could apply to more than those scribblers in Paris. But other factors were intervening. One day when about a dozen or so were playing around our backcourt, milling about with the ball, without any end result in sight, a man appeared with a bundle of papers under his arm. He strode into the middle of us, and we halted, thinking he might be from the plain-clothes division. I tried to think if I had paid for my broken biscuits at the wee shop near us. We did not shoplift, but we were forgetful at times. Bald, with a long trench coat, he said, 'Any of you lads like to help us out?'

He was looking for volunteers to put leaflets through letter-boxes along the whole length of the tenements on either side of Shettleston Road. 'I'll stand you all ice-cream in Matteo's,' he added. Such an inducement from adult to child nowadays would probably constitute an offence, but then in the age of innocence, bartering was both moral and legal for us. Six of us held out for him to foot the bill for a McCallum each at the nearby Italian cafe. A McCallum was to me, then, what a Piedmontese truffle would be to an epicure. It was a blob of ice cream smothered in raspberry sauce. Succulent. Unbeatable. He paid his dues to the 'Tally' and said he would supervise us later and left us to gobble, with the leaflets piled up in front of us. It was the age of trustworthiness. But, while we were in the process of demolishing the treat, a neighbour walked in and spotted us. A wee man with tumbler specs, he lifted one of the leaflets, to which we had paid scant attention, except that there was a man's face on it and an X somewhere at the bottom of the print.

'Whit are these fur?' he asked. We told him.

'Jesus Christ,' I recall him uttering. 'These are for the Tories. Whit wid your faither say?' he asked me directly. The McCallum was still tasting the same, but I did realise that I had now been bribed into taking some part in the 1945 General Election to help promote the local Tory candidate, W. G. Bennett. That was his face staring up at us now from the leaflets with new signif-icance. Even about the age of eleven or so, I was fully aware that not too many people in the East End of Glasgow liked the Tories. Indeed, from as far back as I can remember I was listening to political discussion that was pointedly dismissive of them. But, thankfully, for flirting with the enemy I was not cast into the wilderness, nor did I get a cuff behind the ear, for I came from a family who did have a sense of humour and thought that if I carried on aiding the Tory machine in a like manner, with the McCallums, I would end up like Billy Bunter. We were honourable, and shoved these pamphlets through letterboxes, knowing full well that the vast majority would end up hung on a nail inside the 'stairheid lavvy', as the age of austerity, and old habits, had stunted the production of toilet paper. But I do recall thinking that it was odd that everybody I knew wanted rid of the great saviour of the war Winston Churchill. We had seen him pass by us in an open-topped limousine, bulky in his black coat and hat, V-signing at my mother and me, looking as if his cheeks had been painted, and we felt proud to have seen this war hero. Nobody was spelling out to me the reasons why they were all behind that little man Clem Attlee, who seemed, through his newspaper photographs and in his radio broadcasts, to be as charismatic as the Co-op undertaker. My paternal grandmother revered Churchill. And I revered her, in return, for having the wisdom and integrity of Hopalong Cassidy, my Saturday film-club hero. But, here were people running about the streets with red-coloured leaflets, shouting the odds at street corners, sticking up posters with Attlee's prim face smirking at us. I thought there was something very odd in the air.

The transition from that bewilderment to a clearer understanding of what had motivated the great immediate post-war surge for Labour is hazy in recollection, but it happened. Politically I put the McCallum right-wing tendency well behind me. I had socialism, if not in the veins, at least as a memory of an age when I loved to be with people who told me that the pronouncements on the class struggle were as relevant as the Sermon on the Mount. I grew up listening to political debate in Shettleston, amongst mostly Christian socialists, who were largely self-educated people, impassioned in their belief that they must help a succeeding generation grab the opportunities they never had themselves. There was an honesty and simplicity to their message that resonates through the ages to me, like hearing an old familiar hymn tune being played again on a foot-pedalled organ.

From what I can recall there were never any doubts in the minds of my relatives that a socialist Utopia was perfectly attainable. As my father was a voter, but did not engage me much on politics, the biggest influence on me was that uncle again, Jim Black. He would take me to political meetings in the Shettleston Co-op Halls, where I heard a whole range of left-wing speakers, the first of which was John McGovern, who in the late forties, was an ILP MP for the area, although later he was to join the Labour Party and eventually went rather odd, and became ensnared in the Moral Re-armament Oxford Movement. A heavily built man, who had a rolling gait because of a leg problem, he would limp through the hall as his supporters rose to their feet and acclaimed him, climb unsteadily on to the platform and then release his thunderous voice at the Tories, not one of whom was within a country mile of the hall. There was an evangelical wrath about his condemnations which was augmented by a bassoon-like voice which seemed to come from some extraterrestrial force, since he was not a large man. He applied the classical oratorical technique of that generation, by starting to raise his voice significantly about six sentences or so from his conclusion, then raising it to a level which indicated that only a few words were left, which the crowd could rightly and easily anticipate, and were on their feet applauding before he had completed the sentence.

I warmed to all of this. I was in awe of a man who had the courage to stand alone without notes in front of a packed hall (which in those days was the norm) and by sleight of words enslave his audience. He was not a major political figure. But he really introduced me to the power of oratory, with a style

15

which has become outmoded in the current political generation of scripted soundbites. I never hear Pavarotti's version of
'Nessun Dorma' at the Italian World Cup in 1990 without
thinking of McGovern's similar climactic rapport with an audience.

Of course McGovern was adhering to a different libretto. I
was more fascinated by the messenger than the message itself.
Just before my teens, I was not fully aware of the strength of
argument but was exhilarated by the sound of what appeared
to be justifiable moral indignation. I just took it for granted that
the Tories were a squalid bunch who had no respect for the
working class, and were against any progress that liberated the
disadvantaged from their oppression. Alternative views were
as rare as Eton collars in our streets. Tories you could recognise at election times quite easily. They came from outside. They
looked, well . . . clean-cut, unrough, no glottal stops in their
speech, different. And we did occasionally go to hear what they
had to say.

One night in the local primary school hall in Wellshot Road,
a tall straight-backed Tory candidate with an impressive stiff
white shirt collar and dark military-looking tie was addressing
a healthy-sized audience which was surprisingly docile, given
the rough treatment that I had heard meted out to Tories in the
past. But, during one very articulate purple passage about how
only the Conservative party could encourage proper economic
growth and the creation of more jobs, which even at my age of
about twelve and with an added inducement of another gorging
of McCallums I would have found difficult to swallow, a man
interjected from the middle of the seated audience. He not only
interrupted, but let flow a flood of statistics at the candidate
with his finger pointing, in unison with the cadences of contempt,
which rose and swelled in impressive crescendo. The shocked
candidate suddenly shouted back, 'Look here, my man!'

Now, 'My man!' was not a salutation widely used in my neighbourhood. 'Haw, you' would have sounded more equitable and less socially hierarchical. God knows where the candidate came from or what job he did, but it was certainly far nor'-nor'-west of the East End, judging by his laird-to-gamekeeper gambit. The man in the audience exploded. He got to his feet and began a spiralling attack on the Tories with such eloquent vehemence that it was quite breathtaking.

'He's a shop steward at the Forge,' I was told by a man sitting beside us. 'He's a Commie.'

Ah, so that was a Communist. The nearest I thought I had been to them was through another uncle on my mother's side, who barely did a day's work in his life but who kept a Stalin biography in his bedroom and was to advise me to read about the great leader in later years. But, of course, I believed he could not really have been a Communist, for he was family after all, a bevvier and a gambler, and Communists, as I was led to believe, did not do such things, but led such incorruptible lives as to make us all seem quite decadent.

So this might have been my first real sighting of your genuine article. But even as the meeting broke up in some disorder, as the man was led from the hall with even more eloquent denunciations of the capitalist system, I must admit something had clicked. I felt there was something radical and bold about what had happened, and although the facts and figures of the man's colourful and highly articulate attack on the candidate were quite beyond me, I liked the sheer controlled vehemence and audacity, fuelled as it had been by an utterly convincing sound to young ears. How could a man with such controlled fury possibly be wrong about this iniquitous system called capitalism? I started to copy some of the phrases used and went through Tollcross Park occasionally bawling my head off about injustice, with the rhododendron bushes showing total indifference.

So now in my mid-teens I felt quite thrilled to be flirting with the idea of being a Communist. I didn't actually want to break cover, but just to let it reside within, like a noble ideal. The only outward display, at first, involved a short walk to Shettleston Public Library, and the patience to wait my turn behind the old men there, to read the *Daily Worker* in the hush of the reading room. I was a private Communist. I was slowly departing from the old faiths presented by people near and dear to me. But I was so discreet that I would turn the pages of the *Daily Worker* with barely a rustle, for fear of some ethereal message being conveyed back to my unsuspecting family.

All the periodicals were tethered to the sloping reading desks around the large room, in case of theft, and in an effort at what I thought might be respectability, I would walk round the perimeter, deliberately stopping to read the *Illustrated London News* and *Tatler* as well, for I was conscious of being watched by the old men who would sit there for hours just watching folk over the tops of their newspapers, habitually, like retired spies. My guilt at becoming a fellow-traveller, as I supposed myself to be, was slightly assuaged by the fact that I did enjoy these two glossy magazines with their displays of the high life, showing pictures of elegant women in particular, who seemed to be conveying a simple if brutal message which the *Daily Worker*, for all its perceived purity, for me could not contest, that to be of the beautiful people you would first have to be rich.

Anyway being rich did not seem such a bad thing, even within my family circle, devoted as they clearly were to the coming of a new age of equality. So I admitted my feelings about Communism to our family millionaire, Willie, who at that stage was living in a single-end in Wellshot Road and just getting his business instincts up to speed. He was clearly not an 'ism' man. No ideology, except a loyalty to Labour, just the practicality of 'getting on', letting no bugger get in your way, which he certainly didn't, by eventually taking all the business from an English firm for which he had worked for years, in a sudden overnight coup, which landed him huge contracts to build and maintain furnaces at the entire new oil complex at Grangemouth. He ruled over their furnaces like a clan chieftain.

As a teenager I used to babysit for him as he went out for the night to carouse after a hard day's slog, during which somewhere along the line he was taking somebody to the cleaners, for he was one hard bastard. But I long admired him for that, and indeed saw him as a model of how to take on the world with scant resources, and push ahead regardless. There was many a moment, especially in London and Paris in later life, when the world seemed to be ganging up on me, but I seemed to be bolstered by the past and the fact that I had rubbed shoulders with a man who had granite in his make-up, and by the idea that perhaps I had been smitten by his virus. Perhaps my temperament was actually his. So tough was he that he ultimately sued his own son for thousands of pounds in a family business feud that ended up in the law courts in London. You simply didn't mess with him. My cousin, his daughter, whom I used to bounce on my knee when she was a child, became a fine actress. Jennifer Black became more prominently known through playing the hotelier's wife alongside Burt Lancaster in Bill Forsyth's *Local Hero*. I sat there in a crowded cinema on the Champs Elysées many years later, watching that film for the first time and felt immensely proud of her, and wanting to rush round the French audience telling them of the relationship. I knew that in the precarious theatrical business the Black genes would be of great benefit to her.

So the texture, the warp and woof of social life was a mix of social concern and deep individual ambition which surrounded me. But it is true to say I had my head filled with pictures of the political heroes of the left, rather than egocentric

19

businessmen. They were simply flesh and blood local heroes of the class struggle. The two names most mentioned were John Wheatley and Jimmy Maxton. These names were spoken with reverence. Even though both had long since died when I was starting to take an interest in politics, they were talked about glowingly, as if they still strode the streets of the East End doing good works. In the socialist tradition they would have related to New Labour the way Jesus did to the usurers in the Temple. Wheatley, who held the Shettleston seat for Labour, had a special bonding influence, for as a Catholic he had bravely taken on the church over certain issues and that had gone down well with those who worried about the influence of the pulpit. Maxton was regarded as an orator of the greatest power and to this day I regret never hearing him, so vivid were the descriptions I was given of his majestic powers on the platform.

But I did hear and witness one of the last great speakers of that group, ultimately described as forming the Red Clydeside, when I sat in the front row at a memorable debate in the Methodist Church in Shettleston in the late forties. His name was Guy Aldred. He was an Englishman who had come to Glasgow in the earlier part of the twentieth century and stayed on to make a name for himself as an out-and-out political rebel. He was an anarchist, an atheist, an early proponent of birth control and abortion. He was the very antithesis of the god-fearing people who surrounded me, and was seen as a sort of devil incarnate.

As some outrageous comments by him, about organised religion, had appeared in the press at that time, the local minister decided to have it out with him and invited him to a public debate on Aldred's straightforward denial of the existence of God. Make no mistake, the minister and my religious uncle wanted to recreate the famous Wilberforce–Huxley evolution debate of Oxford University in 1860, when Huxley said of his opponent, the bishop, that he would not be ashamed to have

20

a monkey as his ancestor but would be ashamed to be connected to a man who used his great gifts to obscure the truth. Aldred himself had often referred to that debate. Outside, on the pavement, the anarchists were handing out pamphlets. I was scared to take one. At that moment, and probably for the last time, I was on the side of the angels.

Inside, the hall was packed with folk accustomed to sedate religious nostrums. They were not really aware of what they had let themselves in for. In Aldred came. In truth, he did appear scary to my tender eyes. He was a squat man with long hair, streaked with grey and hanging around his shoulders like steel shards. He had brooding dark eyebrows and a double-chinned grey complexion, and the inflexible set of his face suggested the imminence of thunder. By odd contrast, he was wearing plus-fours, almost as if he had just come off the links. He flayed the minister immediately with a sortie of facts and figures relating religions to wars, corruption, hypocrisy and myth. Here was a street-corner bruiser who had been jailed for his beliefs and who could devour hecklers like a lizard tonguing an insect. The minister, such a nice man, was no match, as he was pulverised by the deep, assured tone of a voice which was overwhelming a stunned audience who never in their lives had heard such brutal irreverence.

Then a storm broke. My uncle Jim, who had been squirming uncomfortably beside me, leapt to his feet, his face puce with rage, to fulminate at Aldred, who had made another disconcerting remark about the 'so-called' Son of God. It was a passionate rant which seemed to go on for minutes, and almost terrified I stiffened, waiting for the Aldred response. Jim sat down trembling, both with anger and the effort he had gone through defending his religion. The audience, who needed something to lift their spirits, cheered him. The hall rang with Christian certitude. Aldred, though, looked down at his new opponent, and with a scorn which suggested not a dent had been made on him, coldly bludgeoned my uncle with a rebuttal, which, I recall, climaxed in a thundering denunciation of bishops who blessed bombers during wars, and which ended with him thumping the table in front of him. The audience started to shout at him, as if my uncle's interruption had broken the oratorical spell Aldred had held them under, and it became rowdy. It also disturbed me, for I felt I was failing a loyalty test. Here I was, beside my own kin, a man for whom I had great affection, but I was finding myself enthralled by Aldred. He even began to seem heroic. He was outnumbered, surrounded. He was John Wayne in *Stagecoach* and, to me, arrow-proof. Perhaps I was attracted to the loner who stuck out from the others. In any case I knew I was thinking ideas which would have appalled the family. That debate was a defining moment for me.

I stuck with the public library *Daily Worker* for many months, although I became more and more excited by those beautiful, exotic creatures photographed at various Hunt Balls, for example, which you could find in the *Illustrated London News* or the *Tatler*, and, being honest with myself, even then, I was becoming more and more interested in how you got on in life within this dastardly system called capitalism, and how I might shape up as a debonair escort at a debutantes' coming-out ball. Never mind that I never had enough money to buy a McCallum when I wanted, my fantasies were almost exclusively devoted to my life as a wanton procurer of society women rather than as an orator at the corner of some street advocating revolt by the masses. Gene Tierney, from the silver screen, had come into my life. Lenin had become boring. The *Daily Worker*'s coverage of sport was naff anyway. And on the Saturday of that week of the debate I went to see my first Scotland international at Hampden Park, where youthful fanaticism was the only 'ism' you needed.

3

SEEING THE LIGHT

Hampden introduced my generation to excess. Big crowds, in a towering vastness which shrank you to insignificance. To a cry of 'Mind the wean!', you could be passed down from the top of the terracing to the trackside wall over the heads of the Glasgow public, who stuck up benevolent hands to propel you further downwards, in a series of lifts underneath the bum, securely but robustly aiding your passage to the front, where you could crouch with other weans on the trackside of the wall like orphans of the storm. Not until many decades later, when I stood at the top of the ski-slope in Calgary, ready to film the intrepid Eddie the Eagle in the Winter Olympics, did I experience the imminence of overwhelming vertigo, as when my father would say to me, as the crush was getting worse at the top, 'Wait for me. I'll come down and get you at the end', and would lift me high above his shoulder, and I'd look down this congested slope with the stomach looping-the-loop, wondering if I would make it.

It never failed. The Glasgow crowd could take care of its own. You weren't a strange little boy being deserted. You were one of them. Tradition kept you safe. And your father always turned up at the end. At least mine did. So I look back on its

utter, insane recklessness with affection. I didn't even have a
rethink about that, the night I witnessed the bodies lined up
along the inside track at Ibrox, just a few hours after the disaster
of 1971, caused by people on a staircase creating a human
Corryvrechan as the lives were sucked out of them in the vortex
of tripping, stumbling and trampling that only an uncoordi-
nated steeply descending crowd could create. We simply had
been lucky, or blessed in our day, in an age when only miners
seemed to have disasters.

My mother didn't like Hampden. For a start, it was too far
away. And she never knew what went on. She had interrogated
me about this sordid business that she had heard about, of
being sold as a hostage to fortune by being deserted by a father
and handed over to strange people. I never let on. Not because
I had some sort of pact with my father. Instinct dictated. If you
welshed you might not get back. It was a man thing. So I lied
and she never really believed me. That is why she never offered
any objections to me going to see the local side, Shettleston
Juniors, at Greenfield Park. All my friends went. The ground
backed on to the bottleworks that employed so many of their
fathers. The ash-pitch was black, the Shettleston shirts were
white, the ground usually packed in those days. It was the
heyday of junior football. It provided only an illusion of pros-
perity, though. Money was scarce, junior football was not.
Poverty was there, all around, but we were shielded from it.
Access to football helped. The grounds were filled largely by
people who had little else to do of a Saturday afternoon. Junior
football was convenient and cheap and provided an escape
from the tedium of five and a half days of slog at the work-
bench or the foundry. Apart from that, my Macpherson grand-
father would take me on the long roundabout trip from south
Carntyne where he lived, on the 22 bus, to watch on alternate
weeks, Queen's Park, and particularly Third Lanark, in the days

24

of the great inside forward Jimmy Mason, of whom my grand-father spoke in tones of affection that he normally reserved for Robert Burns.

I wasn't so much learning about football and how a game ought or ought not to be played. That was going over my head. I was becoming steadily conscious of the fact that it seemed to act as an indispensable catalyst for so much of the social life around me; of relationships, identities, aspirations, arguments, fights, and that if you could command a grasp of why football meant so much to people, then you had a chance of grasping the overall meaning of life itself. But there were counter balances to all of that. And I was lucky. Family life in our household in the early fifties was cosily and safely built round a fit, athletic and helpful – but always sharply critical – father, who never did fully accept that a son of his could be so bad at arithmetic, when he himself would successfully negotiate the answers to my maths tests by scribbling them down the side of his *Noon Record*, the local racing newspaper, before pencilling in his projected bets for that day; an ambitious and meticulously caring mother; and one sister, to be joined by another several years later. That was the core. But Jim Black, my uncle, truly unlocked much of the world for me. I appreciated that most forcibly when he was responsible for Sir Harry Lauder entering our family life.

The great Scottish knight, who on one of his twenty-one trips to the States met the American media on the deck of the *Queen Mary* and to a newsreel camera made a remark which stamped his imprimatur on the entire Scottish identity. He had announced that he had given up golf. 'Because I lost my ball!' he explained. Thus was firmly established an image of the parsimonious Scot, the skinflint, around which have been engendered a million jokes, slurs, calumnies and brought me often to the verge of vigilante retribution in various parts of the world. You could conclude, therefore, that Sir Harry had heaped much of that warped heritage upon us, almost like a biblical curse. But he was a global star whose name was uttered with reverence amongst us, and never did a social evening pass in our house without an airing of one of his songs. He was a hero, but a distant one. Then one day that changed. The first I heard about it was when I heard my mother say to my father, 'Sir Harry has invited Jim to Lauder Ha'.'

A few years earlier Jim Black had started sending a poem every year to the Scots entertainer to celebrate his birthday. They were Glasgow narrative poems, in the vernacular, with highly inventive rhymes which comically explored the ups and downs of a native Glaswegian. He would read them out at parties around the area, to great merriment. One morning a letter came through the post from Sir Harry's niece Greta, who looked after the ageing entertainer in their large estate in Strathaven. It was read out proudly to me, eventually, by Jim himself. It was full of lavish praise for his work and said that the great star wanted to meet this young man who had kept him greatly amused every birthday. We were all rather bemused and initially disbelieving. Suddenly a family entertainer was to be fêted by a man who at one stage was the highest paid stage act in the world, the first British artist to have sold over a million records, and once described by Winston Churchill as 'Scotland's greatest ambassador'. Overnight Jim had been transformed in my eyes; the same interesting, stimulating man, but with a new strange allure. Somebody outside our tiny world had recognised a talent which I suppose, to us, had seemed purely as domestic and limited in appeal as the kitchen sink.

For now I imagined I was rubbing shoulders with a celebrity, not a mere uncle. Greta had alerted the Scottish press about this visit and the *Scottish Sunday Mail* duly published photographs of the pair of them at Lauder Ha', and printed the poem he had sent. He would pay visits to Sir Harry frequently from then on, to read him his poems, right up until this noble old man died in 1950. Thereafter, if I knew Jim was taking the air around Shettleston, I would take it with him and bask in some kind of reflected glory. For on Sundays I would make it a habit to accompany him on Shettleston Road's version of the *passeggiata*, when it was the custom to start walking all the way along one side, for a mile or so, heading east towards Eastbank Academy, then crossing and strolling down the other. This you would repeat until you were exhausted. Until the Sir Harry interlude, this could have been accomplished, or, indeed, you could have expired along the way, without anybody noticing. But after the publicity, people stopped and stared, as they sing in *My Fair Lady* – 'That's him, isn't it?' You would hear that.

In later life Rikki Fulton was to involve me in a sketch on BBC Television's *Scotch and Wry*, which sent up celebrity oglers and pompous celebrities, and which ended in the indignity of preening myself in front of my hovering admirer, only to have been mistaken for Bamber Gascoigne. It reminded me of those Sunday walks, and the fluttering sensation of being with someone who was more than just another man in the street. I could tell Jim enjoyed it, but no more so than myself, overwhelmed by this association with a local celebrity. Even by proxy I was experiencing the first powerful, intoxicating, seductive excitement of public recognition, but not yet, at that early stage, the obverse side, hostility.

For on top of that exposure came another, and odder one, which greatly enhanced his reputation and took me into areas which had so far been beyond bounds. It stemmed from the interest a famous journalist and broadcaster took in Jim. He was Archie McCulloch, who wrote principally for the *Scottish Sunday Mail*. He was a large man with a prominent nose upon which you could have landed a Piper Comanche, as I recollect, and a booming way of expressing himself which indicated great self-confidence. His wife was the singer Kathy Kay, who had been popularised through the Billy Cotton Show on radio, then eventually on television. So, he was up there with the high and mighty in showbusiness. He sailed into our tenement like a Spanish galleon attempting tiny Crail Harbour. He just seemed too big and noisy for us, walking about the three rooms and lobby, arms flapping, as if he wanted to push out the walls to accommodate himself more. 'He's gallus,' my granny said, under her breath. He would command the photographer to take this and that picture, including myself, in a family group snap, all gathered around Jim. We were overwhelmed by this man's celebrity status, and as he beamed prolific compliments to Jim, and the slavish photographer snapped until his fingers must have been tingling, I do believe that it passed through my mind that 771 Shettleston Road would attain the status of that humble thatched cottage down there in Alloway. Not the ploughman poet. This time it was to be the 'brickie' poet. Only one photograph appeared in the paper – Jim with pen in hand – implying that the rest of us deserved to remain in obscurity. 'Told you!' my granny said, given that her efforts with curlers and tongs had come to naught.

For McCulloch had another motive for promoting Jim in his newspaper. Just about that time speedway racing had established itself in Glasgow and became highly popular. McCulloch took a fancy to that, as a new and challenging alternative for his football-obsessed city, and promoted it as much as he could. It occurred to him that what the speedway team, the Glasgow Tigers, needed to catch the ear of the city was a jazzy signature tune. After all, a song of identity was *de rigueur* in our fair city, with 'The Sash' and 'The Wild Colonial Boy' directing you both to Irish history and to two stadiums on either side of the sectarian divide. McCulloch was looking for a frisky lyric to match a catchy tune that he himself would write, utterly in contrast to the football ditties. He chose Jim to collaborate. In a sense this surprised me because the family poet was no devotee of any sport. But the impetus of his new-found celebrity and a bit of cash was enough to spur him on. Off we went this particular night to the White City Stadium, near Ibrox Park, where our ears were to be assailed by an entirely new noise. The terracing was packed. It was the first time I had been to a so-called sporting event that didn't require kicking a ball. I was also beginning to hear that this new sport would divert crowds away from football, and that the old-fashioned leather-ball game was doomed. From the size and enthusiasm of the crowd that did not seem such an outrageous proposition. Of course it does now.

Even from the off I never took to it. I found it noisy, smelly and too brief, with the race virtually over by the first bend. But before the event the new signature tune was aired. To this day I can still hear Jim's words being sung, booming out over the PA system, and felt thrilled to be his kin. It ended jauntily with the ultimate accolade trilled out in the last refrain, over and over again, 'The rippety-roaring Tigers, from the track beside the Clyde.' Rodgers and Hammerstein it wasn't, but it was catchy and bounced along as if you were on the seat of a roaring bike. The following morning Jim donned his brown dungarees to go to work, trowel in hand, lining furnaces at the Stewarts and Lloyds works. Never could I have envisaged that one day he would end up working on BBC radio with me at Queen Margaret Drive.

Where I felt I was perhaps losing touch with him was over religion. The West of Scotland tribalist version of it dogged my footsteps since the day I first put mouth to microphone. It was not something I could lay aside as an irrelevance. People really did want to know which foot I kicked with, as they would put it so delicately. My upbringing and my own strengthening views on religion made me realise how significant it was to people, either in their intrinsic beliefs or, perhaps just as importantly, as helping to define their social identity. Jim Black was not an evangelistic Bible-thumper, and apart from rare bursts of temper, as in his joust with Guy Aldred, he was a sensitive believer in the Good Book. So I was sucked into his Methodist circle, meeting ministers and lay people who sensibly converted belief into pragmatic social commitment. For instance, he introduced me to the Reverend Nelson Gray, who was later to become head of religious programmes at Scottish Television, and who was in the late fifties a leading figure in CND. I recall him saying to me, in summing up his attitude towards the bomb, 'We are all guilty, all of us, if we don't demonstrate against this evil. Will you join us?' I never did. I cannot recollect why I dodged walking all the way to the submarine base at Faslane on the Holy Loch. Perhaps I thought it was pointless. But dodge it I did, and made some excuse or other, which I am sure was feeble and dishonest, given my admiration for his sincerity. But there was never any pressure exerted on me to follow any particular religious path, except of course in the conventional parental ritual of dressing you up, making you appear bright and bushy-tailed, and packing you off to Sunday School.

I went through the dutiful process of attending Sunday School. But it was there, sitting on those small stools listening to tales of the Holy Land, that I discovered a diversion from the spir-itual callisthenics we were engaged in. She was Mrs Craig, a brunette in her early twenties I believe, my Sunday School teacher, and I thought she was delectable. She would sit on a very low seat, put her Bible in her lap, then cross her legs. I was about ten and her expanse of thigh was having a strange effect on me. Sometimes I felt as if my stomach would churn out of control. But there was something else. I wouldn't have known what an impure thought was at that age, but a very strange phenomenon was occurring down near my groin every time she sat down and crossed her legs. It wasn't just that I was smitten, it was that I had also discovered the creepy pleasure that could overtake you just by using your eyes. Was pleasure to be attained in such a simple visual way as that? Look, no hands, I suppose I was saying to myself. At least not at that stage. This was truly divine.

Double pneumonia would not have held me back from attending every Sunday, after she made her first appearance. My mother was delighted, not to say slightly surprised, at the religious zealot she now had as a young son. I still wonder if, during that spell, she was thinking that I was getting the call, and that the ministry was beckoning for me. Previously she would have had to use her considerable powers of persuasion to get me to go. Now I even brushed my teeth before I went. There Mrs Craig would sit, normally under a large print on the wall of Holman Hunt's *The Light of the World*, with the glowing face of Jesus approving of us all. There have been other more profound moments which caused me to jump the religious ship, but I carbon-date my unease with the supernatural from about the moment I trembled at the sight of earthly flesh sitting seductively on the small stool, whilst remaining indifferent to that elongated figure with the lamp in his hand.

The poet Richard Church in his autobiography *Over the Bridge* writes about the sense of melancholy that descended on him whenever he heard the local church bells pealing for evensong of a Sunday evening. For me that similar feeling, on hearing them, lapsed into something like a sense of dread. The notion of my ain folk being duped into believing there was a hereafter actually scared me. So I greeted Monday morning's secular activities like a return to the real world. However, my antagonism towards religious belief, was, at that stage, I now admit,

31

so laced with prejudice that I would shoot from the hip without thinking. From the Vatican to the Wee Frees, all was a conspiracy to prevent rational thought. Rangers and Celtic were the proof of that, with the decadent appeal to tribalism which sprang from their historical backgrounds. We were all enslaved, and weren't aware of it. Then, as if I needed specific ammunition to point a finger at religion, it was handed to me by a man of the cloth.

4

PRIDE AND PREJUDICES

I look back on it as the dog-collar incident. It happened just after I had left school and was in my first year as a student with the intention of becoming a teacher. It was in the spring of 1953. There had been ups and downs. Clem Atlee and the Labour government had gone. Post-war austerity and the onslaught of the right-wing press had done for them. I had come to hate the *Daily Express* with a vengeance. Arthur Christiansen, their admittedly brilliant editor, had unleashed the dogs of war on the Attlee government, particularly through the drawings of the brilliant cartoonist Cummings, with his sinister figure Mr Rising Price mocking Labour. I was more staunchly pro-government then than I have ever been since, as I was enjoying, with so many others, the growing benefits of the embryonic welfare state. Why couldn't people understand that? But I was bumping into new Tories. They had glottal stops. Where had the snobs gone? The working class, I was discovering, could be treacherous. And a real hero of mine, the brilliantly eloquent Democrat Adlai Stevenson, had lost the presidential election in the States to a Republican war hero but political stooge, Ike. The world was going right-wing, but it was too nice a place, as a whole, to want to get off.

A GAME OF TWO HALVES

The family hung out the flags for the Coronation that year but others refused to do so, and you could walk along Shettleston Road picking out the religious differences that existed, by spotting who did and who didn't. It was an event overshadowed by my increasing fondness for the opposite sex – draughty closes for privacy, back row of the State Cinema for sheer bravado: success rate, moderate.

Then, suddenly, inhabiting cinemas, which would produce withdrawal symptoms if missed for a week, had a rival. In May of that year I had inveigled myself into the house of a local chemist, who was a distant relative of the man from Donegal my aunt had married. He was rich and the only man within many square miles to own this new-fangled object, a television set. There I witnessed, in slightly flickering black and white, Stanley Matthews's brilliant dribbles late on in the game to win the FA Cup for Blackpool in 1953. The name of the commentator meant nothing to me at the time. It was Kenneth Wolstenholme. In later years I was to meet both him and Sir Stanley, as he became. I accompanied Wolstenholme in the commentary position in Lisbon in 1967, in my first overseas broadcast, and a decade later, doing commentary for a Canadian soccer tournament, I joined the great knight on a training jog through the streets of Toronto, followed by a ten-lengths swim in the hotel pool, when he was in his mid-sixties. The knight of the realm was ruggedly fit and hugely modest. 'It wasn't my final,' Sir Stan told me, holding up three fingers, 'It was Stanley Mortensen's. Hat-trick in a final? Can't do better than that!' Although I could not have realised it, my future was shaping itself in front of my eyes in the flickering television screen.

Myself, I was no Stanley Matthews. I was playing amateur football at Lochwinnoch in Renfrewshire and in 1953 was realising I would never make a professional like my father, who

34

had played for a selection of junior clubs, and King's Park, which eventually became Stirling Albion. I had a spell training at Hampden under Queen's Park but never got further than one of their lower manifestations, the Hampden XI. I was fast. I had won many sprint competitions over the years at Lanarkshire county competitions. The problem was the ball. The veritable spin of the world on its axis was enough to ensure that by the time I reached the penalty area, the ball was no longer there. I was the maestro of the vanishing end-product. I was learning what it meant to play to your limitations, which I suppose were so many that I might have been born for the players' bench. Thus were established the credentials for becoming a professional critic, as defined by drama critic Kenneth Tynan once, as someone who knows the way but can't drive the car. But if you were in the least interested in football, and hardly any virile male wasn't, then you had to know chapter and verse on the Old Firm.

In that year of 1953, for instance, you could still start a fight in an empty house in Shettleston by referring to the great Cox–Tully incident in the Old Firm game, four years previously, on 27 August 1949. Dear God, you could still feel something of the aftermath of that thirty years later in foreign parts with some of the old-timers I came across in Kearney, New Jersey, where, to a certain extent, time has stood still for expatriates, and old controversies are welcomed like food parcels for the needy.

Sammy Cox and Charlie Tully became embroiled in a vicious incident on the field which prompted terracing demonstrations at the Celtic end of Ibrox. Cox kicked Tully, blatantly and openly, and yet stayed on the field. He pled provocation, and insisted he had been kicked in the ankle first, and told me in Canada many years later, 'I kicked him just above the shin-guard and said, "Don't do that to me again!"' No matter the provocation, he should have been sent off, but wasn't, and that started an uproar at the Celtic end. As one report had it, 'Bottles were merrily doing their "Pennies from Heaven" act'. Fights broke out amongst supporters of the same colours, probably as some protested at the self-inflicted danger of flying bottles. Jack McGinn, who was later to become chairman of Celtic, was in the crowd as a young teenager. 'The sky was black with flying glass. We just had to duck and hope for the best', he later told me. The late John McPhail, Celtic's main attacker, was standing beside his great opponent Willie Woodburn, the Rangers centre-half: 'I said to Ben [Woodburn's nickname], "In the name of God! If they get on the park I bet I can beat you to the dressing room." ' Nothing was done about Cox, and the feeling of blatant injustice amongst the Celtic following lingered for many years, and was brought up frequently as the definitive example of institutional prejudice against their club, especially as the SFA produced a benign report on the incident which offered only a mild rebuke on all concerned.

So, we lived with this separation of minds, in which intolerance was the theme of much of what Celtic people had to talk about, as opposed to an almost smug feeling of entrenched superiority by their rivals. Although attachment to the Old Firm was a reflection of social divisions, I actually revelled in the gutsiness of it. This was serious stuff. These conflicts and tensions were beyond philosophical explanation. We were salt of the earth people, living with an issue that was exclusively ours, and if you didn't understand the implications of an Old Firm result, one way or the other, then 'Haud yer weesht', as my granny would say, to silence an ignorant interjection by somebody who didn't know what he was talking about.

You did not need to live on a high moral plane to recognise the potential for violence that this fixture contained. To be honest, we turned deaf ears to those who damned it and called for its banning. We saw them merely as do-gooders who could not fathom the powerful inspirations derived from this tribalism, which, as I was to discover in later years, gave positive, meaningful spur even to those who attained some of the highest offices in the land. I have encountered politicians, lawyers, doctors, teachers, professors, priests, ministers, whom you might not associate with the blunt incantations of an Old Firm fixture, but whose passion for identification with either club was a major influence on their professional lives and contributed in no small measure to shaping a purpose in life. Monday morning triumphalism stocked self-confidence.

We were then, however, working-class folk joined at the hip over the sectarian divide. But we conveniently turned a blind eye to those powerful instruments of division, the church and the school, and consequently suffered mutual incomprehension of each other's beliefs. That's just the way it was. On my side of the divide I visited church only out of respect for my grandmother Black, who was an exemplary Christian and whom I loved dearly, but it was she who inadvertently caused the dog-collar incident when I was eighteen and in my first year as a student teacher.

It happened in the vestry of the Methodist Church in Shettleston Road. The soot-stained church stood defiantly amidst the tenements and shops, in a tight squeeze that left little margin between Mammon and spirituality. It was a midweek early evening in spring, and the man who sat in front of me, legs crossed, one hand in pocket, was grey in appearance, his flat, monotonous voice a contrast to many of the Methodist firebrands I had heard in my time. He had replaced the man who had taken on Aldred. The sallowness of his demeanour conveyed utter joylessness. He looked rather blankly at you through horn-rimmed spectacles. His opening gambit was avuncular and calculated to make me feel at ease as I sat there wondering how

37

this morbid-looking figure could inspire anybody. He had requested a meeting with me.

'Have you seen *High Noon*?' he asked. Three times over I had, queuing up at the local Odeon cinema, watching Gary Cooper waiting for that fateful train to arrive, then going back outside to join the new queue for the later showing.

'Don't you think the Sheriff is like Christ in the wilderness, as he paces the streets, on his own, apparently spurned by everybody, but determined to resist the temptation to run away and hide? Then triumphs.'

I hadn't, if truth be told, but not wishing to give the impression that I could not appreciate the difference between a classic and a Lassie movie, and wishing to convey that I knew a thing or two about symbolism, I fed his ego by showing appreciation of his enlightening interpretation of Gary Cooper with a six-gun, as the man in rope sandals being invited to jump from a precipice and survive. Jesus certainly had chucked some tables about in anger from time to time, but as far as I knew the only bruising he would have inflicted on anybody was by accidentally rubbing too hard in washing all those feet he apparently washed. But I played along.

'Yes,' I said. 'Now that you put it like that, it does bring to mind the fight against evil.'

'The fight against Temptation. Above all Temptation,' I can recall him saying, the hand in his pocket, I noted, becoming more agitated, as if he were masking a Parkinson's tremor.

'Temptation is all around us.'

Here we go. At that juncture I thought he might have something on me, of which I was unaware, and that he was on the verge of a confrontation. I ran possible scenarios through my mind with the speed of an electron in an atom smasher, knowing that I was in the clear about my activities in the back row of the State cinema, since he would have been preparing his sermon on a Saturday evening and could not possibly have been in the vicinity. Unless someone of the fairer sex had blabbed, of course. And in any case I was now preparing a polite exit strategy, for I was only there because of an obligation to granny and I didn't believe a blind word that any church spoke anyway. But he then began to move into the territory he really did want to cover.

'Moral and spiritual decline always starts with self,' he said softly, eyeing me. 'Self-control is essential before you start out in life, to meet the temptations abounding. But self-control needs to be taught. Sometimes it needs to be imposed. There are ways in which that is possible and very effective. There is one curse which has to be obliterated before we can develop spiritual strength to combat the temptations. Do you masturbate?'

Eh? No adult had ever uttered such a word in my presence. And hardly any of my own generation, whose preferred descriptions were 'wanking' or 'tossing-off'. But, then, sex was never discussed openly anywhere in that period of the early fifties. Not in the home, not in school, not in the church except for broad sweeping statements about immorality that would ignore any juicy references to the details of how immoral you could be, if you so wished. Perhaps in confessionals, and in seeking aid from a minister, there might have been intimate conversations on sexual problems. But other than that it was generally a taboo subject. I remember his blank, unmoving eyes staring at me and the hand movement in his pocket like he was trying to capture a butterfly within. I suddenly twigged. He wasn't taking a census. But after a mental blink or two I responded.

'Yes,' I said. 'I do.' Not sheepishly, but with a kind of 'What the hell!' feeling.

I could have added that I was as adept at handling myself as Artie Shaw was with his clarinet, but I preferred to limit the response to see where this was leading. He seemed to take some encouragement from my admission, which coming from a six-foot eighteen-year-old lad of healthy sexual appetite ought not to have startled even my own granny. He had guessed correctly all along, I was in the throes of moral turpitude.

'We want to rid young men of this practice and I think I can help you,' he continued. Perhaps I could have short-circuited this by telling him that not even under the threat of having my teeth extracted by pliers would I desist from a practice over which I had no hang-ups.

'I have had great success in other parishes with this and I am sure you will benefit from the experience. I would not suggest this, had I not the success rate I have achieved with this particular method. What I do is use this cane.' He reached behind the table and produced this snappy piece of what looked like bamboo, which was as thin as a rapier. 'To drive out the urges from within we have to create some kind of remembrance of punishment. There is no other way. It's very simple. So what I would ask you to do is lower your trousers and underpants, bend over the chair and I will apply the punishment to you. I can assure you it will be greatly to your benefit. The therapeutic effect is that it cleanses the mind.'

Disbelief gave way to an almost irresistible urge to giggle at the preposterousness of it all. Gary Cooper, on the other hand, would have shot him between the eyes there and then. But he was the man with the dog collar and I was experiencing more bewilderment than revulsion, in that he thought I could fall for something that would have been considered a joke, even at Dotheboys Hall. Alternatively, I was about twelve stone and quite capable of looking after myself. One touch, and dog collar or no, he was going to get it. His pocket agitation was increasing. There is nothing so deflating as seeing a figure of authority and respect dissolve, in front of your very eyes, into a sexual creep. But he could see I was discomfited and was actually prepared for that and pursued the matter quietly, insisting that trauma was a part of preparation for life, and reminded me of parameters within which you must remain. He went on and on in that vein for some time. I had had enough. But I remained polite.

'It's very good of you to want to help out,' I said. 'But no thanks. I have to go. I've got some studies.'

'No, please wait,' he implored as I rose. 'Your virility is in no doubt. But it has to be channelled properly. I assure you it works. Please, you can strip over there in the corner.'

That was the cue to depart. As I rose and made for the door, he uttered the words rapidly to me which clearly defined his venality.

'Of course what we have spoken about is private. I think it would be better if we could keep these matters to ourselves. I attend my ministry with great compassion, you know. I must help young men rid themselves of harmful urges. That is all I intend. God bless.'

Sadly, I have had to admit to the good folk who were committed and sincere Christians that that benediction, which to them was a distillation of all their beliefs, thereafter rang in my ears like the salutation of hypocrisy. A caning on the bare backside? I certainly was to learn later that corporal punishment was part of the disciplinary tradition of religious organisations, and that in Ireland some Christian Brothers employed methods which would have been approved by Miss Whiplash, rather than John the Baptist. Since the church meant little to me, my first instinct was to use this incident in support of my mistrust of religion. But I also reasoned with myself that the whole Christian ethic could hardly be dismissed because I had come across one pervert who was obviously exploiting his position. More relevantly, I knew how important this institution was to the Black family, and that I had to express any feelings purely through them. My granny had once acted the Virgin Mary in a nativity play I had been forced to watch in church once. Dame Judy Dench could not have been more convincing. How would she react then?

'The bastard! That bloody bastard!' declared the former Virgin Mary. She was now Dame Judy again, but this time in her Oscar-winning role playing Good Queen Bess going ballistic. This human response made me want to put my arms around her and welcome her back to reality, except that I could not get near her, for she was pacing up and down the kitchen, arms flailing, like she was being pursued by a swarm of bees, but probably had fixed in her mind some unimaginable things she was doing to the man with the cane. After all, 'Sado-masochism in Methodism' was not something they had factored into their beliefs.

We had a crisis therefore. Not a personal one, because although I hoped the man would be tarred and feathered along the length of Shettleston Road, I had really experienced no great trauma. But certainly there was a communal crisis. Uncle Jim was in the throes of putting on his jacket and running up the road to confront the man and 'do the bastard in' and had to be helped back from the door by granny and me because she didn't want it handled that way. I felt sorry for the pair of them. A bond of great meaning to them had been breached. In their world, getting your bare arse ritually skelped had nothing to do with the carpenter from Galilee. Watching them in despair I wondered whether I should have kept silent, except I kept seeing the sallow pastiness of the face I had left behind, a portrait of moral decay despite the dog collar, and the turbulence he was working so blatantly in his pocket, and I knew that he had to be targeted. Granny was distraught and bewildered. A good woman let down. But icily, coldly determined on retribution.

She got it. They hauled the man in front of a specially convened meeting of the elders and waded into him. I was not called as a witness for the prosecution, for in fact they discovered that he had been skelping his way through young parishioners like the Colorado beetle through a potato field, wreaking havoc, with sufficient evidence for a keel-hauling, even though, as I suspected, masturbation would not be lapsing into general decline in the East End. And whether it was Christian charity which prevailed, or, much more likely, that they wished to avoid embarrassment to the church, they didn't throw him out on to the street, but kept it from the public domain, and ensured he was moved to another parish, as if that would have been therapy in itself. Judging by what we know of such things, and the cover-ups which have been used by all churches, it is a safe bet that he would have erred again.

I was left to wonder what other sexual misdemeanours or perversions might be going on under the surface of a strongly macho area, where the culture was so obviously male-dominated and that to boast about getting the leg-over, whether true or not, gave you status as the red-blooded male nature intended you to be. But were there other kinds out there, amongst us? It was the first hint of a much more complex world of relationships and behaviour than we imagined in the perceived certainties of our orthodox living. It's not a thought that lasted all that long and it might have gone away entirely had it not been for the Lord Montagu case arising shortly afterwards, when he was accused of interfering with boys.

Amongst my student body, we reached that ambivalent position as regards what we considered perversion, by expressing disgust, but in a lighthearted way, in singing to the tune of the Frankie Laine melody 'Answer me, oh my love' a ditty about the Montagu sex case. 'Answer me, Lord Montagu / Just how many boys have you been through.' We were macho and arrogant, in the belief that our lifestyle was the only one.

For a little while my own fumblings in the back row of the State cinema or in a draughty close seemed to be assuring myself of my own normality. But information and news about alternative lifestyles was beginning then to seep into our consciousness, even though we dismissed them as irrelevant to us. Years later I chaired the *Sport in Question* panel on Scottish Television and interviewed the gay footballer Justin Fashanu. I found him arrogant and aggressive, and wondered if, in thinking that, it was a residual prejudice, consolidated by the memory of the Methodist vestry. But, in essence, I think he was just plain arrogant and aggressive, and that outside of that, he had to be admired for 'coming out' in a footballing world which is still staunchly homophobic.

I certainly spoke not a word about this to my parents, neither of whom went to church. I found it easier to talk about such a thing outside our own household. They were more concerned about what kind of future I was developing for myself, and although they had wanted me to leave school early and take up tools to bring some money into a household that was never destitute but never flush with money, they supported me valiantly through my ups and downs in Coatbridge High School. In that sense it was my mother who really drove me on. My father had an agile brain, with a great memory which enabled him to quote reams of Burns and long swatches of *Marmion*, at the drop of a hat. I think he also suspected that in writing awful poems and short stories that would never see the light of day, as I did prolifically from my mid-teens onwards, I was a bit odd myself. The agony for me was that here was a good man, from whose lips I never heard any kind of obscenity, prevalent though that tendency was all around us, and who taught me what the competitive spirit really ought to be, by beating me, without mercy, at any game we played against each other. And yet, I knew I was growing away from his world. In my later teens we rarely had conversations of any length. An occasional chat about football remained the binding factor. And, typically, he did not say much when I told him of my clear ambition, at the age of eighteen, to enter a profession. A profession which, on the very first day I walked into a school some years later, confronted me with an implement made of leather, about 18 inches in length, 2 inches in width, an inch thick and which in the hands of a sadist, like the Methodist caner, could have driven the notion of sex out of the head of Casanova.

5

CLASS WAR

To a family whose men, through the generations, had come home from work with grimy hands and sweaty dungarees as brickies, or labourers in factories, to have a bath in the kitchen sink, becoming a teacher was seen, by my mother at least, as almost an elevation to a clean-limbed priesthood. To me, at first, it was merely a job which offered long holidays. It wasn't until I had sampled what I thought were the serious flaws of the educational system then, that I developed a distinct sense of purpose and idealism in my career choice. And certainly my mood changed early on, when I was given an odd tutorial on my first day at Garrowhill Primary School, as a trainee teacher in 1957. I had trained at Jordanhill College, first in the Scottish School of Physical Education and then in the graduate course for primary education. I approached this first assignment tentatively, knowing I would only be there for a short period but was looking forward to entering a profession which by definition, ought to have been a powerful, civilising force for enlightenment. But then I met Mr John Hamilton, the headmaster. I was about to receive an introduction to the profession which seemed as civilising as replacing anaesthetic with an amputational saw.

As one of his first steps he introduced me to that infamous piece of leather that has given a kind of tarnished name to that village in Fife, Lochgelly. He knew how to use the tawse and was determined that I had to as well. The school was in an area which you would not have associated with violence of any kind. Garrowhill, in the suburbs of Glasgow, both exuded respectability and at the same time suggested there was more to it than meets the eye, with some of its social critics summing up the middle-class enclave, albeit rather enviously, in a phrase I heard a few times – 'All fur coat and nae knickers.' Not exactly a Marxist analysis, but indicating that pretension was in the air there. Undoubtedly it was the school in the middle of the estate that caused most envy, as it was considered one of the model primary schools in Lanarkshire, and people would seriously consider moving house into the catchment area just to get access to it. So there I was, a trainee teacher, brimming with optimism.

Hamilton was a suave man, immaculately dressed, Brylcreemed to a fault, liberally splashed with aftershave, who practised a lingering two-handed shake with women which suggested his home life was in need of extra-curricular supplementing. He frequently expressed contempt for the 'Reds' in the council who ran educational policy. He had invited me to his office to have a chat and meet the local councillor, who uncannily mirrored Hamilton, except in accent. He was always addressed formally as Mr Eamond: a 'gentle, parfait knight' of an Englishman who helped run Henry Boot, the major house-building firm which had developed Garrowhill. He was pleasant and courteous and softly but insistently spoken, with a slight Yorkshire accent reminiscent of that Tory grandee from the past, Marcus Fox. I suppose he was part of that now apparently deceased breed of one-nation Toryism.

'This is the kind of man to know if you want to get on,' Hamilton said to me. 'You have to get to know the cooncillors.

47

Never mind John S. MacEwan [the Director of Education for Lanarkshire], it's the cooncillors who'll get you on.' But even then I suspected that in Red Lanarkshire Eamond, an Independent by name, Tory by intent, would have as much access to the seat of political power as the inmate of a padded cell to the key of the door. From the contempt with which they spoke about the political set-up in Lanarkshire, both he and the head seemed concerned that the Bolsheviks in the County Buildings in Hamilton would eventually come storming though the privet-hedged serenity of Garrowhill and insist on the Lord's Prayer being replaced by the Internationale, and the cub scouts by the Young Socialists. Altogether, that first morning was quite startling.

I believe the first tableau was stage-managed for the benefit of the councillor. Hamilton walked behind his large desk, opened a drawer and took out the belt. He held the stiff tawse up in front of me. It stood rigid, unbending, unflinching in his hand, defying gravitational pull. 'Hold that,' he said. It felt like I was being ritually empowered. I had never held one before, but had had considerable experience of being at the receiving end. So, having this medieval instrument in your hand was the dawn of enlightenment, according to Mr Hamilton? But what was I supposed to do with it there and then? Hamilton moved back to the office door, half-opened it, then stood holding the handle on one side of the door.

'Right, I want you to belt the door handle,' he commanded. The councillor, probably having seen this ritual before, never moved so much as a muscle and lay back with his soft hat tilted towards the back of his head, his rimless glasses looking eerily opaque.

'You want me to belt that?' I asked.

'Go ahead,' he said, admittedly with a slight smirk.

So I widened my legs, gripped the leather rod and let fly. I missed. For on the down-swing he jerked the door back using the other handle with a defiant but gleeful look on his face.

'Try again. Come on! Hit it!'

I swung and missed as the door was jerked away again. Next, I feinted to swing and got a quick reaction but when I lashed down again trying to get through his defensive tactic, his mastery of door-handle manipulation made me almost fall into the carpet in swiping at thin air again. Those who will remember that brilliant amateur boxer Dick McTaggart will recall how skilful he was in back-pedalling and counter-attacking. Hamilton seemed to be the McTaggart of door-handle evasion. I looked back at the 'cooncillor' in growing embarrassment, but he was merely sitting back with a smug smile on his face, as if he had seen it all before. About six or seven times I tried, but never yet made contact, as he anticipated the swipe with elusive jerks from the other door handle. Now I cannot pretend that I was so charged with educational idealism that I did not require some down-to-earth practical advice on how to take the first faltering steps in handling a class. But here were three men ensconced in a room, one making wild lunges with a leather thong, another wristily manipulating a door handle with accompanying climactic hoots of pleasure, the other lounging back with the almost depraved look of the voyeur. At least it was free. They pay for that sort of thing in S&M parlours in Soho.

The headmaster was smug with triumph, the councillor wearily amused.

'You see,' Hamilton said. 'That's what you're up against. Don't expect them to hold their hands still when you belt them. Be prepared for the moving hand at all times. The little buggers will always try to take the sting out of it.'

Belts and councillors. The former are now banned, the latter not yet. I certainly had not expected a lecture on current educational theory, but what I had been handed was a tutorial on how to sneak your way through the educational system in acknowledging patronage, and how to hammer the living daylights out of those who refused to be enlightened. Door handles never looked the same after that. But although Hamilton did try to appoint me full-time to his school, he failed in his first attempt. I was to go further away than the Glasgow suburbs. When I eventually graduated I was sent up-country.

They were still mining for clay in the pits when I arrived in the small community of Glenboig, in August 1957, in my first official teaching post. With post-war estates on the fringes it was too sprawling to be called a village, although at the heart of it was the main street, the centre of the old village before the expansion of housing. About a couple of miles away to the east was Annathill, the coal-mining village for the Bedlay coal pit. Very famously, one terraced row in that village produced the core of the defence for Scotland in their triumph over England at Hampden in the Victory International in 1946, Jock Shaw and his brother David, and the big man who eventually became a folk hero in Newcastle, Frank Brennan. Even from a rival area the folk in Glenboig spoke with pride of Annathill's favourite sons, and indeed one of them, Jock, the captain of Rangers in the days of their Iron Curtain defence in the forties, had established a shop in Glenboig main street. He was a popular man in a community where Protestants and Catholics still live amicably, side by side, but in distinct awareness of each other's tribal associations.

There were no outrageous, massive displays of bigotry. It was a commendable area of honest working-class people, most of whom in sociological jargon would have been considered upwardly mobile, and indeed, some of my pupils, who came from homes where they had to scrape together to make ends meet to ensure their offspring got the best out of life, ended up achieving very successful professional lives.

There were three focal points – two schools and a pub. It would be difficult to assess which of the three made the greatest impact on the generations of Glenboig folk, for the social affirmations of the pub and the mulling over of values at a bar can never be overestimated. But, the schools and the pub had something inflexibly in common. They both practised separatism. In the pub there were two entrances. Protestants used one, Catholics the other. Not just sometimes, but always. Regulars simply did not breach that code. As Tevye sang in *Fiddler on the Roof* to justify the intransigence of particular ways of life, 'Tradition! Tradition!' It was not that the pub was a powderkeg waiting to explode. It was nothing of the kind. It was just a reflection of the way the two strands wished to co-exist; peacefully, but steadfastly refusing to merge identities. Indeed, it was apparently an important strand of ensuring you displayed your particular identity. If there was such a thing as benign intolerance then it was practised here. And they were proud of it. They boasted about it. They were never slow to tell you about the separate doors. To a civilised outsider this seemed absurd. But, equally, it was prudent to hold your tongue on the issue and certainly not mock it.

But they didn't mock the even more preposterous situation of this small area having separate schools. The white-painted public primary school stood prominently on a hill to the south, and nearer the centre of the village itself was the Catholic school. This was the norm. The ethos was simply Shettleston all over again, but with fewer people. I despised religious indoctrination, of course, and felt that religion should be studied as a subject, if it had to be in a school at all, and should not be actively promoted as the only system of belief. There is now more discussion on segregated schools than there ever has been before, but in the sixties if you dared bring the matter up professionally, amongst teachers of the different faiths, you were summarily dismissed as being something of a bigot. That was the principal get-out for those who cherished church schools, in my experience at the time. There was very little mature debate around.

So here, in a village that more accurately could have been called Ballyglenboig, was a reflection of many of the divisions across the Irish Sea. Depending on which door you went through at the pub, or which playground you frequented, you could have a Protestant lager or a Catholic long-division sum. I was learning in this superficially harmonious community that people go to great lengths to make life more complex than it really ought to be. Which door of the pub did I go in? I didn't. I drank elsewhere. As the local teacher I had summed up the perils of association-by-door fairly quickly so all my information of that place came second-hand. But my whole experience of Glenboig was to focus, as I never had before, on the deep splits in our society and especially on those fomented by segregated schools.

In 1957 the primary school was small, with only five classes. The headmaster, George McFadzean, was a meticulous man who carried himself with great authority, and who was eventually to lead Scotland's teachers as the president of the Educational Institute of Scotland, the teachers' union. He was not only a brilliant teacher but also a man with the common touch. In keeping with what I have already said about the pervasive influence of the Old Firm, he travelled every week with the local Rangers supporters' bus, all round the country, wearing the colours, and on occasion could be seen weaving his way woozily home of a Saturday evening, eating a fish supper out of a newspaper wrapping. But by Monday morning, this spruce man would appear, ready for the teaching fray, as if all he had done at the weekend was the *Glasgow Herald* crossword.

The great loves of his life were family and Jim Baxter, the Ranger with genius in his left leg. We would discuss the games before the bell at 9 o'clock. After that it was action stations, as he ran the school with military precision and nothing escaped his notice, particularly my late-coming. When you missed the requisite bus at Coatbridge you had problems, as the bus timetable to Glenboig would bear unfavourable comparison with the rate of camel traffic on the silk route to Samarkand. You had to depend on Good Samaritans giving you a lift, amongst which were a baker's van, an AA patrol vehicle, a tractor, a coal lorry, a police van and on one occasion a hearse (empty, it has to be said). The journey was awkward but worthwhile. For it was in that village that my whole life blossomed, first when I met my prospective wife and second when I witnessed something very briefly one afternoon which was to change my life utterly. One warm, sultry afternoon, I spied something in the village which caused me to write a short story. I simply put it in a drawer, not knowing then what it had in store for me.

I spent almost two formative years there before receiving word in 1959 that I was to be transferred to Garrowhill School, where I had been a trainee, much to the chagrin of McFadzean, who knew that Hamilton, the headmaster there, had been using his powers of persuasion with the authorities to achieve that. I said my sad farewells, realising I was in for an entirely different experience. Garrowhill Primary was the Sandhurst of rote learning. Beautifully uniformed, neatly presented by parents, nurtured by conscientious teachers, all the pupils were products of a process that was like minting coins, with the bad ones thrown away as being of no use. Garrowhill had its reputation to live up to as a finishing school for young boys and girls of fortunate circumstances. At least for the vast majority of them. You were supposed to consider yourself privileged to be on the staff there. It had many of the characteristics of a private 'crammer' school within the public system. The whole *raison d'être* of the school was to prepare for, and make sure pupils passed, the 'quali' or to give it its *nouvelle cuisine* name, the 11 Plus exam. If you passed that you would go to the secondary schools of note. Hamilton Grammar was the ultimate glittering prize, then came Coatbridge High, and further down the pecking order but still immensely desirable, Uddingston Grammar.

And then there was the nearby Baillieston Junior Secondary. If you did not pass the 'quali' and your verbal reasoning tests were sub-standard, that's where they sent you. It was regarded by middle-class Garrowhill as something akin to a leper colony. How were they going to be able to talk to the neighbours over the privet hedges when Alex over the other side of their immaculate lawn was doing Latin at Hamilton Grammar, while their wee Sam was making a fruit bowl in a woodwork class in Baillieston? Such indignity. They would rather flit than suffer that. It is hard to credit such a thing nowadays, but I am talking about the Ice Age of primary education, when life-altering decisions were being made about kids before they had their first bout of acne. Some folk dipped into their pockets and forked out for a private education in one of the Glasgow schools, where the bank book was obviously more important than the IQ. Private education in those circumstances only pumped up the ego of parents and did virtually nothing for some poor souls whose academic flaws, within the admittedly unfair state system of early examination, were hardly likely to qualify them as fellows of Magdalene College, Oxford. So naturally the pressure on many of those pupils was immense, actually obscene when I think back to it.

So the contrast with Glenboig could not have been more extreme. I was now teaching future readers of the *Daily Mail*, many of whom would eventually grow up to be beguiled into voting New Labour. I was in an elitist school whose pupils in the early sixties would be some of the first in the land to enjoy a package holiday to Spain, or a Volvo or a patio or central heating or knew then what *tiramisu* meant. This was a whole new culture to be dealt with and it did not require too much effort. The children were so keen to get on, the internal system so competitive, the school blueprint for 400 or so kids laid out so well, in their progression through the age ranges, that you could have gone on to auto-pilot for most of the time. In that particular sense, they were brilliantly taught by superb teachers.

I became lazy. That reformist zeal I began to feel in Glenboig began to seep away as I indulged in the luxury of dealing with children most of whom found no real challenge in the work they did, and who for that reason were intelligent under-achievers. They simply were not asked to do more than the orthodox norm. Spell correctly and add up sums properly. There was no place for those who seemed, well, different.

A wee boy, immaculately turned out, his hair combed so neatly you felt it was a work of art, sat in my class producing indifferent work, hardly opening his mouth, and from what I had heard, some other teachers frowned on him as one of the 'no-hopers'. Just before the Christmas holidays one year I asked the class if they would like to contribute to a class concert. Up came this lad, humping a music-case almost bigger than himself. Out he came for his turn, slapped a guitar on his knee, as he sat on a stool, and proceeded to enthral us with a rendition of Cliff Richard's 'Living Doll'. It was so professional it was diffi-cult to take in at first. Here was this little mouse of a boy revealing a mature talent well beyond his years. In one swift moment his status soared. Think of Susan Boyle, of *Britain's Got Talent* fame, and the thrill of the unexpected emerging from an unlikely source and you might understand how we felt. They did have a school concert every year, but the songs and lyrics were written by a teacher and the pupils efficiently, but mechan-ically, went through their paces. This was original talent. So I went to fetch the headmaster to listen to him, as the kid did a few encores. This po-faced man, who had replaced Hamilton by that time, simply listened for a moment then said, 'Pleasant' and turned on his heel and walked out, as if I was wasting his time. In a nutshell the talent that the kid was displaying was an irrelevance in the grand scheme of how to pass the quali. It didn't seem to matter. You ought not to spend time in unearthing talent. Get them to parse a sentence properly, that's the thing.

The kid plucking the strings that day became one of Scotland's successful cabaret acts, as a singer and impersonator. He was Alan Stewart. The last time I heard him he was imitating Pavarotti, would you believe, hitting the high notes in front of a rapturous audience. He didn't need to parse sentences properly to get to that level. He certainly did not get any real encouragement in that school. I still have in my possession a recording of his first public appearance in that class. In that admittedly effective, orthodox, but in many ways stultifying school, his song resonates like the song of liberty.

But, they damn well knew how to get the kids to pass their tests. It was a case of teaching them the right kinds of tricks. The senior teacher, Miss Reid, a smart, able, no-nonsense teacher, used to coach her class on how to cope with the IQ tests. This was something completely against the purpose of those tests, which were supposed to evaluate the raw material of intelligence, and a practice which was quite illicit. This was supposed to give them a head start on others in the county and was palpably unfair. But the teachers were caught up in the frantic business of getting good marks to maintain the school's reputation, forcing them into practices which were essentially unethical. All slaves to the quali.

The various types in the staffroom had one thing in common. They all disliked inspectors and any Labour politician. Hamilton, the headmaster, would come into the staffroom to address them as though he had to vent spleen from time to time. His typical rant was, 'You know these bloody miners want to rule us all. They want to bring us all down to their level, the common five-eight. All this nonsense about abolishing the quali. What do you put in its place, for God's sake? If you cannae select what can you do? These numpties can't even use the Queen's English properly and yet they're trying to tell us what we're supposed to do with our kids. They'd love to walk in here and tell me what to do. Over my dead body.'

I thought there could only be one affirmative action for me to take, and that was to move from sympathiser and supporter, to actually join the Labour Party. The local Labour MP Jimmy Hamilton, his namesake, would occasionally visit the school, and whilst they were politically poles apart, I think Jimmy treated Hamilton the head, as I did, as a man whose time was running out anyway, and not to be taken too seriously. But then Jimmy had a knack of being able to swing between social extremes, as he did when, later in his career, he paid his weekly visits to the Queen as the representative of the Westminster backbenchers, and in a few years' time, in 1967, was almost wholly responsible for my being given permission to leave my headmaster's post to travel to Lisbon, to assist in commentary on that famous occasion of the European Cup Final.

Then came what I thought was a turning point for me. That new headmaster had come in. I thought he would change things. In fact he was a quali diehard. Separating the sheep from the goats at the age of eleven was what he was born for. Jimmy Hamilton came into the staffrom for a cup of tea one day. It was crowded. They treated him with a distant reserve. There was a babble of conversation, as if, after acknowledging his presence they wanted to drown him out. But he turned to me at one point and said to me quite innocently, 'Glad to hear you've joined the party. Labour could do with more in Garrowhill.' Silence fell on that staffrom, like they had heard the miners were now clamouring at the gates. Perhaps it was discontent with my lot at the time but I went home that same night and remembered the short story I had written about a Sikh brush-salesman trying to sell his products, humping a large suitcase around the houses in Glenboig, and his relationship with a local boy who helped him make his only sale. I took it out of the drawer, tidied it up, and in the morning posted it away to the BBC.

6

THUMPING THE TUB

'Comrades!' I intoned, one evening shortly afterwards, with the kind of forced sincerity of someone who simply felt uncomfortable using that form of traditional salutation. I was in the mood for a bit of rabble-rousing that would paint the renowned Garrowhill School in less favourable colours, and pour damnation on selection at the age of eleven. The word 'Comrades' was, at the very least, to signify traditional togetherness in front of the weekly meeting of the Budhill and Springboig Labour party, an area only a stone's throw from Shettleston, but part of the Lanarkshire Bothwell parliamentary constituency. We were not much of a crowd, for the average evening attendance of the faithful there was hardly ever more than about eight. A really exciting event, like discussing what we should do for a Christmas Party, would edge us into double figures, just. That of course did not negate the need to be passionate, indignant, and angry, and fulminate against those who we thought had heaped up iniquities against us, the oppressed upholders of social justice. However, the era of Shettlestonian evangelical oratory was well behind us now. Crowds encourage real orators, and crowds we certainly did not have. The uplifting, soaring voices of the past which would raise an assembly to its feet seemed to have disappeared from political life. Prattle and sound bites seemed to be taking over. Nevertheless, that night I took a deep breath and called on the tradition of my boyhood political mentors, and ranted on about the deeply unjust selection system of education, trying to raise my voice at the pertinent climaxes, which in the Co-op Halls in the past used to have them standing on their feet cheering.

A JCB wouldn't have lifted these worthies from their backsides. They were the stuff that political parties are made of, though, the evergreens of the garden of political righteousness. They were largely ancient. We had a Welshman, Bert Griffiths, who said that, as a boy, he had known Nye Bevan, the founder of the NHS, and so was treated like he had touched the Holy Grail. Only one other person commanded as much respect, the local librarian, Annie Murdoch. In her fifties, she fashioned her pure-white hair in a pageboy style, the effect of which was to accurately convey the impression of smartness, and of a previously attractive youthfulness that she was obviously reluctant to leave behind. Smart she certainly was. She ran us all, as secretary. You needed to convince her first of all, if you wanted anything done. That night I saw her interest waning in what I was saying, with a 'Heard-it-all-before' look on her face. So I launched into the incident which really brought about my separation from one of Lanarkshire's model primary schools.

I am teaching one morning when I hear a gentle knock on the classroom door. When I open it a woman is standing there. She is blonde, dressed to kill, high heels, short cream coat, with a pert little black hat perched on the side of her head. Her smile to greet me is wider than the Mississippi delta. Perhaps her intoxicating presence is enhanced by the fact that I have just been embroiled in the drudgery of teaching the value of the adverbial clause. She is, nonetheless, a stunner. She tells me she is concerned about the progress of her ten-year-old boy and she wonders if I would be interested in calling in at the house for personal tuition for him, as her husband travels the world and will be away for a couple of months in Australia. As her high heels scuffle on the tiles of the corridor it does flash through my mind that this might be a 'come-on'. Perhaps I had been reading, at that time, too much of John Updike and his chronicles of sexual shenanigans in New England, but an illicit thought does dwell in the mind for a minute or two, until I become aware that her mood is changing. The charm offensive lasts but a minute or two until, suddenly, she is transformed into a distraught, nervy, twitching individual spilling out her fears. She is crumbling before my eyes. Anguish surfaces like a sudden adverse skin reaction to Max Factor.

It is all about her son, who is not performing at school as she would have liked and she is concerned that he might fail the quali with all its social implications, like flitting to the Outer Hebrides to avoid the stigma. It is true her son is not one of the brightest, and equally true that his chances of performing well are decidedly slim. At the age of eleven nobody is a failure, I try to tell her. She is not convinced. I point out that the answer is not initially an educational one, but a political one. I tell her that if Harold Wilson wins the next election (as he was to in 1964) then he would implement changes to end selection and introduce comprehensive schools. I add that Garrowhill School did not challenge the status quo, but pandered to it. So go see your MP. Complain! That's the route to take, I advise her. It is not what she expected. She shakes my hand with long purple-hued nails which could have scratched a hippo's back into ecstasy, and I watch her clip-clopping attractively down the corridor away from me, thinking that she is returning to her tranquillisers, and I am, once again, alarmed about how this iniquitous system of selection affects people. About twenty minutes later I discover that her next port of call has, in fact, been the headmaster's office. And she has blabbed about my comments on the school.

This Darth Vader of the 3Rs strides in with a bark: 'I want to see you.' When the door is closed behind us he doesn't wait for his office but starts to bellow in the corridor. 'What right have you to bring up politics in this school?' he shouts and I know that kids and teachers along that stretch of the school will hear every word. 'Who do you think you are, criticising what this school does? How dare you speak out of turn to a parent as if you think we are letting their children down? And telling this woman to complain to her MP. That is outrageous!' Now those who thrilled to the spectacle of Maggie Smith, shouting her defiance at her headmistress to defend her political views in *The Prime of Miss Jean Brodie*, would have been disappointed with this confrontation. I didn't possess Jean Brodie's genteel muscularity.

Then and there I realise that a screaming match in a school corridor is a waste of time. It would be about power, not about educational theory. He would win hands down. In any case the public rebuke will seep throughout the school. I imagine some of the older kids will be telling tales out of school, of the day I was dressed down, and that the incident will be luridly magnified throughout the locality where we have to live, shop and eat. The immediate effect is to place me in some kind of unofficial quarantine with the rest of the staff. They suddenly become decorously formal and polite, and pointedly avoid the kind of small-talk which makes the intervals in the staffroom oddly bearable. The quaint spinster infant-mistress, who dresses as if she came from the flapper era and could have claimed she danced with a man who danced with a girl who danced with the Prince of Wales, and who plasters her face with more make-up than Norma Desmond in *Sunset Boulevard* and wears large pendant earrings an Olympic gymnast could have swung on, and who, as a wonderful gossiper, normally shares with me private, intimate views on the rest of the staff, pointedly becomes more distant. I have to guess that they will not wish to be seen being so chummy with someone who the head-master thinks is a traitor. Time to get out. Although that is never going to be easy.

When I finished my speech to our party that night, with that pointed anecdote about the human misery caused by this bloody test, I noted I had not reduced the Budhill and Springboig Labour party to tears. The polite applause was really what I had expected, nothing much more, since the only time I had seen them animated was when Labour central office sent out a speaker to talk about foreign policy. He was a QC from Edinburgh, wearing the black jacket and pinstripe trousers of his trade, as if straight from court, and probably persuaded to come in the belief that if you could interest the Budhill and Springboig party in the repressive Gaullist policies in Algeria then becoming Solicitor-General was a dawdle. He came in with the aroma of a few malt whiskies around his person, and before he spoke asked for the toilet. When he returned we noticed he had not done up his flies and a fragment of white shirt could be seen peeking through his lower regions, like a small flag of surrender from a Flanders trench. We were privileged to be given a peek at something a judge in the high court in Edinburgh would not have observed; although in retrospect, having learned more about the private lives of legal dignitaries since, you couldn't take even that for granted. But our group then went into quiv-ering titters, which went on for some time, as they barely looked at the man's face and seemed to think that something dramatic was about to occur down there.

I could only take it that the alcohol had made him immune to what was going on. Then one lady, who could stand it no longer, broke ranks, snorted as her repressed giggles became sounds of strangulation, rose and made for the exit, outside of which we heard screams of unrestrained laughter. The poor fellow, denouncing the French colonists for all his worth and ending up with a rallying call for them to be driven into the Mediterranean, did not realise he was the first speaker ever to make anybody in the Budhill and Springboig party rise to their feet in some sort of acclamation. So polite applause was what I expected, and got. What I didn't, was Annie Murdoch's response.

'You should put your money where your mouth is,' she said challengingly. 'If you feel that way about schools why don't we put you up for election to the council?' It was Annie's way of not asking, but really telling me that that was what was going to happen. But the level she had in mind was not one that would give much opportunity for dialectical debating; it was the lowest species of political life, district councillor. At the time I was not aware of the duties of the district councillor as opposed to county councillor, except that I thought that they made sure that signs were put up in public parks warning of the penalties for littering. Keir Hardie had said nothing about dog shit in parks, but in true socialist concern for the environment Annie pointed out, wistfully, 'You have to start somewhere.'

She was a realist. That also covered her feelings about winning such an election, since although the Bothwell constituency was a safe Labour seat, that part of it in our area always returned either Independent or Conservative councillors. As starts go in political life, this would be like taking on Everest wearing sandals. Still, with trouble-at-mill, as it were, I felt like striking out and trying something different, anything. A few weeks later it was officially announced that I was to be a candidate for district councillor, although the neighbourhood took as much heed of that news as they would of being informed of a rickshaw collision in Shanghai. Still, if you are going to do it, it's as well you think you are an Abe Lincoln emerging from the log cabin to change the course of epochal events.

They stuck my election poster up on a tree beside a burn, in a small park in the middle of Springboig. On the first night somebody drew spectacles on my face. On the second night a moustache and a goatee beard appeared. By the third night I was beginning to look like a disguised KGB defector. The fourth night the tree was still there, the poster was not. I wondered if it would be a metaphor for a brief political career. Teaching during the day and handing out leaflets in the evening became the steady diet over the next couple of weeks, and as the pace of rushing around doors increased, so I became aware of hostility towards political parties and individuals of a kind I had never thought possible. At school it was different. They had become aware of what I was doing and whilst the head there ignored that fact altogether and had given me up as a lost cause anyway, the others were far too polite and genteel to be nasty. But they were not slow to be thrashing poor Harold Wilson whenever I was there, for his new-fangled ideas that would lead the country to disaster, as they saw it. And that hoary old, and completely unfounded, notion kept surfacing, in its different forms, that politics and education should be kept separate. Retaining the status quo, which they saw as vital, was itself an undiluted political act.

Of course I had to keep my feet on the ground in this elec-tioneering business. I discovered that the man I was running against was none other than John Deans, who owned Deans's pub in Shettleston, in which many of my relatives had spent many happy hours during my childhood. He was, it could be said, a popular man. Somehow I had to convince some I was not a prohibitionist. Still, out canvassing, on what might loosely have been described as the hustings, it wasn't so much what you were standing for but whom you represented that aroused feelings. Fooled by the notion that all I would have to worry about was apathy, I was caught unawares by a figure one night who stopped me in my casual tracks, a former school friend who expressed his astonishment that I should be associated with 'them'. I knew what he meant by 'them'. He didn't mean just the Labour Party. He meant what he saw as a Catholic Mafia controlling the constituency. The pulpit ruled. Not this bloody nonsense again, I thought.

I had simply ignored such a factor, one way or the other. What I did know was that the people I dealt with were genuine upholders of the need to defend the aspirations of the working class whatever their religious beliefs. But not just then, in the early sixties, but through the succeeding years, I worked with and lived amongst people who expressed their astonishment that I not only voted Labour but would argue with myself in an empty room on their behalf. I wasn't exactly pinned with the champagne socialist tag, but it just happened that as we became more prosperous we were always politically in the minority in our sphere of acquaintances and friends, which thankfully turned some dinner parties of vacuous banter into steaming verbal barneys, with me fighting my way to the exits, thinking I had said enough to be banned from ever again being invited on to the golf course to make up a foursome.

Add the conceptions, or the misconceptions, of religion to the equation and you get a heady mix likely to unhinge even the most mundane approach to relationships. A good long-standing friend of my father who seemed a sensible enough man, with reasonable views on life, became neanderthal when the word Catholic was ever mentioned in his presence. They were succinctly disposed of again as 'them'. He put it to me graphically and memorably one day, after hearing of my modest step into politics. He knew, as well, I was working hard to have Catholic

66

Jimmy Hamilton re-elected to the Bothwell constituency for Labour, which wasn't all that much of a struggle overall, for one of my granny's wally dugs could have won the seat for the party. However, I was turning in the hours for him during a general election period, and this gnarled individual addressing me about religious influence was, incredibly, a Labour man who disliked the Tories. But he put it to me this way, with brutal frankness, telling of what he had experienced at one general election.

'Honest. I walked up to the school with every intention of voting Labour. But I didn't. I walked out without voting. I got to the table where you sign in and the girl there was wearing a big crucifix round her neck and the sight of that put me off. I couldn't give Hamilton my vote. You know who dictates to them what to do! I just couldn't do it. I just walked out again. I never voted.'

I think if you are aware of the depth of sectarian feeling in your own community you are never as shocked about it as some outsiders to our culture are. You exist, in a curious way, unshocked, desensitised, complacent, until you feel, as I did then, that you are being shaken out of a deep sleep. Of course this was appalling, and I never did view this man again in the same light. But, at the same time, in the context that my colleague Annie Murdoch suggested, I knew that the Catholic influence inside the Labour Party in my part of the world was significant. This was not so surprising to anybody who paid attention to the real world. For, after all, the socialist movement in the East End could not have succeeded in building up such momentum throughout the last century had not Catholics converted their rightful struggle against intolerance into a defined political shape and in the main adopted the ILP and the Labour party eventually as the main conduit. Some, of course, had even left religion altogether and joined the Communist party. A man for whose election, in future years, I worked hard, the former cabinet minister John Reid, now chairman of Celtic Football Club, was a prime example of someone who trod that particular extreme left-wing path, only to return to the fold eventually.

So from my early days in the Bothwell constituency I was aware that Jimmy Hamilton, who could not have been more sincere in his work for everyone in the community, nevertheless knew he could bank on the Catholic vote as the core of his continued electoral successes. On the one hand, that seemed perfectly obvious and logical. On the other hand, to the suspicious, not to say perverted mind, it meant rule by biretta. The feeling hasn't gone away. Of course it was far from a straight sectarian divide in the manner of voting, but my experience was that many Protestants would have voted Labour if Hamilton had not been a Catholic, and that it was widely known that he enjoyed most Saturday afternoons basking in Celtic's success as a guest in the Parkhead directors' box.

Even in the immediate aftermath of a social catastrophe, the sensitivity of political–religious relationships surfaced. On the evening of the Ibrox disaster in 1971 I interviewed the then Lord Provost of Glasgow Donald Liddle. In an aside afterwards in the BBC offices, Eric Hamilton, the permanent secretary of Provosts at the City Chambers whispered to me, 'There goes the last Protestant Provost of the city of Glasgow.' I have no idea whether that could now be confirmed or not, nor do I care. But what it again revealed was the suspicion that a party had been taken over by one section of the community, and with it came an unhealthy cynicism. On the other side, the late Jock Stein once described to me a future Lord Provost of Glasgow, of the ruling Labour Party, as one of the biggest bigots in the city. Stein had a habit of abruptly speaking about somebody, as if he was fully aware he would be shocking you with a revelation, even about those who supported his club.

This factor resurfacing did shake me, though. I bruised easily in those days. To be honest, I was never able to take public criticism all that well, even in later years, but at that time as a young idealist, convinced I was as pure as the driven snow, I found it hard to come to terms with that distaste which was aroused by simply wearing a red rosette. I didn't need to knock on doors. I could have shoved the leaflets through letterboxes and run. But I wanted to press flesh. How could you be a politician without pressing flesh? I did try to communicate. I knew that trying to explain my support for comprehensive schools would be as relevant as discussing the current state of astrophysics in the world. The fact that I can recall the banter on the doorsteps during the election period so vividly is purely because it so took me aback, me who wanted to change the world while others obviously didn't.

It is a semi-detached in Springboig. I knock the door.

'Who's that?' says a wheezy female voice eventually from behind an unopened door. 'Labour Party. Archie Macpherson. I'm your Labour candidate for the district council.'

'You don't have a fag on you, do you?' the voice asked.

'Sorry, I haven't.'

'See the wumman next door – are you gonnae go and ask her for a fag for me? Tell her it's for Agnes.'

So I go next door, I'm a candidate after all.

'Her,' says the woman next door on her doorstep thrusting an ample bosom in my direction. 'That old bitch? You know, she threw her tea dregs on to our dug a couple a days ago. She said it was an accident. I know better. She claims the dug's been peeing on her grass at the back. That's a lie. You tell her frae me that she can get stuffed. She shouldnae be smokin' at her age any roads.'

I move back to the first door.

'She hasn't got a cigarette on her at the moment.'

'Eh? She smokes like a lum. She's havin' you on. Away and tell her that my knee is playin' up and I cannae get out to the shops. And if she's no' gaunae, if a gied you the money could you nip down tae the chip shop at Budhill Square and get ten Capstan for me?'

It is time to vanish. They did sound as if they could be Labour voters but their territorial dispute over where a dog should pee is beyond my remit. Then a man cutting his grass asks me to help him heave a bag of weeds up a path to a bin at the back, and as I retreat I see him put my leaflet into the same bin without so much as a glance.

But silence mostly, as you put the leaflet in their hands. Not a word, not even a smile. Sometimes the bum steer.

'Jesus, the chip-pan's on fire I think. Sorry son!' says another aggressive woman before rushing back inside and closing the door. By that time I was so sensitive to rejection I began to wonder if somebody would actually go to the extent of inventing a chip-pan fire just to get rid of me.

Up and down the stairs of the supposedly much more friendly Labour-oriented tenements of Budhill I got this. Young boy comes to door. Adult voice from behind him. 'Who's at the door?' Boy shouts back. 'A man from the Labour Party with a leaflet.' Voice from within. 'Tell him tae stick it!'

If I couldn't command some respect in a Labour stronghold what chance would I have, I thought.

'Whit election?' an old man says honestly to me as he respectfully looks at the leaflet as if it was written in Sanskrit. He looks as if he had been around when Keir Hardie still trod the land.

'I'm sure you're a Labour supporter,' I venture bravely.

'Used to be!' he growls. Now that was a phrase I heard a lot. At first it didn't matter; then even in pursuit of a humble role in politics it did cause concern. What happened to the great '45 post-war revolution when it looked as if a new age was dawning for the masses, I used to think. Why the massive defections? Were Labour now born losers? In any case I was discovering political door-stepping was an intrusion into folk's private apathy.

I vowed to keep the chip-pan fire excuse as a way of rebuffing door-step Jehovah's Witnesses and Mormons. Then, after all the rebuffs, came the day of the count. Suddenly you don't want a count. A count could mean humiliation. Who talked me into this, I was thinking, as if I had had my arm twisted, which of course I hadn't. I left Annie to take care of the count as I, thankfully, was teaching. In the evening I walked from home to the Labour hall to learn the outcome. Annie was sitting there at the side of the small stage sipping tea. 'There's the result,' she said pointing to a scrap of paper beside her. By her body language I wouldn't have needed to look at the result, but I had to.

Mr J. B. Deans 1,232, Mr A. Macpherson 720.

It was a defeat Screaming Lord Sutch might have been satisfied with, and in its modest way, in both turnout and losing margin, it meant that my mother would not now require to shop at the local Co-op disguised as the bearded lady from the circus, to avoid what could have been acute embarrassment. I didn't like losing. In fact, I felt particularly pissed off with the electorate, however humble a station in political life I was seeking initially. There is little doubt that the experience confirmed me as a very bad loser indeed. In later life, though, I enjoyed the company of many prominent men who, like me, seemed pursued by the hounds of hell when things didn't go their way. One in particular. A giant of a man. Curiously, his name had cropped up only four weeks prior to the election in the context of a success of his, not a defeat. His name, Stein.

For one night, after having gathered our electioneering wits together and as we came out of the hall, in the dying light of evening, a bus came sweeping down the hill towards Budhill

Square. There was a lot of shouting and carousing coming from within and a man poked his head out of the window shouting for directions, as he said they were lost getting back on the road to the east. Could we point them in the right direction, since they were heading back to Dunfermline? Glasgow's East End maze of streets had defeated them. But they were ebullient. For they were supporters of Dunfermline Athletic who had just beaten Celtic 2–0, in the replayed Scottish Cup Final, as they were gleefully informing us from inside the bus. Tom Tait, a strong Celtic fan and a stalwart of the local party, took the pipe from his mouth and muttered, 'How could Stein do that to us?', referring to the Dunfermline manager whose career had been salvaged by Celtic, bringing him back from the almost mummified precincts of Welsh non-league football at Llanelli, before he left the club for his managerial post in Fife. 'Celtic fans will never forgive him,' he said with an obviously heavy heart. He was as wrong about that as I was in thinking that, in my parochial political world, from small acorns mighty trees inevitably grow.

7

PROMOTION

I waited for some reply from the BBC for that short story. Nothing came even weeks later. I prepared for the rejection slip. I had grown accustomed to them, after sending out a stream of short stories to different publications. As James Thurber once said, they could come back at you like ping-pong balls from the other side of the net. But what had encouraged me to try them out was one day opening the Glasgow *Evening Times*, on 12 March 1960, and discovering a short story I had written, in their early Saturday edition, staring me in the face. It was like watching your first-born. Nothing that ever happened to me in later years in public life could quite equal that moment. Acceptance. At that time I was using the pen-name Alan Marshall, largely because I did not want my Garrowhill School colleagues to know I was sort of moonlighting. It was stupid, but that's the way it was. Eventually I put the thought of a BBC reply out of my mind and concentrated on teaching and succumbing even more to my addiction to football.

In between trawling the country, watching games, I would find myself fascinated by the broadcasting voices of the day. As a kid I used to climb on a wall just outside Shettleston, in a more affluent area, and watch this immaculate lawn on which people were playing a strange game, where you knocked wooden balls through hoops. They laughed and clacked away with their long hammers, and occasionally someone would bring drinks, and another would whip off a dressing-robe and jump into a small round swimming pool they had. Almost straight out of *The Go-Between*, you would think, but even then I knew this was class. This was privilege. It would be nice to have a bit of this. They would shoo us off the wall, eventually, with a bounding hound of the Baskervilles leaping up at us.

I was sitting on that wall again, overlooking another scene of privilege, listening to the voices of the BBC commentators, from cricket to rugby to football, marvelling at their aristocratic status. How do you jump over the wall? How on earth could you leap into that parallel world? The more you thought about it, the more, perversely, it seemed to recede as a possibility. So we soaked up the journalism of the prominent writers, which opened the eyes of the public to the events and personalities of the day, much more so than the flickering images of embryonic black and white television. Sports writing was immune then from the pervasive influence of television's ubiquity. The writers chronicled events and personalities, with the self-confidence and flair of men who had not yet taken on board the possible influence the cathode-ray tube would have on their craft, and as it certainly would do eventually. They wrote as they saw it, unhindered by the necessity to cater for a public which eventually would see as much as they would, through television. We read, then discussed or argued and fell out and became enraged and went back to read them again. They were the indispensables.

The more you were reading during that period, the more you knew that any red-blooded Scotsman would think they could do it just as well; one of the outrageous presumptions that made us, even then, before the era of radio phone-ins, perhaps the most contentious, cantankerous footballing community of all. But it was all so distant. And if you are holding down a post amidst an educational ethos with which you feel more than slightly disenchanted, and among teachers hopping up and down in extreme discomfort on that afternoon of Friday 16 October 1964, as the results were coming from the general election, and my hero Harold Wilson was about to become Prime Minister, albeit with a wafer-thin four-seat majority, and they were greeting it in the school corridors like the Red Army had just occupied the Post Office in George Square, you feel rooted to the spot, unable to make a career change of any kind, with the increasing feeling of being merely the school's pet insurrectionist.

Then, although my feeling of alienation was not as bad, admittedly, as Papillon's sense of isolation, came the timely wave that pushed the boat out in the right direction to freedom. I was informed by the headmaster one day that the education authority was looking for someone to become temporary head teacher of a small school in the mining village of Calderbank. Would I be interested? Fighting the Vietcong all the way out to mid-Lanarkshire would not have deterred me. Thus it was that I walked into this staid, grey building a week later. Victorian children must have thought it was the last word in modernity but now, in 1964, it seemed utterly insulated from any progress. Until the kids came in. And until you saw the outstanding work which was being done by them, inspired by the departing headmaster, who had embraced new ideas so foreign to the school I had just left. It was a model of how to mitigate the sternness of the surroundings by mounting enterprising ideas and projects which opened the world to the kids, who could so easily have been enslaved by tradition.

Outside the school walls, the kids lived in a village not unlike the one I had left behind in Glenboig, with the same sectarian wall built, metaphorically, right down the main street. Thus it was that I experienced the first feeling of independence and power, however temporary it was going to be. Thus it was that my first major test of that power was as far removed from developing young minds as nude mud-wrestling is from the *corps de ballet* of the Bolshoi. For within a few days of settling in I was confronted by a woman with a man problem.

She was the school dinner lady. Dressed in her neat white uniform, she was a white-haired, neatly built, middle-aged spinster. She entered the office nervously and I could see right away that it was not concern about the quality of Brussels sprouts that had driven her in. She cut to the chase.

'I have a complaint to make about the janitor,' she said. ' I am at my wits' end.' Tears welled and I noticed the knotted handkerchief twisting in her hands. How often had I seen that in the cinema? Bette Davis at her best. 'You are the only person I can turn to and I hope you can help me. It's just that . . . It's difficult to say the words. But I have to. He . . . he exposes himself to me.'

'Exposes himself?' I asked. 'You mean . . . ?'

She nodded. And in case I was still fumbling around puzzled, and couldn't decode what she meant, she added, 'You know . . . he . . . well . . . has his trousers . . . well . . . open . . . down there. You know! He shows it.' I remember that last phrase well. We looked at each other for a silent moment or two as images, unquestionably, interplayed between us. They weren't pretty. It was clear her better days were behind her, and the man in question would have been quarantined in Skid Row. He would have made Blackadder's assistant, Baldrick, seem like George Clooney. This had apparently been going on for months, she went on to tell me. The janitor, on the other hand, had tried to impress himself on me as a man's man, with his admitted love of football, racing, greyhounds and booze, believing that being chronically unshaven and wearing his janitor's cap, to cover his white baldness, at a preposterously jaunty angle, as if he was Calderbank's resident boulevardier, suited the persona. As for her, I thought I detected a smugness when I expressed some sympathy. Was I truly believing her? I don't think I was initially. I have often wondered if this is some deep-rooted bias in the male culture which women have to face after making accusations of sexual harassment. I should have regarded her, I suppose, as a poor soul who needed protection, and yet despite myself, I was dubious about her. So much so that I sweated overnight about it before confronting the man. The next day I came prepared with a sensitively thought out exploratory request for his explanation, with words delicately chosen for a discreet approach that could not possibly cause initial offence. But when he sat down and smiled at me like a buddy in a pub, I found myself asking, 'Have you ever taken your cock out and shown it to the dinner lady?'

On the Richter scale his reaction was definitely on the level of the great San Francisco earthquake of 1906. All the lines of his much-lined face seemed to rupture upwards in protest, and a noise came from deep in his throat that rumbled, and then spat out a furious 'Whit?' What then followed was a long, bellowing and spluttering denial that sounded incoherently evasive. His line of defence was that this stripling of a woman was really a siren, luring the innocents on to the deadly rocks of her nearly anorexic body, by flaunting herself brazenly at him, but that, upstandingly moral as he was, he had resolutely resisted and that this accusation was her revenge, in the vein of hell hath no fury like a woman scorned. He itemised smiles, *doubles entendres* (he alleged she had said something about 'peeling-off', with a suggestive leer, when she was putting potatoes into the skinning machine once, which threw that vegetable into a new light as a conductor of sexual arousal), the short

skirts and high heels and swinging her legs at him when she
sat on a high stool in the kitchen, and so on. Forsooth, he
protesteth too much, I thought. I realised I was taking sides.
Gut instinct. I let that take over. Which it did, for a bit.

'Stay away from that woman,' I told him. 'I'm not going to
be here long. There will be a new man coming soon. But I have
given her my home telephone number and if she so much as
gives me one hint of anything improper you do again I'll have
you up before the beaks and you won't be able to hold your
head up in this village again.'

'Sir,' he said, addressing me for the first time with such
formality. 'You're making a big mistake. She's a bitch. She's
conned you. She's made this all up. I'll put my hand on the
Bible and swear that I did no such thing.' As soon as he said
that, I felt I was changing sides again. I recalled that smug smile
on her lips. I would rather have dealt with an irate parent
attacking the school with a machete than adjudicate on lust
amongst the pit-bings. Her word against his. I suppose I was
betraying that male tendency in these matters to assume that
there is no smoke without fire. Indecision not only set in but it
also began to anger me that I was being sidetracked by an issue
that was really distracting me from settling down as an apprentice headmaster.

He never spoke to me again after that and skulked around
the school doing his normal duties with his face mournful and
grim. She, still resplendent in her starched white uniform and
high heels, would give me beaming smiles, after I had told her
the matter was in hand and there would be no further occur-
rences of the venting of lust. Not that I was entirely sure about
that, but I tried to sound convincing, and she acted as if she
had just been selected belle of the ball, all fluttery and cooing
and grateful, and seemed almost on the verge of throwing her
arms around me for a hug, which might have lessened the case

for the prosecution, as even then I began to wonder. In fact, I said nothing to anybody else about this. Not because I felt it distasteful to repeat, but because, frankly, I felt embarrassed that I did not know how to proceed to a conclusion on the matter. Then, a couple of weeks later, with me luridly imagining, and fearing of hearing, that she had taken a cleaver and solved the problem herself by turning him into Lanarkshire's *castrato* janitor, came salvation. I was informed that I would be on the short leet for the headmastership of a small school in North Lanarkshire and would be interviewed the following week. The way I felt, I would have taken a job as tutor to the 150,000 gannets nesting on the Bass Rock. It was no longer a case of being fussy about where you might end up. This one I had to go after, even though I had little inkling of what was in store for me.

Now I was to play the political game. It wasn't an ecclesiastical court I was to address in the selection process, it was the Council. The game was this: first you had to lower your notion that councillors were driven by principles established along the shores of Galilee. You had to concede that they were subject to that other more worldly motivation of 'Scratch my back and I'll scratch yours', to put it euphemistically. Some, of course, through the years took the scratching to extremes and became guests of Her Majesty, as the record shows. But they did like to be approached – by phone, by pub encounter, by being bumped into 'accidentally'. They liked to be recognised. The problem is that I only knew, at that stage, one man on the education committee – Eamond from Garrowhill, and of no influence.

I certainly didn't want to bother my MP, Jimmy Hamilton, to use his influence, simply because he struck me as a man who wouldn't take kindly to such a naked approach. But touting for support went on to such an extent that some short leets were simply shams, with a job already earmarked for someone in particular. Hence the bizarre nature of the interview, held in the County Building in Hamilton, in front of a largely un-interested group of councillors who looked as if they had feasted on the fatted lamb at lunch and were slumped in their seats, like those dead bodies propped up around the ramparts of the desert fort in *Beau Geste*, to confuse besiegers into thinking they were indeed a force to be reckoned with.

Only the chairman spoke to me. Not one question was asked, not even by him. All he was doing was ascertaining that I wasn't an impostor. And there was I, primed to give the speech of a lifetime, involving every possible solution to our educa-tional dilemmas, excluding, of course, how to encourage male staff to keep their flies zipped up. I was in there for no more than a couple of minutes, sat outside for another minute or so, and was called back in for the chairman to say, 'I am pleased to say, Mr Macpherson, you are now the headmaster of Swinton School. The education department will be in touch. Congratulations.' In a time perhaps even shorter than it took to brush my teeth, I was now feeling as if I had been retooled for the rest of life, at the age of thirty-one.

I did know that the school I was to inherit was in close prox-imity to Easterhouse, which then had a reputation akin to that of Al Capone's southside Chicago, and had yet to benefit from the publicity surrounding singer Frankie Vaughan's efforts to help subdue the gangs which effectively dominated the area. I knew that Swinton still retained the geographical position of the weavers' village it had originally been, and although Glasgow was reaching outwards toward it, with Easterhouse only a few minutes' walk away, that surely would be an entirely different environment. I knew it was tiny by comparison with others, although I was so keen to get it that I hardly cared about the numbers of pupils there were. It would be a stepping stone,

I explained to others, without knowing to where exactly. So I returned to Calderbank School and tried hard to say farewell to the staff without making it too obvious that I was relieved to be escaping from the sexual intrigue that was taking place under their noses. On my last day there the janitor was nowhere to be seen, although I guessed he was in the pub. The lady in white brought me my lunch in the office, on a tray, with a packet of Wills's Whiffs lying beside the plate of rice pudding.

'Just a wee thank-you for helping out,' she said, pointing to the cigars which she knew I occasionally puffed. 'You have lifted a burden off my back. You don't know how relieved I am. He's not come near me since.'

I smoked her cigars uneasily, but smoked them nevertheless, even though I had failed to solve or bring any kind of closure to the problem. For what would happen when I left? I approached my headmastership of Swinton School, nervously, but imbued with the zeal of a determined innovator, and with the hope that the relationship of janitor and dinner lady in my new school would be based on mutual celibacy.

8

IN CHARGE

I rang the school bell for the first time at Swinton School on Monday, 22 March 1965. It was not an electric bell, but one which worked on the lever principle. You pulled one end to allow the hammer to clang against the metal. The sound, though, coming from a little alcove just outside the small headmaster's office, was dull and lacked reverberation. I wondered if anybody could actually hear it even just outside the door. I clanged it four times, then waited. The natural response to the electric bells in the other schools was one of raised kids' voices, laughter, screams, running feet and then a babble of conversation. Of that I was hearing none. I clanged again, harder. Nothing much happened. It was then that the janitor appeared, a big hulking man with a mop of white hair and the ruddy complexion of high blood pressure, or the tanking he gave his liver.

'Mr Macpherson,' he said. 'You only need to ring it twice. They hear it OK.'

I could hear very little response, though.

'Why is this bell not electric?' I asked.

He shrugged. I was to get to know that shrug well in the next few years.

Then, at last, came the slight slapping of footsteps and I walked out to the cloakroom and saw the first kids. Perhaps it was the paucity of numbers, but they all seemed so correct and docile. Perhaps they had also been warned about my coming, because I knew they were staring at me, and then, when I would catch their look, they would quickly bow their heads and pretend I wasn't there. The school roll then was approximately ninety, with three class teachers, in a school that had originally been built for three times that number. But Swinton, as a village, was cut off by the main Glasgow–Edinburgh road, from the populous area of Baillieston, whose primary schools were bulging at the seams, only a mile or so away from what is now known, by burdened travellers, as the Maryville Interchange, Lanarkshire's Spaghetti Junction.

So, even before Maryville loomed, the Glasgow–Edinburgh route was an effective barrier between the Swinton area and Baillieston. In the accepted demarcation areas of education, when the village population got older and diminished, with no new house-building taking place and fewer young families moving in, the roll of the local school had been decimated. The intake of kids largely disappeared. There was no way they were going to send young ones to travel over that main artery to Swinton. This meant there were three classrooms lying completely empty. These empty rooms brought me face to face with the same virus that had affected me in virtually every professional situation, and which I thought, by coming to what was a tiny outpost on Lanarkshire's educational map, I would elude: sectarianism. For only some weeks after I arrived, being a new headmaster, I was visited by a group of local councillors and a motley collection of those outside the council who were on the education committee, to see what I had in mind for any changes or improvements. Amongst them was the local Roman Catholic priest. What caught his eye were the empty classrooms. He quizzed me about them and asked me about the viability of keeping a small school operating in such a situation. In his conversation with me he pointed out the crowded conditions of the school to which he was chaplain. I just listened and said nothing. But the conversation was overheard by somebody or other in the visiting party, and putting a nefarious two and two together, the word got out that the Catholics were contemplating a takeover. Parents came knocking at my door concerned that they were going to lose their school. Whatever assurances I tried to give failed to convince. About a couple of weeks after that, I received a visit from a man who did not beat about the bush.

'I'm in the ludge,' he said. 'If you need any support to prevent this school falling into the hands of the Church of Rome, then you will get backing from us.' I had noticed that that phrase, 'the Church of Rome', was sometimes solemnly used by those militantly against the institution, to convey some sort of gravity, and that they had some deeply convinced theological position from which to denounce. It was their preferred mode of reference, when they attempted to dignify their position. At least it was preferable to their other mode of reference, in other circumstances, 'Fenian bastards' or 'Papes'. He was indeed from the local Orange community, and he was in little doubt that some dastardly scheme was afoot which would end decades of Protestant schooling in the village. I assured him that no such move was being made, and that the story had been greatly exaggerated. I didn't exactly endear myself to him, though, by pointing out that I would like to see a mixed school where kids of any religion could attend, without clerical interference of any sort. He didn't quite get that point, given that suggesting such a thing in Scotland in the mid-sixties was like advocating the benefits of leprosy. Of course this blew over, and no such move took place, but it was a warning to me that I was rarely going to escape the clutches of sectarian strife.

When you don't have enough staff even to play a hand of bridge, your thinking is shaped by how you are going to deploy any strategy, with only three teachers to spread over the wide range of ages from five to eleven. Tricky. But small schools, particularly in rural areas, had triumphed over such apparent adversity through the centuries of Scottish education, and guided many a lad o' pairts to go on to great accomplishments, in many walks of life. So there was no reason for anybody to come to Swinton and feel inferior, although I wasn't kidding myself that it would be easy to get replacement teachers for the two I had, if they were ever to leave. Smaller schools with such a range of ages in a classroom are really for the very dedicated teacher. And there was another factor. Teachers were so scarce, at that time, that some headmasters patrolled the streets, with the vigour of a press-gang, looking for anybody with even the minimum qualification. It was that bad. My wife, at one stage, had to come in and teach the infants for a period, accompanied by our own two kids.

And although anybody visiting the school would have felt as if they had come to an isolated outpost, with its open corridors and stretches of lawn, both outside and in the middle of the school, we were also aware of the invasive presence of Easterhouse, just over the hill. Indeed, in my first couple of years there, we were broken into so often that we felt that our school was being used in an apprentice scheme for those who would go on to higher targets, like banks. On the other hand, I had got lucky.

In that very year, 1965, the Scottish Office produced a revolutionary document on primary education which was later to be known as the Primary Memorandum. It became my bible. There it was, laid out for all to see: the old ways had to go. Effectively, no longer would it be sufficient to tutor children towards the passing of exams, but methods had to be deployed which would allow children to progress at their own pace in classes of mixed ability. It could have been written for the type of school I was now in. The other two teachers were suspicious of this, at first, since they had come through their training college with little appreciation of what changes in the curriculum lay in store for them. But I made it clear that there would be no diverging from what I had in mind. It wasn't as declamatory or dramatic as Obama's 'Yes We Can!', but they were left under no illusions. I was going to do it my way, and my way was to be different from anything they had experienced before.

The dreaded quali was still in existence, but in the same year, 1965, Anthony Crosland, the Labour Education Secretary, a public school product himself but a fervent supporter of change in the state system, laid down the grounds for the wholesale introduction of comprehensive education which would effectively abolish selection throughout the land at the age of eleven. It was one thing to be heartened, politically, about that. It was another thing to implement the changes in a practical and realistic way. I had abhorred some of the 3R's rote learning of schools I had been at, which I think was so narrowly focused that it failed to unlock the depths of talent that existed among the kids. So, to break the ice, as it were, I decided to institute regular meetings with parents to try to explain to them what all this meant, and what I was about with my new methods.

So, at Swinton, parents would troop in of an evening, looking awkward and bemused by this experience. And, probably, after my very first lecture on progress and the introduction of new methods, were just as puzzled. Parents, at root, are conservative. They need to be assured that their offspring will go through the primary system and get to the right school, and as the old system of selection was still in place they certainly were not wanting their kids messed around by some fanciful ideas. I thought it prudent to assure them that the Scottish Education

Department supported my ideas. But I could tell they were far from convinced. The heating had failed in the school on that particular night and they were wrapped up in coats. I should have known that creature comfort can aid innovation and probably ought to have cancelled that first meeting. So there was undoubted scepticism as to what I had in mind, but no outright objections.

One day, some two years after I had arrived, one of the wee boys who had been sent out to count the traffic passing the school in order to make a graph for a class exercise, came back and told me that he had seen a strange man walking around the school. I went outside to the corridor and saw a man looking into the infants' room, stroking his chin in a rather contemplative manner. He was dapperly dressed in an elegant pin-striped suit, which was not the customary mid-afternoon mode of dress for any of the locals. Now, in these pre-Dunblane-tragedy days, Dracula could have entered the school without prior permission. So there was no sense of alarm, just curiosity. This moustachioed gentleman came ambling towards me, held out his hand, uttered his name and then said, 'I'm an inspector.' The sense of dread which that title had elicited from other teachers during my time in Garrowhill for a fleeting moment seemed to possess me, when he suddenly added something to that pronouncement, with a smile, which, although it didn't relax me, put him in the same bracket as others, from kids to parents, to friends, to bores, to strangers in the street, which placed him more humanly and simply as a mere member of the community of the television-viewing public. He said, 'You look rather different in real life.'

For something significant had changed. On one of my last days at Garrowhill School, a year previously, the BBC had responded to my short story. In came a letter accepting my effort about a small boy trying to help a Sikh brush salesman sell a brush to indifferent villagers. I was invited to Queen Margaret Drive, in the West End of Glasgow, by James Crampsey, the uncle of the late Bob Crampsey, to discuss the story. He was exactly as I imagined a BBC producer would be. A middle-aged man, slightly greying at the temples, of dignified bearing and a velvety baritone voice, all of which made him seem so venerable and properly Reithian. He liked what I had written and told me he would hire the actor Michael Elder to read the story for me. When eventually it was broadcast I felt that the rather plummy tones of the speaker made it sound stilted and artificial, and definitely not North Lanarkshire. Just after that I had a short script accepted for Radio Scotland's breakfast programme, about a school nativity play I had organised which went awry, and ended up with the Virgin Mary and one of the Wise Men departing from the Gospel message, and producing a flow of vitriol about each other which was more Quentin Tarantino than New Testament. The producer John Gray, with whom I was to build up a very productive relationship in future years, asked me to read it myself, which I duly did. I can remember facing the microphone with two predominant emotions. There was the fear of the unknown – stage fright you might have called it. But there was another element. In that stark studio, with the mechanics of broadcasting, the microphone looking gloomily at me from the middle of the table, like some eyeless creature from another planet, the red and green lights beside it blinking alternately on and off, the faces of engineers and producers staring at me through a glass panel – all of that suddenly induced a sensation of being endowed with great power: the power simply to put your voice to this appliance in front of you, and you could be heard throughout the land. Beautifully, seductively simple. Just as after the first tanglings with sex, I thought that having a lot more of this would be no bad thing. So, when I submitted my next short

story, I asked if I could read it myself. Crampsey unaggres-
sively disagreed, and suggested he could get an actor to do it
and said, frankly, that such a person might do it greater service.
I persisted, he relented and I read my story throughout the UK
in the Morning Story series.

After that, with scant reason for thinking so, I felt I had my
foot in the BBC door, and that there was a compelling need
to further burrow my way in there. Having grown up with
short stories from the *New Yorker* in particular filling my head
with fantasies of living in an apartment in the Upper East Side
of New York, lobbing the odd gem of a story to that great
magazine, in between sipping dry martinis in the Oyster Bar
at Grand Central Station, as my short-story idol Irwin Shaw
used to do, I was now gripped by this hopelessly ill-founded,
but nevertheless burgeoning ambition to write for a living.
But a re-routing took place. I received a telephone call from
someone in their sports department who, learning of my
interest in football, and having heard my broadcast, asked if
I would like to go to a game and come back and report on it,
as an audition for regular reporting. I did and they liked it.
And that was that. In the space of a few weeks, from reading
a short story on what was known then as the BBC Light
Programme, I was on weekly radio, and then television,
reporting football matches. In between I was still a headmaster. This was the parallel existence, at last, and crossing
from one to the other was like taking part in a quick-change
act in old-fashioned vaudeville. I delivered the reports in front
of camera, bundled up with tension, but also with a sense of
disbelief permeating the whole experience. So when a small
boy came up to me in the school one Monday morning and,
without a trace of nervousness, delivered to me a critique of
my Saturday television report, I knew life would never be the
same again.

'Sir, my dad said you made a mistake on Saturday,' this little lad said, uncoweringly, to me. 'He told me to tell you that you said Thistle had won two games in a row. It was three.'

He held up three fingers, in case I hadn't quite got the point. You can probably see what is happening. Here is the headie being put in his place by an urchin whose reproof is exposing a chink in the armour. The loftiness of authority was being diluted because I was, in a way, public property now. Would any other teacher in the land, any headmaster, any professor at any establishment throughout the educational regime have a child holding up three, and blessedly not two, fingers at him, as an admonishment? A parent visiting the school one day, to discuss the work that was going on, said to me, 'Bill spotted a grammatical mistake you made on Saturday.'

'Really?' I replied with feigned indifference.

'Yes, you said the "the team ARE winning" instead of "the team IS winning". He spotted that.'

Whatever my honourable intentions, and hard work, in establishing liberal child-centred education, were my fleeting appearances on television actually encouraging a school of parental smart-arses? Certainly in these early days of exposure I was very conscious of the fact that although I might accurately sum up an Old Firm match with verve and passion, I might have hell to pay on Monday morning in Swinton if I were to split an infinitive. Bright-eyed and bushy-tailed they would pile in of a Monday morning, bristling with good intentions, these hard-working kids, but I found myself thinking, which of the little buggers is harbouring some comment or other from their parents this morning? Here were the tables being turned, where the minutiae of correction, normally through the red pen of the master, were now also in the eager hands of those whose futures I was hopefully moulding into respectable shape. I tried hard to give the impression that the man they had seen on Saturday was quite another person. And of course, he was another person. That is the nature of the parallel existence. When a worker digging a drain in the road just outside the school recognised me and hailed me with, 'Hey, Macpherson. Is that a wig yiv goat oan?', referring to my bush of red hair, I could see the boys in the playground, within earshot of this charming repartee, cowering with suppressed mirth. So much for headmasterial omnipotence. However, it has to be said that by the mid-sixties the status of the teacher had largely been eroded anyway, from that of the traditional, awesome dominie, to no more than that of a moderately useful public servant, in a profession for which you seemed to need a special calling, as for the cloth, since you had to come to terms with penury. The power of the pound in other professions and industry culled real talent from teaching and at the same time lessened the teacher's social authority.

On the other hand, in this particular case, there was no lack of fascination with me for all of those reasons. When I introduced regular parents' nights, to explain the theory behind the new methods, I first had to discuss the value of Baxter to Rangers or Johnstone to Celtic with some of the men before we got down to business. That was useful. It was a way of establishing contact with people who were bemused by being invited into the school for such meetings. But I had a case to put. I needed them on my side. So, as I reached out to shake the hand of Her Majesty's Inspector of Schools that day, I knew, about two years into my reign, I was about to be given some kind of verdict.

9

JUGGLING TWO WORLDS

The inspector walked around the school humming Beethoven. The lilting 'Pastoral' movement. He said nothing other than hailing the teachers pleasantly enough and then, hands behind back, slowly paced around the desks as if he was looking for a missing cufflink from his immaculate white shirt. What was he seeing? He was seeing movement. There were no serried ranks of desks any longer, no hierarchical positioning of pupils, but groups, even of different ages, clustered for the sake of mutual support. To encourage individual work by the children I created tasks for them on a single card which led them, hopefully, down the path of discovery. I had toiled for months devising these for the kids to read and follow. It was my attempt to place the pupil in a process which might be called self-learning, under supervision of course. It was a radical departure from conventional teaching, but I had my bible to hand (the Primary Memorandum). The tasks were all-involving. Reading, writing and arithmetic, the 3Rs, in a different atmosphere, which was one of informality and relaxation. At least, that is what I hoped. I had set out deliberately to remove myself as far as I could from the slick, chalk and talk lectures of Garrowhill Primary. And since I knew selection, the quali, was on the way out, the slavish devotion to coaching to pass these tests was about to become an irrelevance.

But was I right? I debate that constantly with myself, even yet, as I realise with the passing of time that perhaps I over-reacted to orthodoxy, in a bid to prove my virility in education, having been frustrated for so long with what I was seeing. And it is true that the other two members of staff were not greatly enthusiastic about the path I was treading. Apart from any ideological opposition, I had to admit that these methods required the teacher to work much harder. It is physically easier to stand at a blackboard all the time, pointer in hand, deliv-ering facts, or to sit at a desk with a queue of kids waiting to have their work corrected. It is quite another thing to be involved in such 'discovery' learning, which requires huge preparation and constant attention to individuals, rather than supervise and lead the class as a whole. I knew I was not going to have an easy time over this.

The verdict? It came in cryptic words.

'Very interesting, very interesting.'

Words which leave you dangling, wondering.

'I think I'll pay another visit very soon,' he said. 'Very inter-esting. Yes, I'll come back soon.'

But he didn't. Instead he sent someone else. The head of the inspectorate, a Mr Forbes, a slightly rotund and less enigmatic figure than the previous visitor, who spent a couple of hours at the school before telling me candidly,

'I love the work going on here. I think your intentions are admirable. We really will have to draw attention to it.'

I wasn't exactly sure what he meant by that, nor did I care at that stage. I had passed muster. That was enough. What happened next I am, admittedly, a little hazy about. I can't recall whether the suggestion came from me, or from Forbes or someone within the BBC. But not long after his visit and his enthusiasm about what he had seen, I found myself charged with the responsibility of writing, and fronting, a definitive radio documentary on the transformation of Scottish primary education, produced by John Gray. I threw myself enthusiastically into this project. We travelled around the country gathering information from large and small schools, educational experts, parents, children, in a total sweep of all those affected. All this was endorsed by Forbes, and while I was in my element in both working on this for the BBC and running the school, little did I realise I was building up trouble for myself. I hit a brick wall.

In the first place, parents were beginning to rebel at the amount of time I was out of the school. I did always get a replacement, including my wife, but I could tell by the various comments reaching my ears that some people were querying my strength of commitment to the school. On top of the radio documentary came the request by the BBC for me to travel to Lisbon to assist Kenneth Wolstenholme with the 1967 European Cup Final. The director of education, John S. McEwan, flatly rejected leave of absence, and whilst I was frustrated at first, I felt a certain relief, knowing that such a trip would not go down well with some parents. But when my friend Jimmy Hamilton MP turned up at the school, and heard about the official refusal, he swung into action, being a fervent Celtic supporter, and within a couple of days of his visit I was booking my passage to Lisbon. Jimmy had intervened strongly.

Then there was my staff, who were undoubtedly cheesed off with my recurring ventures outside the school, which I think aggravated their growing concern about the work that was being piled upon them with these new methods. They were now boldly offering criticisms of some of the work they were involved in. I was increasingly having to defend the system I had established, even though there was little option for them to do anything, other than get on with it. The laborious preparation work, the tension involved in trying to juggle so many activities, the feeling of losing touch with the parents whose support I deeply craved, an increasingly sullen staff – all that, I believed, I could take in my stride, and did so, until one night I was stopped abruptly in my tracks. Helping to shove a piano up a ramp with some parents, I suddenly felt a sharp pain in my groin. Like a dagger thrust deeply in. By the time I got home and lay on a couch I desperately wanted to admit something to my wife, but I couldn't bring myself to do so. I wanted to tell her that I had got it into my head I had an incurable disease. I didn't know what. It didn't matter what. It was a death sentence I was heaping on myself.

Depression didn't creep up on me. It seemed to have delivered a sucker punch. Perhaps there had been something more gradual that I was unaware of. But from that night onwards I went through a period of years feeling as if I was playing hide-and-seek with a phantom vampire that sucked vitality from you when you thought you had escaped its clutches, toying with you, supplanting self-confidence and self-esteem with a coruscating belief that you were a chancer, not worth anything to anybody. Churchill called his depressions 'The Black Dog'. Bestial imagery seems dead right. What perhaps sent me over the edge then was an illness of my younger son, who was struck down with diabetes when he was only eighteen months old, which necessitated us injecting him with insulin, sometimes three times a day. It was a deeply painful necessity to do that to someone so young. But in the process of his hospitalisation at the Edward Unit of Stobhill hospital, which was the children's ward, we actually felt a certain kind of relief that the diagnosis was diabetes, and not what some of the other children had there, leukaemia. In a bed opposite my son's cot was a boy of about five. His name was Arthur. Over the space of a couple of weeks or so, we saw him dying slowly. He had the ruddy complexion and the rotund, beatific face of a child pumped full of cortisone. He loved Celtic and in particular Jimmy Johnstone, and like his idol he had a mop of curly red hair. I made it my purpose to get a signed Celtic jersey from Jimmy, and presented it to the wee boy. It was the least I could do. By then Arthur was lying on his back, with life-supporting tubes sprouting from him. But the broad radiant smile on receiving the message from his hero seemed cruelly healthy, a kid in ecstasy, with lots more to come, it seemed to be telling us. A deeply felt smile like that has future life all over it. But he was, in fact, doomed. On our last visit to collect our son, who in over forty years since then has triumphed over his adversity, Arthur was no longer there. He had died the day before. Even though we were gratified that Banting and Best's great insulin discovery in Canada had offered a full life to our son, albeit a lifetime of some considerable inconvenience, but, we were numbed by Arthur's death, and I recall driving back home thinking of what other cruel trick might be played on another innocent child by that all-knowing, all-loving, all-benevolent God.

It certainly exacerbated the depression. It wasn't going to lift, whatever I tried. On the one hand you want to know the truth, but on the other you don't want to go down the route when the fateful words are spelled out that you are doomed. You live with chaotic clashes between the inordinate desire to know and the unwillingness to face up to the possibility of being told that your days are numbered. So you don't investigate the way you ought to. You let it be, to fester in a fog of uncertainty about the future and how to cope. And anybody to whom you might mention that the pink spot on the chest is perhaps the onset of leukaemia and who ridicules it, you feel is merely part of a conspiracy to hide the truth from you. You trust nobody. I was able, on the whole, to separate the private hell from the public professional commitments. Only my doctor really knew what was afoot. I didn't need to be told by anybody that one of the ways of escaping the tentacles of depression was to throw yourself into work. I could feel that way myself. The radio documentary became a form of therapy.

It helped. One day I arrived at a small one-teacher school at the tiny, isolated hamlet of Kirkurd in a valley in Peeblesshire, to record an interview for my radio documentary with the headmistress, who went picturesquely by the name Miss Tawse. We had heard, on the grapevine, that she was doing interesting things with the kids. I marvelled at what I saw. She actually had this one class, in ages ranging from five to eleven, into film-making. They could talk technicalities with you. They were positive and articulate, and you felt her methods were lifting these rural children from traditional wariness of the world into productive self-confidence. Her classroom revealed the splendour of the interplay between the class within and the world outside. The walls were festooned with the evidence of projects of all kinds. This tiny patch was, in fact, an educational powerhouse belying its rural isolation. Watching this one-class school of kids, humming with energy, bright and happy, industrious, helping each other over the wide age range, writing and spelling coherently in their notes, explaining to me how they created a film, was like watching a masterclass on how to overcome adversity. But it was not just for educational reasons I was impressed. I felt I was being smitten by Miss Tawse's optimism and the examples of her pupils' work scattered around that classroom. Driving through the valley, away from Kirkurd, I felt a blissful relaxation I hadn't experienced in weeks. Religion and pills were handing me no solace. So I wondered if the way out of the fog was in rubbing shoulders with heroes, which is what she was in her humble way – of witnessing simple human triumph. Miss Tawse, the pioneer, helped me that day. The lifting of the fog, and the feeling that life was worthwhile, only lasted a few days before I began the spiral downwards into dark thoughts about mortality again. But that was the pattern, the hide-and-seek game you play with the vampire. It chased me as well in the parallel world of broadcasting, as I was more and more in demand at the Beeb. Here was I, thinking at times that life was hardly worth living, haunted by nothing you could explain away rationally, at the same time as I was being intro-duced to the public, by way of the microphone and the televi-sion screen. In the first couple of years I had been simply involved in short reports for both radio and television. Now I was involved for ninety minutes at a time. I was now a commentator, wondering increasingly whether it was broadcasting on the side, or education.

One of the early jobs was a League Cup semi-final at Hampden between Rangers and Kilmarnock in 1965. I had made sure there would be no self-induced calamities and kept the pills out of the system before setting off. That evening was a dark, gloomy evening and the original floodlights at Hampden were so poor that to recognise players from our ground-level pos-ition was a task more onerous than trying to spot a Yeti on the north col of Everest. When Tommy McLean and George McLean, of different shapes, and wearing different coloured shirts, look like one and the same person, careering down the far wing, it was never going to be easy to cultivate an intimate feeling for that match.

Then there was the other factor. Technology. It was primi-tive. We filmed in those days with 16mm film. Two cameras running for ten minutes a reel, alternately, with the cameraman having to skip daintily from one to the other every ten minutes, in the dingy dungeon that was the old south enclosure at Hampden. The final result that night in front of a crowd of

53,900 was 6–4 to Rangers, with Tommy McLean scoring a hat-trick for Killie in the last twenty minutes. What the viewer saw was a game played by furtive, shadowy figures which ended in a 1–1 draw. We had lost eight goals. We even missed a penalty goal by George McLean. This is a hard feat to achieve, you would think. Not in that day and age. Not if you have cameras which go on the huff occasionally, refusing to start on command, and with the film to be dispatched to the other side of Glasgow, developed, edited, sound-checked and then later that evening, with nobody having the time to check out the final product, put on the air.

No matter. In those days the public had a certain affection for the flaws of sports coverage, like a well-loved family car which keeps breaking down but which you can't afford to get rid of. I met the assistant cameraman of that evening on a trans-atlantic flight years later. He came out of first class to chat to me. He was off to Hollywood to discuss the making of a movie. His name was Bill Forsyth. I did chide him playfully with a new sort of praise for his masterpiece, *Gregory's Girl*. 'At least we saw the ball in that film,' I suggested to him. Given his great success, and probable wealth, he could afford to offer me a chuckle in reply.

So although we were not deeply conscious of it, we were coming through the pioneering days of black and white television as a whole. There was a television drama produced by BBC Scotland, just before I started broadcasting, which had a biblical theme about Joseph and his coat of many colours. It was transmitted live and the viewers saw stagehands walking across the set and actors missing lines, and the whole effort was like watching something performed by the women's guild in a church. But it was television. It was in its rudimentary, if not entirely embryonic, state and the public were certainly irri-tated, but largely tolerant of the new-fangled output. That is why the recurring breakdowns in football coverage, which would nowadays cause riots, were simply accepted as routine. Often Peter Thomson, the first presenter of BBC's *Sportsreel*, would sit in front of the cameras offering apologies for goals not appearing on the screen. And the editing of film, being so rushed and crude, in the limited time to get from game to screen, caused mayhem occasionally. There was one match in which sound was lost on the film. We needed something in the background to fill in the gap. The technician, who knew nothing about football lore, hastened off to the sound library to pick up the noise of a crowd celebrating a goal. It was slipped into the edit. So we saw the Celtic goal against Hibs at Easter Road. We saw the green and white masses bouncing up and down, but the sound the engineer had picked was from a Rangers game at Ibrox and in the background there was an easily discernible sound of 'We'll Guard Old Derry's Walls'. Superimposed on a jubilant Celtic support, it might have led the public to believe that a new-found zeal for ecumenism was surfacing at Parkhead.

The big fear was of losing a goal in an Old Firm match. But it could happen. I witnessed a scene of corporate mental breakdown when, waiting for the film of a game which Celtic had won 1–0 to emerge from editing, we learned that the only goal of the game had gone missing. Although nobody said so at the time, you could tell from the strained faces surrounding me that they would have to brace themselves for accusations of an Orange plot. At that time BBC Scotland's standing amongst the Celtic's faithful was akin to the respect they would show for a lodge down the Shankill. It is a relationship I will explore later, but for now I can specify it was largely based on the fact that in the famous Scottish League Cup Final of 1957, which Celtic won 7–1, perhaps their most famous victory in history outside Lisbon of '67, the BBC only showed the recorded game up to half-time, when the score was 2–0. The rout of Rangers in the second half was never shown on public television, although an amateur film of it did surface some years later. The conspiracy theorists plundered this. The explanation the BBC gave seemed simple enough, at least technically. A London engineer, charged with filming the game from a television set, as they did rather crudely in those days, went off for a cup of tea at half-time, put a dust-cover over his camera and, when he returned, he started the camera again but forgot to take off the cover. Yes, that stretches credibility to the point where you also would have to believe that Fidel Castro was up there in the Texas Book Depository as well. But that was what happened, so they say. Thomson's apology that night only increased the unease of the man, who was never comfortable in front of a camera, to the point where I thought he might break down altogether.

So on two fronts I was involved in innovation. In the classroom and in broadcasting. And the two commitments were beginning to clash. The radio documentary on the new age of primary education went down well. But, again, some of the parents at Swinton were wondering just how often I could keep the fronts going, especially since I was away from school so often. They were certainly pleased to know that officially Swinton School was well geared up for the new methods, and I wasn't slow in passing on to them the plaudits I had received from the inspectorate, even though I knew there was a degree of scepticism about my methods amongst some of them. The kids were easy to discipline and enjoyed the tasks we set them. The parents did support our ventures outside to see the world, in taking them to Belgium, to London (where we had the audacity to lead twenty-five kids ten minutes late into a West End theatre to see *Oliver!*, which almost caused the production on the stage to come to a halt, so great was the commotion in the stalls) and to a variety of local industries to see what jobs actually meant to people, all of which nowadays would seem quite normal, but which then was unusual policy for far too many schools.

So I am still proud of my efforts, even at the same time as admitting that not everybody agreed with the course I was pursuing. In short, the pressure of juggling two major commitments was telling on me as I felt, whether as an illusory part of my depression or not, that I was becoming more and more remote even from my own family. And then, if not exactly out of the blue, but certainly with a speed that did almost take the breath away, the man who was the brains behind the ground-breaking BBC programme *That Was The Week That Was*, Alasdair Milne, the bagpipe-playing Controller of BBC Scotland, intervened. His secretary phoned the school one day and asked if I could come in, late that afternoon, to see him. When eventually I climbed the stairs at Queen Margaret Drive I still had no inkling of what this was about. He sat pale-faced behind his desk, his dark hair slicked back, like a Johnny Haynes Brylcreem ad. I had been told he was a man who didn't mess about. He didn't. After a shake of hands he quite simply said, in that clipped Oxbridge enunciation, 'We'd like you to come and join us here at the BBC full-time. Yes or no?'

10

AUNTIE AND I

'Sir, this is for you'. It was a wee boy with a small brown parcel. 'My mum sent it. She says to thank you.' It turned out to be aftershave. I had puzzled some, I had pleased some, I probably had angered a few. Had I got it right all the time in trying to establish new methods? Perhaps not. Innovation can sometimes lead to excesses. But I felt genuinely privileged to have been even a very minor part of a radical change in primary education, which although subsequent checks and balances have produced a more balanced, less open-ended approach than that of the sixties, had been irrevocably re-routed. But, in general, the parents' consensus view on my tenure, after I had decided to accept the BBC's offer, manifested itself in a special evening they held for me, with a more formal presentation of a gift. It fell well short of *Goodbye, Mr Chips*, but what it did do, that evening, was scare me. I had left the certainties of life for something of the unknown.

I knew the BBC could be known colloquially as 'Auntie', conveying that double image of both primness and solidity, but it was still scary to think of what I was giving up. Trying to balance what I certainly wanted to do against what I really should have done had left me in that sweltering, swithering state, even after a decision had been made. It was too late for cold feet. I tried to convince myself that few men are given the opportunity to switch professional lifestyles so completely, other than by being sacked. For I had already rejected an offer, whilst I was still in teaching, to go to London and work for the *Sports Report* programme, which was then introduced by Eamonn Andrews. I did go down to hear what they had to say, but was wholly put off by the advice given me by the late Brian Moore, that excellent commentator, who was then with BBC Radio and told me not to touch the job with a bargepole and to stay in Scotland, which would 'be better for your health'. It had been offered by Angus Mackay, formerly with the *Scotsman* newspaper, who although a fêted producer was also greatly feared and at times drove some men to desperation. Later I was to learn from BBC sources that he was going to give me a run at introducing *Sports Report* in place of Andrews, who was then moving to ITV. The man he eventually recruited lasted only a year. His name was Liam Nolan. I met this Irishman, years later, on a plane, and he admitted to me that he had told his parish priest that he actually felt like killing the man, such was his hatred for Mackay, who first promised him the earth, then dumped him on the scrap-heap inside a year. In a way I felt relieved hearing that, because I did have lingering regrets about not accepting the offer to work in London. So Milne's offer simply could not be refused. The assistant director of education for Lanarkshire did come out to see me and assure me that I was a certainty for promotion to a bigger school, as an inducement for me to stay on, but the deed had been done. I left teaching with the wholly predictable regrets of someone who loved, nay, was obsessed by, the job.

And so to Queen Margaret Drive, in the West End of Glasgow, and that grand Victorian building which was established as the women's college of Glasgow University in 1892, and which Queen

Victoria visited briefly in 1888 as a mark of interest in the early venture in women's education, and which now was the hub of Scottish broadcasting. The stately building seemed possessed by a sense of its own significance, quiet, lofty, inducing a lowering of voices to a reverential tone. The red lights above doors, though, whether on or not, indicated studios and men at work: the clearest sign that even with the all-pervading sense of restraint and of subdued tone, this building possessed the loudest voice in Scottish society. And given the general mood at that time amongst too many broadcasting executives, that sport was simply a necessary evil, you got the impression that, within its almost civil service-like structure, the sports department I was about to join full-time was equated to the Ministry of Silly Walks.

On my first day in the BBC office I found myself missing the school bell ringing out the end-of-day to classes, and the stampede of feet running down a school playground. It was then that I had to make the effort to shake myself and turn away from the past. In that, I was speedily assisted by a remarkable meeting with Milne again, in which he made it clear to me that I was being brought in specifically to replace Peter Thomson as the main presenter of BBC Scotland's sports programmes. Thomson, a man who had risen from being the internal-mail delivery boy and server of tea to his superiors to becoming the head of sport, I was deeply indebted to, for recognising and adopting me in the first place. It was part of the proud boast of the BBC that within its own ranks the sky was the limit for promotion. He seemed to exemplify that better than most. But I was soon to discover that he was a man fraught with all kinds of anxieties and fears, and he once admitted to me that one day, when he was doing a commentary on Scotland against England, he was so confused mentally that he couldn't tell whether he was at Wembley or Hampden Park. I didn't reveal to him my own private terrors, sympathising with him over his mental turmoil and for having the courage to spill the beans to me. Which is more than I could do in return. But I had barely joined his office when I realised that our relationship had altered. He had embraced me enthusiastically when I had first appeared on the scene as an occasional contributor. But, after the Milne meeting, a subtle change took place in the relationship. After that he saw me as the man who had been brought in to replace him. Within a few weeks, and without any fanfare, or indeed a special edict, it was clear to everybody that he was being ousted.

Now a television camera-lens, to an ego, is like a fix to a junkie. Eventually you feel you cannot do without it. You need the surge. You crave the attention. You feel withdrawal symptoms the longer you are away from it. I know, for that is exactly how, in later years, I developed myself and I now understand the feeling Thomson had about being apparently usurped. So, while on the surface there was help, and politeness, there is little doubt that he was not enjoying this transition, and every step I took in the department in these first few months was scrutinised, not so much by him, but by his loyal, devoted secretary, who ferociously protected him and made it clear that she felt that he was being treated rather unfairly. Her office ethic did not seem to stem from secretarial college, but more from the works of Machiavelli. She effectively ran the department for him. Nothing was accepted unless it was passed by her. She was the first woman I had come across to exercise such power amongst a group of men. It indicated a weakness in Thomson himself. I simply accepted this and got on with it.

All that was of less significance than actually being there. The BBC was unique. Certainly ITV had been established in 1954, along with the competing news of the death of Grace Archer in *The Archers* on BBC, with Scottish Television coming into being in 1957, and soon Arthur Montford would appear for the first time, fronting a new programme called *Scotsport*, which established itself as a strong communicator for the foot-balling public. So no longer was there a BBC monopoly. But it was still the Establishment in broadcasting. Lord Thomson's statement that his STV franchise, based in the Cowcaddens in Glasgow, was a licence to print money, might have been accu-rate enough at the time, but I got the general impression within the BBC that his comments were viewed simply as the bombastic claim of a man of vulgar wealth and not worthy of significance. In short, there was a degree of corporate arrogance abroad, within the corridors of Queen Margaret Drive, that cultivated the belief that they really did not have any competition to worry about, and that commercial television was simply for the plebs. It was only in later years that I could sense a growing aware-ness that we had to compete for audiences, and not assume that they were ours to command.

The man who did more, initially, to help me come to terms with this huge institution was Archie Hendry, who technically was a continuity announcer but also occasionally introduced the main sports programme. His immaculately turned out attire, his faultless delivery of the Received Pronunciation of the BBC, with a voice that sounded like gentle cooing at times, gave you the impression that the Beeb was still a place where announcers on radio were required to dress formally in dinner suits before reading the news. In fact these days might have long gone, but Hendry, in the most acceptable way, seemed to convey the lingering legacy of the rigid Reithian days. His problem, in the sports or football context, was that he came across, on the screen, with all the animation of a mannequin in Burton's shop window. But he certainly did not want me to feel that I had joined an institution that was as inert as Madame Tussaud's, and that even the great austere Reith, who established the stern ethical commandments of the Beeb, was not, as many thought, totally inhuman.

To illustrate this, Archie Hendry told me the story of how Reith had walked into the office of a famous announcer one day and discovered him under the desk exploring the anatomy of his female secretary. He went out in a blind rage, calling down damnation on the man. He wanted him sacked. His executives after many hours persuaded Reith to retain the man but punish him in some way. 'All right,' said Reith, 'he never announces the Epilogue again.' Banishment from the God slot was deemed worse than a public flogging. But Hendry also indicated that announcers like himself, were not exactly slaves to orthodoxy. He mentioned that in his broadcasting training he was taken to London to 'shadow' the famous announcer Wallace Greenslade, who had attained great popularity with audiences for his straight-voiced interjections in the *Goon Show*, his immaculate voice becoming as recognisable as Spike Milligan's or Harry Secombe's or Peter Sellers's. He was nevertheless a continuity announcer who did, in fact, introduce some of the God slots, late at night, and throughout Hendry's stay down there brought broadcasting to an end for the night, in a way that was a sort of astonishing, broadcasting Russian roulette. Perhaps it was the Goons influence acting on him, in an entirely inappropriate context. He watched Greenslade do it every single night, with that soothing, velvety voice, the same way, relying on the red light on the desk to indicate when he would be off the air. He would say, 'That's all from the BBC for tonight. We hope you enjoyed your listening today and we'd like to welcome you back tomorrow morning. So from all of us here in Broadcasting House, goodnight, a very good night.' And then when the red light went on to indicate he was off the air, he added, almost in the same breath, 'You shower of fucking bastards.' Greenslade was too pleasant and popular for the sound engineers to succumb to the compelling temptation to keep him on the air, when he thought he had finished, or not even the Goons' stature would have saved him. I suppose Hendry was trying to make me recognise that the perceived formality, the studious, meticulous nature of BBC broadcasting, ought not to dehumanise people. But, at the same time, not to take crazy risks with so-called 'dead' microphones. If only I had told that story to a man whose company I thoroughly enjoyed, Ron Atkinson, and whose *faux pas* in front of a 'live' mic that he thought was 'dead' cost him his career with ITV.

The only factor which really did make Peter Thomson fret was our relationship with Celtic. He didn't like Celtic. Much of his unease about how we treated them was based on the fact that he really would not have shed a tear had an earthquake consumed Celtic Park. But he tried manfully to lend a neutral posture, publicly. This, I am sure, pained him. It is not that I took any particular census on the matter, but merely assumed from listening to all around me that Thomson employed nobody who, as they say, 'kicked with the other foot'. It wasn't that I was uneasy about that at that time. I just didn't care. I just wanted to get on with broadcasting. What I didn't appreciate then, and had to work at in future years, was that within the minds of decent people our credibility was in question, for that reason.

I recall listening to a straight-faced discussion among some of the men in the department about the way Catholics pronounced the word 'there', with emphasis on the 'err' sound, which made it different from the white Anglo-Saxon Protestant pronunciation, and that it probably stemmed from something to do with celebrating Mass. Not a *Monty Python* sketch but an actual conversation amongst men who believed it was another way they could work out how different they were from the 'others'. Again, several decades on, I was to experience, if not to the same degree, the very opposite of that tendency, within STV, which I will address later.

There was one man, outside of all of that, who wouldn't have needed a census to make up his mind about us. It was Jock Stein, the Celtic manager. He had come to Celtic not just to manage them, but to battle for them. In that sense he had an instinct to identify, uncannily, those who were for him, and those agin. That was important to him. He gave the terrifying impression that he knew of conversations held in the Maldives the night before. Men were known to look over their shoulders when they said anything detrimental about him in case word got back. A journalist once said facetiously, so he thought, in the Hampden press box, as he watched a helicopter land on the pitch at half-time in some exhibition for some deserving cause in a game in which Celtic were involved, that if the 'copter crashed he trusted it would crash into the Celtic end. Before the day was out Stein had heard about that and had given the journalist a dressing down that would have made the Fergie hairdryer technique seem like being sprinkled with icing sugar. It was not that he was unjustified in being angered by an outrageous remark, but that whereas in the past a certain sanctity existed in the press box which fostered a fair degree of banter, risqué or otherwise but insulated from others, Stein's powerful influence had now breached it, through, one assumes, his network of informers.

His very name put the fear of death into Thomson. Not that it happened all that often in those early days, but when Celtic were defeated Thomson used to bound into the office with unbridled joy, as if he had heard of the demise of the devil. In those moments he didn't seem to care that Stein would get to know about it. He assumed that Stein simply played by the same orthodox managerial rules as, say, that of Rangers manager Scot Symon, who made no efforts to cultivate the media, other than largely to treat them with contempt. Thomson had not come to terms with the fact that he was now dealing with a revolutionary, one of the shrewdest political operators ever to don a tracksuit and who was no longer going to play by the old rules. He bent the ear of one journalist in particular, who worked for the BBC occasionally as reporter and analyst, John Blair of the *Sunday People.* Thomson did not seem to realise that Blair, as Stein was to admit to me later, was a carrier of titbits back to Parkhead and played the role of double-agent immaculately, because, as a journalist realising the burgeoning influence of Stein, he knew which side his bread was buttered on. And the Celtic manager knew that his tirades against the BBC fell on fertile ground amongst the press, which generally speaking was hostile to the Corporation. In the first place football coverage on television, whilst crude and stilted, as it was in those days, was perceived to contain a threat to the written press. The general feeling was that we were pariahs providing pictures to the public which would drive people from football grounds into their armchairs, and make their job as reporters redundant. What was so brilliantly astute about Stein was his exploitation of that feeling. He helped them direct much of their aggro towards the reviled BBC, at the same time realising, better than anyone else in the business, just how valuable television was, as a way of getting messages across – his messages. And, no matter his mistrust of the Beeb, I cannot recall a single instance when he spurned an interview. But we were manifestly in hostile territory in dealing with Celtic, which is why Lisbon in May 1967, the European Cup Final against Inter, was so torrid.

The game itself was exhilarating. Sitting, bathed in sunshine, behind a huge television set that was acting as our monitor and which we could only peek over, Kenneth Wolstenholme and I savoured, in full, this unique triumph. It might have been Europe's most prestigious final, but in ways it looked like an exhibition game, ushering out the old, and heralding the new.

There was certainly tension, especially as Celtic went behind, and Herrera's *catenaccio* threatened to turn the match into a routine win. Easy enough to say now, but I never saw Celtic losing that match. They were simply irresistible. Celtic flooded *catenaccio* out of existence that day. Stein knew very little about me personally then. In future decades I would travel the world with him, talking to the great insomniac into the wee sma' hours on many a trip, as he loved to gossip and savour a whiff of scandal about anybody, and I would sometimes elicit some astonishing revelations from this immensely private man, especially about his near-death images of his car crash in 1975. But in Portugal I was simply identified as a Thomson product, from the stable of intolerance, and that was enough to put me beyond the pale. This manifested itself in a clash at the post-match banquet, with the European Cup swathed in green ribbons standing proudly at the top table and Stein leaving his seat and heading for me, his face almost purple with rage.

It had been a great day up till then. However, the night before, I was in the commentator Kenneth Wolstenholme's bedroom as he negotiated, as a go-between for an agent, with Stein about the proposed match with Real Madrid for Alfredo Di Stefano's testimonial. At one point Wolstenholme told Stein I was there and I was going to speak, but when I took the receiver I discovered he had just put the phone down on me at the other end, sharply, thus hinting that even in the event of a triumph, a warm embrace between us was only a remote possibility. I should have taken the hint. The closeness I got to him was first pre-game, when I sat in the palatial surroundings of the Palácio Hotel in Estoril as he barked a sharp rebuke at his reserve goalkeeper John Fallon for sitting at a window where the sun could strike him. Then when mayhem ensued on the field at the end of the match, and thousands of Celtic supporters had invaded the pitch and I had to try to get him for interview, he was losing his temper at the supporters for pulling at Tommy Gemmell in particular, who looked as if he was going to have his arms pulled from their sockets. Stein had just won the greatest of all the footballing trophies available to him, but I was seeing a man actually enraged by the chaos which was preventing the presentation of the trophy itself. I would rather have interviewed a fighting bull at that stage. Then, somewhat like a bull, he came for me at the banquet.

I had approached his players who were sitting at a long table simply to congratulate them and, let us just say, they were in a merry mood. The banter was pleasant. Then I saw out of the corner of my eye, just as the banquet was breaking up, this huge figure striding towards me with that characteristic limp, which in a sense carried its own menace when he would break into a fair rate of knots. Before I could say anything he had grabbed me by the arm and pulled me away from the table. I recall his words well. 'Don't talk to my players. You are only a guest here. You never talk to my players at the best of times, so you're not talking to them now. Sit on your arse!' Real venom poured out.

So where exactly are you heading when the greatest manager in Europe has just swatted you aside as if you were a fly on the table? Not all that far, you might think, as I did then. But after Lisbon I began to realise that somehow or other we had, or I had, a serious credibility problem. This was not a tyrant I had to deal with, although his rages would have turned Lot's wife into a pillar of salt, had he been around then, but an intelligent and sometimes ruthless man, who sussed out his environment perceptively. I certainly could not be disloyal to Thomson, who had brought me into the BBC in the first place. But in that single epiphanic moment at the banquet I realised that a barrier to credibility had just been put in place, and had to be crossed. Two years after that incident I was installed as the first full-time broadcaster in sport that BBC Scotland had recruited from outside the Corporation. I was in the hot seat, fronting the programme called *Sportsreel*. I was ousting a famous name from his niche in studio, I was doubling up with commentary work. I was thriving.

And yet I was ill at ease, the vampire was still attacking me, almost daily, and shrouding me in illogical misery. Even more so was the professional problem, treated with alarming indifference by too many of my new colleagues, that we still were perceived, in some important quarters, as a pack of bigots. Hard work had to be done on that image. For this was 1969. Neil Armstrong had bounced around the moon with his well-rehearsed tribute to mankind's ability to look further than its navel. I was stuck with earth-bound suspicion and mistrust.

11

INTO BATTLE

Shortly before he died I sat beside Jim Baxter, the former Rangers and Scotland player, at a large dinner-table in the banqueting hall of a Glasgow hotel which was thronged with people indulging in pre-Christmas revelry at a charity function. Baxter didn't get up to dance. He looked as if the spirit simply wasn't there any longer. He was ashen-faced and subdued, speaking in short staccato bursts in that irreversible Fife accent which sometimes, in itself, seems like an act of irreverence towards the English language. He didn't really want to talk football and after some baleful efforts to try to engage him that way, he would make it clear that he wanted a bit of elbow room, and sat quietly with his partner, completely unaware that I, and others, were appalled to see his decline. He was dying, although at that stage we simply were not aware of the terminal nature of his condition. The liver transplant was not to be the panacea after all.

Four years later I was sitting in a neat villa in Viewpark, Lanarkshire talking to Jimmy Johnstone. He was bright, articulate, in a chirpy mood, making jokes with his wife Aggie in that comically insulting way they had developed, which was almost like a Chic Murray and Maidie double act. It was a strangely uplifting experience, given that Jinky, riven by motor neurone disease, could not lift a cup, unless he held it between his wrists and hoisted a straw to his lips, his fingers dangling helplessly, and sucking with an effort that was like an infant taking his milk quota in class. He could not go to the toilet unless somebody helped him there, and even hold his manhood for him to ensure relief, for his fingers were now like limp string. He sat in his chair as if he would never go anywhere else. This great player, like Baxter, seemed marooned amidst the bewildering physical tricks that nature had played on him, making both of them only husks of the athletes they once were. Where once they influenced, manipulated, dominated and shaped events, they were now brutalised by them, and cruelly unable to fight back, as once they could.

Although many other men and women have suffered and died the same way, unquestionably when you see those who trod the stage so brilliantly, bereft of any alternative other than slow death, it has a special poignancy. It certainly had for me, who could look back on those two men to the days when I was flying solo every Saturday night to present the BBC's main sports programme. Baxter was king then but Jinky was the crown prince, ready to emerge into the limelight through the promptings of Jock Stein, who even before he had officially taken up his post at Parkhead had gone to the toilet at half-time one day in a game Jinky was involved in. They bumped into each other. As they stood there relieving themselves, in a few short, stinging words he told the wee red-haired winger, who had contemplated leaving Celtic at one stage, to waken up to his own abilities. He did. Baxter courted controversy and introduced touches of cabaret to football; his keepie-uppie at Wembley in 1967 would have earned him decent marks in *Britain's Got Talent*. Johnstone became a European name and went on to outdo Baxter's nocturnal capers, of which there were many, and had half the Lanarkshire constabulary chasing him one night in a car chase down a motorway, like in a scene from *Bullitt*.

It is certainly true that Baxter's career was about to turn and wane after leaving Rangers, just as Johnstone's was dramatically taking off about then. But they overlap in my mind as icons of an age which I helped bring to the public through the weekly Saturday-night programme which was first called *Sportsreel* and then *Sportscene*. Their contributions, and the achievements which sprang from them in different ways, created an era that, in my view, could justifiably be described as the Golden Age of Scottish football. I suppose I would say that anyway, since I was a principal part of chronicling events, but it is difficult to deny that between, say, 1967 and 1983, between Lisbon, Barcelona and then on to Gothenburg, we witnessed, recorded, interpreted and analysed achievements that elevated Scottish football to levels of unprecedented credibility throughout Europe. And you couldn't help feeling, at the time, that that status was ours to keep, that it was our niche, that our measure was not in the actual size of the nation compared to others, but in our ability to overcome that relative weakness and astonish the world; that raw talent was on-stream in what could only be an endless supply of skill and brawn; that money had little to do with any of this, and that any commentator of Scottish football would continually have to brush up on his superlatives for the future. A Golden Age, regrettably turning up some fool's gold as well.

However, the sad demise of these two men simply crystallised my appreciation of how that era helped shape my own public identity. For instance, I commentated on Jinky's best ever goal (so I would claim). Ibrox 1967 in the mud. Three weeks before the final in Lisbon. A left-foot drive which turned the heavy ball into something unleashed by Mons Meg and nearly disconnected the top of the net. I rhapsodised over Baxter's greatest performance (so I would claim). It was a friendly and thus probably merited less attention than some of the other more highly charged games he took part in. But it was against Brazil. Hampden 1966. We all came to study Pelé in action. But Baxter's command performance overshadowed everything. His mastery of the ball in the swirl, his threaded passes, his avoidance of tackles, his shift of the hips to wrong-foot opponents in the 1–1 draw, were like being sucked into the improbable inference that this man came from the sands of Copacabana and not from amidst the coal-bings of Fife. Jinky and he, in particular, allowed me to sharpen my teeth on the highest level of performance, and away I went, hopefully on the wings of lyrical description which, to other ears, might have sounded like clunking cliché. But I knew I was in business now. People were listening.

Scot Symon, the manager of Rangers, certainly was. As I came on the scene, he was enjoying remarkable success with a side of talented men who merely had to turn up to win a game. They would beat Celtic at will. They were dominating. Then came Stein. Everything changed. Symon didn't, though. He still wore his trilby whenever he went to training. He still retained that rather gentlemanly but aloof demeanour that was natu-rally his, but stemming also from the conviction that he had the best job in the world, with a club which had an unshake-able belief in its own superiority. And he had made the not entirely mistaken assumption that everybody at the BBC was part of his tug o' war team pulling against Celtic. When Maggie Thatcher was said to have commonly asked 'Is he one of us?', it did bring to mind that Old Firm loyalty Geiger counter, employed discreetly by both sides, to try to find out where sympathies lay. It is true that within the highly sensitive nature of the Scottish footballing environment such admissions were only subtly revealed at that time, although people in the media in the last decade or two are much less inhibited in that area. But, for some, it was held close to the chest, like the love that dare not speak its name. Symon not for one moment doubted that the BBC were allies. However, when he was preposterously sacked in November 1967, when Rangers were actually at the top of the league, I proposed we look at both Symon's and the club's weaknesses on our programme. I might as well have asked Thomson if I could appear in green and white hoops. He baulked. So did his secretary. Which was an even bigger problem than his objection, as she still influenced his thinking. It was out of the question. But I spied an opportunity that would be irresistible for Thomson. I suggested we bring in somebody he admired, Ian McMillan, the deft, intelligent, traditional inside forward of Rangers, who had been affectionately nicknamed by his supporters the Wee Prime Minister, after his namesake Harold. Ian was a gentleman, church-goer, quietly and intelligently spoken. In short, harmless. Or so Thomson thought, as he bought that idea. But he wasn't. The man had hinted to me in advance that he had something interesting to say. Out of his mouth came an astonishing, swingeing criticism of his former manager, made all the more effective by the quiet manner in which he spoke. Think of a bishop telling the one about a fat man with flatulence problems and you might imagine the shock it produced. Even though I knew he wasn't there just to warm the studio seat, I was surprised myself. He spoke about Symon's lack of ability to come to terms with modern tactics, especially in relation to their 1960 European Cup semi-final with Eintracht Frankfurt, who demolished Rangers, and of how at half-time in Germany, with the writing on the wall, Symon offered no advice to his players but stood in the corner of the dressing room, sipping a cup of tea. It was quietly devastating. Thomson saw it as unnecessarily over the top and his only reaction was that it would merely inflate Stein's ego. Without doubt, Stein would be watching since he missed nothing on the box.

I was affected by the fall-out from that in two ways. In the immediate sense, the following day, I travelled to Dundee for a game in the old Fairs Cup, and stopped on the banks of the Tay in Perth for a sandwich in a hotel. I walked into the restaurant and straight into Scot Symon himself, sitting at a table with a couple of friends. There was no way I could avoid him. As I stopped he merely lifted his head and said, 'If my wife had got hold of you on Saturday night she would have torn the eyes out of your head.' And then after a short pause, added, 'However, you are entitled to your opinion.' Dignity, I was discovering, has a cutting edge to it as well. I contrasted that with the vicious reaction Stein had to me in Lisbon, beginning to see it personifying the essential change that was about to convulse Scottish football, and putting Rangers, the club which had dominated since the end of the war, into a more defensive mode. On one side of the city was a scrapper, who did not play by the same rules as the others, but was in effect shaping new ones in his relationship with the world through the media; a man who saw part of his role, crucially, as a political one, to alter the image of Celtic, from being passive outsiders, forever crying 'Foul!' on behalf of a minority community, into a positive, modern force, whose focus was not only on setting new standards on the field of play but also on rendering old prejudices redundant. On the other side, Rangers had been strictly conventional, and until they saw the league slip away from them, and Celtic win in Lisbon in 1967 as they lost in Nuremberg in the Cup Winners' Cup days later, they were forced into the unedifying spectacle of first panicking and then sacking a manager. The chairman, the builder John Lawrence, didn't have the nerve to face him personally but sent out a go-between to do so.

What they couldn't realise then, of course, was that even though they brought in a young, idealistic former manager of Clyde, Davie White, to take over, he was diminutive in comparison with Stein, and in any case they were still going to be lumbered with their narrow recruitment scheme based on which school boys went to. A revolution on one side, a mere refurbishment on the other. In my view, in the longer term, it was going to be no contest. And that produced the other consequence of the McMillan broadcast. For although there were no major rows, as Thomson was certainly not that kind of aggressive man, I could tell he realised I was not going to fall neatly into line with his thinking on matters of opinion and editorial selection. This came to a head when I took an idea to him that caused him then to regard me as some kind of quisling. I proposed that we invite Stein into the studio to be an analyst for a Scotland international game. I recall he looked at me as if I had just spoken in Urdu to him. He was utterly baffled by my suggestion. For we had certainly just been at the receiving end of some of the Celtic manager's most vociferous criticism.

It has to be emphasised that nobody at the BBC actually manipulated programmes to suit Rangers. Nobody doctored film to distort games, since the technology was so primitive in those days, and the exigencies of time so demanding, that nobody was clever enough to do such a thing. Certainly, when you edited a game it could appear that you might favour one against another, and since bias is in the eye of the beholder there was really nothing you could do to allay fears about that. It is true that Rangers benefited by the number of times Thomson preferred to send cameras to their games rather than their rivals, but there was no diabolical plot to distort the record. No, Stein's perception was more fundamental. It was about 'attitudes'. He knew that there was an anti-Celtic cadre at the BBC and from that sprang some of his partly genuine and partly delusional beliefs, that his club was not getting a fair deal. One of the most dramatic blasts from Celtic Park had come at the end of the 1968/69 season. Celtic had won the league. But Rangers had beaten Celtic twice that season. There was nothing we could do to alter that in our summary of the season, which we showed prior to the Scottish Cup Final that year. It was history. Stein would have none of it and claimed that our programme gave the impression Rangers had won the league. It was over the top, and fuelled Thomson's attitude that we were dealing with an unreasonable tyrant. There's no doubt that Stein could summon up that gale to great effect.

On top of that was a scene he had been informed about when we travelled with the SFA to Hamburg for a World Cup qualifier against West Germany in October 1969. Stein was on that official party. One night some of us became involved in a conversation with Willie Waddell, who was a journalist then, working for the *Daily Express*. The former Kilmarnock manager and Rangers player was a severe critic of the Rangers board then, and produced a scathing article headlined 'The Boy David', an acerbic dig at the youthful rawness of the man who had replaced Scot Symon. During that conversation the SFA doctor suddenly turned on Waddell and almost begged him to move into Ibrox and take over. Some other journalists took up this theme and whilst the man himself rebuffed the suggestions with his customary dourness, there is no doubt he was enjoying this. Somebody naturally told Stein, and the following morning, almost before the cock crowed, he was round everybody who had formed that huddle to mock them for trying to organise a rescue party for Rangers. He didn't miss me in his sarcasm that day. I knew this could not go on. Something had to give. The following year, 1970, I travelled to Milan for the European Cup Final, Celtic against Feyenoord. On the evening of the game, the dismally wet weather had provided a pallid scene, compared with the glorious brightness of a spring afternoon in Lisbon, and Celtic's defeat mocked the notion of logic in football, because they had already beaten the highly fancied Leeds side in the semi-final. When we returned to the hotel he was sitting in an almost deserted foyer with his assistant Sean Fallon. I expected some kind of waspish comment. Instead, he simply pointed to a case of champagne which was on the floor beside his chair. His words are etched on my mind. 'They were a better team than us,' he said softly, huskily. 'Look at their support too. They outnumbered us. The Dutch have got more money than us. They can afford to travel to a place like this. How did the broadcast go, by the way? Would you like a drink of champagne? There are bottles of the stuff over there. Help yourself.'

For one brief, shining moment I thought that I had made a breakthrough with this man. But there was still a long way to go. For the following season after they had won the Scottish Cup 2–1 in a midweek replay with Rangers, I went to the dressing-room door seeking an interview with him. He came to the threshold of the room wearing nothing but a towel round his waist, thus revealing that King Billy was not tattooed on his chest, as some demotic rumour had suggested, and berated me for some comments which had been made at the BBC, when some guests we had invited in to watch an Aberdeen–Celtic game noted the jubilation amongst some Corporation staff when Aberdeen scored. They had informed Stein, and this was lodged in his mind, even though the Scottish Cup was in the corner of the dressing room.

'You're nothing but a bunch of bigots,' he said before slamming the door in my face. He eventually did come out to be interviewed, at pitch-side, but by that stage I had made up my mind that some real showdown had to be faced up to. There were others in our department, including other commentators and reporters, who believed it was something we all had to tolerate and that it was just one of the factors you lived with. Thomson's notion was simply to dodge Stein, at all costs, and keep him far removed from anything we did, believing it was best to have nothing to do with him. There was also the thought, gaining strong currency, that too many people in the media had fallen under Stein's sway at that time; that you would be seen to be running scared if you tried to reach out to him. I was prepared to risk all of that when I decided to pay him an unscheduled call shortly after that Cup Final replay. He was surprised to see me.

We were in the boardroom at Celtic Park, he with his back to the fireplace, where eventually he would stand on his last day at the club, in that famous final photograph of him being given a sideways handshake by his chairman, without looking at each other, in a terminal moment of mutual disdain. The man standing in front of me at that time, though, was unassailable. He had on his customary black tracksuit, splattered with the mud of the training-ground. When I brought up this festering sore of an issue between his club and the BBC, he was quick to single out Peter Thomson as the man who set the anti-Celtic agenda and stated that he knew that no Catholics were employed by him. It was difficult to rebut this. We discussed sectarianism for some while and then I think he began to understand that this was a maverick enterprise by me, that I wouldn't have taken the trouble to be there had I not been concerned about the relationship. Almost as if he had read my mind and intentions, he summarised my position for me.

'You're just starting out,' he said. 'If you've got any sense you'll see this is where the real action is going to be. We're going to be in Europe for a long time to come. You've got to get your feet in this club and not treat it like it was inferior or else you're going to be left behind. We've all to forget that old boyhood stuff,' he added, referring to the assumption that we

124

both had emerged from the same tradition. 'That's for your own sake I say that. Times have changed. If you want to come to any training session at Celtic Park at any time, give me a ring in advance. Now, I'm away to have a shower.'

At which he made an abrupt departure. Thomson did not know I had paid that visit. Had he heard the conversation he might have concluded, as others certainly would, that I was now in Stein's back pocket. I wasn't in the slightest bothered about that possible conclusion. Here was a man of the future. Here was the most interesting phenomenon to hit Scottish football in generations, and yet there were some around me who felt that we had to keep him at arm's length, because of the old prejudices. It did not matter to me that the public would not notice, one way or the other, any significant changes in our transmissions just because I had attempted to build a bridge. A feud like this, based on sectarian issues, was simply unhealthy and had to be brought to an end somehow. That is why I took another step, hoping that, for my own sake within our department, it would not be considered a bridge too far. It would be the most tangible evidence of a change in the times. That is why I proposed inviting Stein into a BBC Scotland programme which previously he had shunned.

It certainly does not sound significant now, but I knew that the Celtic manager, appearing live for the first time in one of our broadcasts would cause a stir amongst the rest of the media, who had known of his distaste for our existence. This was not simply overcoming a petulant reaction to anything that had been said on the air, like Sir Alex Ferguson's long-running objection to letting BBC interviewers come anywhere near him, because of opinions aired. This was more visceral. This was related to the deep-rooted sensitivity he had to the divide in our society, which he had crossed over himself, to great effect. Thomson at first would have none of it. But I persisted, with

125

the hint that if it got out publicly that he had objected to using Stein, then the BBC at the highest level would have to justify that, and I knew they couldn't. He relented.

Jock Stein came into our studios for the first time in 1973, watched the international match, made his comments on the air with me and then afterwards sat in our office having a chat and a cup of tea. Compared with the efforts to achieve that, it all seemed so mundane. Except for one element. Thomson didn't show up. 'Where's the boss?' I recall Stein asking me at one point, with a knowing smile on his face. The snub could not have been more obvious. What I could not have known was that this was the beginning of a long relationship with Stein in broadcasting, one whose peak might have been when he was my co-commentator at Anfield on the night Scotland beat Wales to qualify for Argentina in 1977. I knew that my relationship with Thomson would never be the same again. He regarded me simply as disloyal. But at the same time I had broken a mould, and it wasn't until later years that I began to appreciate how I had spent so much of my time in the first few years of my new career forging a political stance, both inside and outside the Corporation, rather than just broadcasting every week. Sitting in front of a camera was the easy bit. Sorting out relationships in an area where sycophancy was perceived to be a prime requirement was much more harrowing. But I had got some return for it. For the first time, BBC Scotland had a decent, working, professional relationship with the nation's two major clubs, on what might have been called a level playing-field. And with that, we had a better chance of competing with a vibrant *Scotsport* on Scottish Television.

12

THE *COLEMANBALLS* ERA

You could hardly miss Arthur Montford in a crowd. Tall, and wearing checked sports jackets which could be spied from outer space, he had a head start on me by having established a new sports programme by the early 1960s which had made BBC's *Sportseel* seem stilted and stiff. Peter Thomson was no match for him. Indeed, it has to be said that STV has never really found anybody to equal Montford's natural abilities in front of a camera. Although he delivered many excellent commentaries, it was sitting in a studio, handling the perils of live television, in the less secure environment of cruder technology then, which commanded respect. In many ways he personified the belief that a good broadcaster can be hoist by his own petard by making it look so easy that you fail to appreciate the skill involved, thus encouraging the belief that almost anybody could do it. He was therefore a formidable opponent in the search for audiences. But whilst the press might have conveyed the impression that Arthur and I were locked in showdowns more akin to that of the OK Corral in Tombstone, the relationship was more like the challenge of two mates playing ping-pong with each other down at the YMCA. We both wanted to win, but at the same time we were aware that what mattered more than anything else in those early days was a need for a bonding of sorts. There was a very basic reason for that. The press saw us both as a couple of pests trying to muscle in on their territory and never failed to seize an opportunity to put the boot in. We gave them plenty to grab.

Breakdowns of our film coverage, missed goals, crude edits, shaky cameras, missing sounds, and the use of some reporters who, in front of a camera, looked so tongue-tied and nervous you would have thought they were about to be waterboarded, too often conveyed the impression of overall incoherence, of not being in command of events. We thought of ourselves as pioneers. They thought we had three wheels on the wagon, and didn't hesitate in saying so. We both knew we were partners in trying to establish television's credibility. Yes, we did want to win the ratings game but always with an eye to appreciating our mutual problems. Arthur, though, grasped an opportunity which we did not. As an ex-journalist himself, he appreciated, better than anyone at the BBC, that a powerful figure from the press, recruited for occasional work, would help his cause. And it did. Amongst others, he brought in Alex Cameron of the *Scottish Daily Mail* who was later to join the *Scottish Daily Record*. 'Candid' Cameron, as he was to become known, was a totally different personality from Arthur. It was like Mike Tyson being brought in to aid the techniques of the Samaritans. He was exactly what television needed. Fiercely opinionated, he stamped a different kind of authority on the programme. His mood swings could be extreme.

One evening I took the air with Cameron round the pleasant harbour of Frederikshavn in Denmark, where we had come to take in a quite harmless Under-21 international. We set off like the ying and yang of the media, cosily dovetailing with cooing self-endorsements, as if we would be like that to the end of our days. Twenty minutes later we were eyeballing each other, and shouting crude threats at one another, like murder was in the air, in front of a crowd of scared little blond Danish boys who must have thought a couple of Martians had arrived to start the War of the Worlds. Candid had taken exception to some view I had expressed and his internal fuse had been lit. They heard Glaswegian expressions which thankfully are beyond the reach of Danish interpretation. An hour later we were downing Remy Martins like we could not live without each other. That's the way it was with Candid. There was no air of neutrality around his personality. He would let fly. If, say, you would wish to berate Marxist philosophy and the totalitarianism of East Germany, and the symbol of oppression which the Berlin Wall was, then you wouldn't pick a bar in a hotel just on the wrong side of Checkpoint Charlie, long before the Wall came down, would you? He did. Loudly. On the day before an East Germany–Scotland international. Some of his colleagues, who did not take well to his occasionally abrasive moods, and despised Candid, were secretly hoping that if he kept that up, surrounded as he was by grim-faced waiters who could not have had that job were they not with the Stasi, he would quietly be slipped a Mickey Finn and we would have heard no more of him, until, perhaps, a postcard arrived at his newspaper, sent from a Siberian gulag. But he thrived and survived on the crest of controversy, and it made me think that the way to insulate yourself from 'the slings and arrows of outrageous fortune', was to employ brazen effrontery as often as possible.

The only time he was treated with disrespect, openly and flagrantly, was when a police horse shunted him out of the way during a live broadcast in front of millions of viewers outside Hampden Park. There would have been a public outcry if the horse had been put down because of that. So, although there were others incorporated into *Scotsport*, the Montford–Cameron

129

duo provided a stern test for me, especially as we did not employ anyone approaching Cameron's status in journalism, and in his dual press and television roles. It was a good, healthy contest which did, at the same time, call for co-operation.

On one notable occasion Arthur travelled to Hungary to commentate on one of Celtic's European ties against Ujpest Dozsa, in November 1972. Candid was left behind to present the programme in the studio with some guests. But a 'stramash', as Arthur used to call it, befell them. A farmer somewhere in the fields of south Tyrol, ploughing merrily in his field, was said to have cut through a communications cable and thus all contact was broken with Arthur. No pictures or sound were coming out of Budapest. Candid had a two-hour programme to fill with nothing to fall back on. At the BBC we sat and watched this in some fascination, because we had a separate radio link to the game, and the commentator there was filling us in with information. We watched until half an hour or thereabouts had gone, as Candid squirmed in his seat, with no ammunition to feed his guests and making largely optimistic guesses about how Celtic were faring, even when they were behind in the match. We could stand it no longer. I phoned STV to let them know I would feed them information for the rest of their programme. At first they thought it was a spoof call. Then, as the waffle in the studio began to sound like Candid was fast approaching the point when he would have to start a game of charades to fill the space, they put me through. For the rest of their programme the BBC talked them through the course of events in Budapest, which they duly reported to their public.

But both of us were at the important transition of film to videotape, and the use of the outside broadcast units. It was the start of an era which would see the burgeoning importance of televised sport and the astonishing transformation of the

press, from outright hostility to a vital co-ordination of interests. Prior to this, Arthur and I had lived under the spell of the
razor blade. That tiny piece of metal, which we used to shave
with every morning, was also a vital tool of the trade. Down
in the edit suites, the film editors, in their white gloves to prevent
them from having their hands soiled by the film, would slice
their way through the edits with cuts that Sweeney Todd would
have commended. Even in the early days of videotape, that
was how they portioned the selected highlights. Film was being
superseded and we felt the better for having those huge elec-
tronic cameras riding to our benefit. The competition was such
that often, to retain our identities, we would roll up to grounds
with our separate huge trucks and cover the same game, something that, in the current era, would never be countenanced.
This was especially so for Scottish Cup Finals, in the days
before exclusivity. Hampden was left crawling with television
technicians as we vied openly for the larger audience that day.
There were times, though, when important games fell exclusively to you for one reason or another. The BBC was delighted
to get its hands on one such, exclusively. But, although the
outside broadcast cameras covered the match, to this day it is
a game that has never been shown in public.

It was 2 January, 1971. The man we called the Ancient Mariner,
George Davidson, a retired sea-captain, who had been one of
the first to land in Yokohama after the great earthquake there
in 1923, was at Ibrox to do the commentary for recorded highlights. I was to present the programme in the studio. The day
was misty and chilling. First, there was the initial shock of
hearing Frank Bough in the *Grandstand* studio announce, with
a degree of incredulity, that he had been informed that twenty-
two people had died in an incident at Ibrox Park. As the actual
enormity of it all sunk in, some hours later, and the news that
sixty-six people had died, I discovered how inadequate our

response to tragedy can be. Although there were powerful, unforgettable images to cope with, especially the sight of the sixty-six body-bags lined up underneath the Ibrox stand, when I eventually got out to the stadium I remember certain words as well. I remember Stein dismissing a journalist with a withering rebuke for having dared to ask him a question about what he thought of the actual game, which ranks with the 'What did you think of the play, Mrs Lincoln?' apocryphal comment, as an example of crass insensitivity. But there was worse to follow, much worse. When we convened an editorial meeting with the top brass of BBC Scotland there, later that evening, to agree on how we should reflect the tragedy, if at all, or whether to cancel the regular programme outright, one comment plumbed almost unreachable depths. In the middle of our discussions I was asked by a senior BBC executive,

'How many people were at the match?'

'Eighty thousand or thereabouts,' I replied.

'Sixty-six dead out of eighty thousand isn't all that many really.'

It came out of his mouth as if he were reciting a statistic from some ancient battle, which time had desensitised for us. Not about the writhing mass of innocent people who had been trampled to death, that very afternoon. It had a stunning effect on all of us. It was not just the insensitivity, it was the temerity. How could any man utter such a statement with impunity? He could, because his executive level meant he was in no fear of being affected by the anger, the rage, that I then directed towards him, which thereafter blemished me in the eyes of management. Indeed, I lost control, and was asked to either calm down or leave the proceedings. Thomson had sat there and said nothing. Somehow the whole tenor of the discussion had taken the turn of the fault being mine, not that of the man who had just demonstrated appalling insensitivity.

Forty or so years later, I still recoil at that memory. I remember, too, words expressed to me many years later, when researching a book, by the man who was in charge of the first police inquiry into the tragedy, Inspector Joe Beattie. Here was a man whose erect height and forthright policing made him feared by Glasgow's gangsters, but when I met up with him years later he was suffering from Crohn's disease, which had shrunk him alarmingly in size. But his memory had not been affected, as he described the ghastly scenes and the disorder that had reigned in the Ibrox boardroom. 'They were like headless chickens, not knowing what to do, or which way to turn,' he told me. 'When I got there Matt Taylor, one of their directors, was actually cracking jokes. To be fair to the man, he probably had snapped by that stage and perhaps he felt he had to lighten the atmosphere. But it was bizarre and completely disorganised. It was like that until Willie Waddell came upstairs and joined in. He took over. Waddell pulled Rangers together in the next few weeks. He saved them from just collapsing into chaos. That was probably Deedle's greatest achievement in football.' The game could not be shown. And one of the paradoxes of that tragic day was that the commentator and the entire outside broadcast team left Ibrox and returned to their base in East Kilbride, completely unaware that a catastrophic accident had taken place. Whilst the world would have wished to see at least some live evidence of the incident, our cameras rolled blissfully back to their depot, with men intent on joining in the New Year celebrations, not knowing that sixty-six people had set out for a football match one day, and had not survived.

The disaster weighed heavily on me. You cannot eradicate such images of death easily. My depressions had certainly lessened, but I still suffered the blank days where nothing seemed worthwhile, even eating. When you are in this fog, a sense of purpose is hard to find and yet I had around me all the inducements for living a stimulating life, which many would envy. It wasn't easy to rationalise that for oneself. That's the damnable nature of this condition. Everything that seems right just doesn't work. Your smile is a feigned smile. You have inner conversations with yourself even as you talk with others at a dinner party. You thumb through *Black's Medical Dictionary* looking for what is next about to strike you. You suddenly decide to go for long walks without knowing where you are heading, like trying to shake off a pursuer. Remember Butch and Sundance looking down from a butte, as the dust signs indicate the unshakeable nature of the posse trailing them. 'Who are these guys?' Butch says, almost in awe of their tenacity. Something like that; the moments when you capitulate to the feeling of the sheer impossibility of shaking off something that won't give up trailing you but not knowing precisely what it is.

What I had seen at Ibrox was hardly a palliative to all of that. But part of the puzzling nature of this confusion is that it can roll away, almost as though you are unaware of what is happening, like becoming conscious of a haar suddenly lifting, as the wind takes a grip of it. I had talked to many doctors about this state and by and large the advice was simply to hang on in, see it through, and it will work its way out eventually. And it did begin to roll away. It is very difficult to put a time and duration on when the blackest days took on a greyer hue, and you became aware that you had not been haunted for a while.

Focusing on sitting in front of a camera every Saturday evening, delivering words as precisely as I could, in itself might have been therapeutic. Who knows? It was stimulating. And there is no doubt that although some might have felt that the pressure of broadcasting in its multiple ways puts enormous stress on you, it is that sense of knowing that you could easily flop that concentrates the mind. It is when you take a 'Look, no hands!' attitude that you sometimes come a cropper. For instance, one night, brimming with confidence I announced to the public, 'Good evening! The two games tonight are from Hambley and Wemden.' There is nothing like a good old-fashioned spoonerism to bring you down to earth. The senior announcer at the BBC at the time was Alistair MacIntyre, who used to introduce *The Kilt is My Delight* in those beautifully mellifluous tones of his. He heard me do this and consoled me with two stories. He told me he had announced a music progamme by saying, 'And now over to the fifing and piddling.' And added that perhaps the worst of all the spoonerism mistakes was committed by the great Henry Longhurst, who preceded Peter Alliss as the doyen of golf commentators, and who looking down the 18th at an Open once, in thankfully a recorded session, tried to say 'Here come Coles and Hunt', but fell right into spoonerism's Black Hole of Calcutta.

All this was before *Colemanballs*. Whatever the intention of those who started that compendium, perhaps even to intimidate anybody going anywhere near a microphone, or simply as a warning not to get carried away with a sense of your own importance, in a way it began to lose its impact on the trade. For eventually, no self-respecting broadcaster would wish to be left out of the list of classic errors. I now even suspect some of 'crafting' a phrase or two. I look, almost affectionately, at probably my most illustrious gaffe, when years later I pronounced on a Turkish team of 100 per cent Islamic background by saying, 'They prefer to be known by their Christian names.'

To rile David Coleman, as I sometimes did, you needed only to bring up the subject of what purportedly came out of his mouth during an Olympic commentary in Montreal in 1986, when describing Alberto Juantorena: 'The big Cuban opened his legs and showed his class.' He disputes that. Who cares whether it was said or not? It sticks. It belongs to the relationship between broadcaster and a public who might now have developed creative interpretations, taking words completely out of context. It has also to be said that to categorise all the gaffes under one man's name, *Colemanballs*, does not cast a slight on his stature. Indeed, the opposite is the case. It merely reflects the influence, power and authority he commanded in his heyday.

Now we have the hoovering up of gaffes, and other things, on YouTube. The world is now the voyeur's oyster. You can be sitting minding your own business and somebody will pass you with a mobile-phone camera, and in a matter of minutes, you can be watched innocently picking your nose, or worse, from one pole to the other. There is a sequence on YouTube, among quite a few, to be honest, which shows me trying to be cool and reliable as some breakdown in one particular programme is causing vitriolic abuse in the background, from the director of the programme. You can hear his voice screaming obscenities as he tries to get order brought back into the proceedings. It sounds as if his tirade is directed to me, and indeed that is the whole point of the excerpt. That is what I mean about context. For in fact he was screaming at the men deep in the bowels of the videotape area for not bringing up the correct items or sequences. We are all fair game in this new dimension. *Colemanballs*, by comparison, now seems as intrusive, and as mocking, as runes on Pictish standing-stones.

That was the other reason Arthur Montford and I bonded, in the kinship of the truly vulnerable. We both knew that the debit side of the 'weel kent face' was constant scrutiny. The *Daily Record* actually informed me that my son was being married over the anvil at Gretna in 1986 before I knew anything about it. There was nothing nefarious about either the circumstances or the way they treated the story, which they did in a light-hearted way with a back-page spread entitled 'Off-Side Archie!' But the constant scrutiny of public figures became more sinister as the years progressed, as a by-product of the tabloid wars. One slip and they would be after you. It felt infinitely worse when you could almost be the architect of your own potential downfall. Such, indeed, was my involvement in an episode when inadvertently we allowed a little monster to come into our lives. He was the son of the great Pelé's agent, a Swede called Borje Lantz.

In Switzerland in 1983 for the original draw for the group stages for the World Cup Finals in Mexico in 1986, I was introduced to the man who, in Sweden in 1958, at the Finals, took on the responsibility of public relations for the largely unfancied Brazilians when few others were interested. Pelé, then the youngest player, at seventeen, to have participated in the Finals, was a sensation. His success and ultimate fame made Lantz a fortune. He not only became the sole agent for Pelé and Brazil's European representative during the subsequent era of their domination, but on the back of it built himself an empire in advertising. He did not need to tell us in so many words that he was then, in the mid-1980s, fabulously rich, for the meal he hosted for Ernie Walker and three others of us in a Swiss hotel, which started out with Dom Perignon and then became even better, would have set him back the equivalent of the GDP of Liechtenstein. I then became friendly with him by meeting up in several locales throughout my sojourns in European football.

Then in 1986 I received an odd phone call from him. He was then domiciled in a huge house in Cascais in Portugal. His tone was desperate. At first I thought he might want me to intercede in some transfer transaction. One always hopes with men like that. But no. His son was in trouble. He had just been expelled from Gordonstoun. The fact that the lad's sponsor (or Guardian as they call them there) at Prince Charles's former school was none other than Sir Stanley Rous, former President of the FA in England and former President of FIFA, indicated that he would not have been shunted out for asking for more scrambled egg at breakfast. I ascertained from his housemaster that his offence was taking knives to younger boys and forcing them into blood rites by cutting their wrists. He had ignored previous warnings. Charming, I thought. But I agreed to take the fifteen-year-old boy, called Gustav, into our home and try to find a new school for him. My two sons looked on in jaw-dropping incredulity as this boy went around our house, in between making calls to his father in Portugal, like a mini-Jeeves, impeccably mannered, clicking his heels whenever he saw my wife, lending her occasional advice in the kitchen, and looking no more threatening than Pollyanna. He talked frankly about his school and, of course, denied that he had been bullying, but did say, somewhat indiscreetly and perhaps to make his own offences seem less intimidating, that he knew of certain distasteful homosexual practices going on there. In a casual conversation with a friend who happened to be a journalist I mentioned that last allegation. And thought nothing more about it.

Eventually, using my influence as Rector of the University of Edinburgh, which I was at that period, I persuaded the head-master of Tony Blair's former school, Fettes College, to take him in. They did, with the pointed warning that my reputation was at stake in endorsing him. Gustav seemed to settle in and was there for several months, until one fateful Sunday morning I received a phone call from the school saying they were expelling him for exactly the same offences he had committed at Gordonstoun. I drove through to the capital with murderous thoughts in mind, but contented myself with being allowed to take him into a room by ourselves, pinned him against the wall and introduced him to language that would even have been out of place in a Shettleston pub. Then, as he visibly shook, I drove directly to the Scots Hotel, on the westerly fringe of Edinburgh, because I was well known there and I had made up my mind that we had done enough for him. At reception I phoned his father, curtly explained the circumstances and got his credit card number to book his son a room for the time being. When that had been agreed I deposited him in the room and told him his father could come for him, if he could manage to drag himself away from the pool in Portugal. It was not the end of the matter, though. About three days later I received a call from a tabloid newspaper. The conversation, after the usual friendly preamble to relax you, went exactly like this.

'Do you know a boy called Gustav Lantz?'

'Yes.'

'Why was he expelled from Gordonstoun?'

'You'd better contact the school!'

'Why was he expelled from Fettes?'

'Contact the school!'

And then it came.

'Was he expelled for homosexual acts . . . and did you book him into a hotel room in Edinburgh?'

There come occasional moments when the earth seems to stop on its axis. This was one of them. I held the phone at arm's length for a moment trying to ponder the diabolical inference of the question and the breathtaking association of ideas which obviously had gone through the tabloid mincing machine. Could they actually think . . . ? For the first time ever I slammed a phone down on a reporter without a further word.

Now, slamming a phone down on a tabloid can sometimes be like inviting red-hot lava to be poured over you. But I felt that the possible inference was so laughable as to allow them to go ahead and print what they liked. Not a word appeared, despite the fact that they were after some sort of story with a malevolent slant on it. I learned from Fettes School later that the little horror, who made the script of *The Omen* not as far-fetched as all that, had phoned a friend, whose mother came to take him from the hotel and promptly phoned the newspaper to complain about my cavalier treatment of this apparently innocent young lad. On top of which the journalist I had casually informed of the lad's allegations of homosexual goings-on at Gordonstoun, which might have been pure fiction on his part, had obviously talked about it in his newsroom. That was enough for the bloodhounds to get to work.

It shook me. Pelé could certainly not have known that his talent had produced wealth for a man to be able to afford to send his offspring to a renowned public school only to display the worst aspects of vulgar wealth. And there was now no going back for me – I regarded even the most benevolent approach by a news reporter as being like the overture of the friendly man who eventually put the ice-pick into Trotsky's head. But I look back on a final in Barcelona in 1972 as the event which showed just how significant television had become, even to the most cynical of the fourth estate.

140

13

FOREIGN EXCHANGES

The Rangers–Moscow Dynamo European Cup Winner's Cup Final in 1972 was the last of the European finals to be refused a live transmission in Scotland, and the last to be covered by black and white cameras. That, of course, is not the only reason we will remember that night. The arcane rules of the SFA, and the general feeling that this competition was not to be taken just as seriously as the European Cup itself, meant that a Scotland–Wales game had been arranged for that same evening, and as a consequence the BBC were banned from covering the game live. It now seems so preposterous. We discussed these issues in our hotel in Castelldefels, on a hilltop just outside Barcelona, three days before the final. Some of the press were gloating at our obvious discomfort at being denied our live broadcast. Others, more discerning, knew that whilst their reports would be the first to reach their sports desks, watching this game live would have been of enormous benefit to sports editors back home. It is not that I make that assertion to doubt the veracity of reporting, but television was now an enormous window to first-hand verification. And it most certainly is now. Dramatic opening paragraphs, like the classic, 'As I sit here in this hate-filled stadium, surrounded by gun-toting carabinieri', can be matched, or perhaps bettered, almost picture by picture, by live cameras. Purple prose can never be replaced by television, but in a sense it can be policed by it. We arrived for the game itself on a pleasant summer's evening, and, to our astonishment, discovered the pitch was already covered by hundreds of Rangers supporters. They were still trying to get used to the fact that one of the greatest stadiums in Europe had no apparent security system. It was like people who had come 'doon the watter' for a stroll along the prom at Rothesay, on one of the days it didn't rain there. It was that casual and relaxed. The 'polis' surveyed this scene in total indifference. They all seemed to be small and stout, and looked as if they wouldn't have been able to apprehend a kid stealing a toffee apple. How inaccurate first images can be.

Rangers won this final after being three up and being hauled back to 3–2, with their legs visibly failing. They held on. Hell broke out, as their supporters, who had twice invaded the pitch thinking the final whistle had gone, were being denied a cup presentation and responded to the first police action of the night. It was brutal. I was becoming conscious of an agitation right in front of us, after having cleared off a Rangers supporter who had tried to sit on my knee, offering me a celebratory slug of Fundador, the basic brandy, which can eradicate dry rot if applied properly. I recall this little martinet of a ranking officer raising his baton and signalling for the attack to take place. They advanced, batons whirling. It became like a threshing machine as the supporters at the front, hemmed in by those at the back, could not get out of the way of the onslaught. If they weren't being struck by the batons, they were being kicked. Stupidly, after reassembling on the other side of the pitch, many of the supporters, armed with parts of the wooden seats they had broken, charged back. 'Any moment now the guns could come out, for God's sake,' a man said gently beside me. He turned out to be the Reuters correspondent in the area. I won't forget what he said, 'What you're seeing down there is the Fascist police in action. That is the only way they can handle a disturbance. They are the experts in ruthless suppression. They are not even local police. They are not Catalans. That is why they are so hated in this city. They are Franco's men. They are recruited from Castile or Murcia. Anywhere but Catalonia. They are principally in this area to maintain a dictatorship. They have regarded these supporters from their very first invasion of the pitch, like an assault on Franco himself. That is how they are conditioned to act. Respond to command, don't think. These supporters do not understand that their lives could now be at risk.'

The fact that the Rangers supporters reacted to the provocation with such sustained violence virtually obliterated any mention of the origin of the trouble. You could also have said it started in the bars and cafés around the city, long before the game started, where cheap booze fuelled passions. But, in essence, it is my belief that had the little officer not signalled for his underlings to attack, and had the authorities allowed John Greig to emerge from the dressing-room dungeon to receive the trophy somewhere in the stand, the riot would not have erupted. It is also in keeping with what my Reuters friend was explaining, that the Spanish television producer decided, perhaps under pressure, to turn his cameras away from the developing skirmishes, and point them to the empty streets outside, as if not wishing to reveal the scale of the police operation. So, nothing was recorded of the worst of the riot. Amidst the sensational accounts of the night in the press, which laid great emphasis on the behaviour of the Rangers support, my efforts to account objectively for the actions of the police as the principal instigators of this were greeted as almost as an apology for hooliganism.

By now I was four years into fronting *Sportscene* and gaining enough confidence to stick my neck out and state opinions. Where that began to pay off was in my relationship with *Grandstand*, which Frank Bough still presented. I would stand at the edge of a pitch and pontificate about one matter or the other about Scottish football for the network audience, virtually every Saturday morning. It was all controlled from London, and while I did think they were patronising us, as only the metropolitan mind can, and I was irked by the tiny amount of time they devoted to Scottish football, I kept my counsel, because it was at least a window of opportunity. I once broadcast in a snowstorm at Easter Road which blew the umbrella out of my hand whilst trying to introduce various snippets of videotape. I managed to stay on script, but the sight of me in a sheepskin jacket fighting the elements produced a request from the south never to take that jacket off, ever again, as they felt it portrayed the kind of edge-of-civilisation life of the Scot. I was a combination of Rob Roy and Captain Scott of the Antarctic. They actually did think like that. And I let them. The sheepskin is now installed in the Scottish Football Museum at Hampden Park.

At a snowbound Tannadice, with the game just having been cancelled, we felt the show must go on, so the producer made a snowman, we dressed it in the sheepskin jacket, and I ventriloquised the piece. My contribution had become such a regular item that when I received a call from the editor, Alan Hart, to find out if I could get hold of Billy Connolly to join me for a special New Year's Day presentation from Ibrox, for *Grandstand*, prior to an Old Firm game in 1976, I didn't want to disappoint, although I knew I would be up against it since the request came at three o'clock on Hogmanay afternoon. Billy had just had a hit with his D.I.V.O.R.C.E song, and he was catching on big in the south. It was also, though, the time when Billy drank, and

144

drank like prohibition was just around the corner. His later sobriety in life was in stark contrast to a man who at that time was a drunk in a manner that would have made Hemingway seem like an advocate of temperance. When I contacted his close friend Brian Wilson, who was then a journalist, and later to become a Labour minister and director of Celtic FC, I was warned that Billy had been on the sauce for most of the day and wouldn't be entirely coherent. But he did answer the call I made to him, and whilst he sounded as if he was on the verge of collapse, I simply took it that he understood what I was after, and when he appeared to accept, slurringly, I put into motion the process to get him to Ibrox by the following morning. I didn't know what I had let myself in for.

I hired a car and with the rest of Scotland in deep sleep or still carousing, at about eight o'clock on New Year's morning I travelled to his large country house, just outside Drymen, to the north of Glasgow. When we arrived on that bleak, frosty day, the large country house was shuttered up. The silence of an uninhabited world prevailed. After some tentative knocks, I eventually kicked and banged on the door to get some response to a place that from the outside was like one of these eerie, spooky mansions without which Stephen King would never have written a book. Eventually we heard somebody dealing with locks on the other side of the door, several of them, of Fort Knox security level, and the door was opened several inches to reveal a face I did recognise well, Billy's then wife Iris, who looked as if she had gone to bed about the same time as Rip Van Winkle. She knew nothing about the *Grandstand* appearance and my heart sank even further when she kindly asked us in, and I saw the carnage – the Culloden of Hogmanay jollity. There were several bodies strewn around, two on a couch and another three on chairs and the floors, thankfully making sounds of gentle snoring. Iris told us she didn't think Billy would be

capable of doing any broadcast that day, as he was in no fit
state even to come downstairs yet. But she allowed us to go
upstairs, where we found him lying flat on his back. His face,
as white as the sheets around him, was garlanded by his John-
the-Baptist hair length, which was strewn around his head like
a sea-anemone floating on the tide. He was 'miroculous' as he
might have said himself.

Ibrox and *Grandstand* seemed like a distant dream and nothing
else. I had promised the editor in the south I would get Billy
on the programme, and by God, I was going to do it. I primed
myself, as one does in these self-motivating situations, to think
that my career as a network presenter would go down the drain
if I didn't get the Big Yin to the church in time, as Alan Lerner
would have put it. So I shook him vigorously, but with no
response. I increased the shaking, with nil results. So, there, in
that room, with no witnesses, I slapped him on the face, then
again, with some force. A fully *compos mentis* Billy would no
doubt have tried to flatten me after such an assault. But he was
beyond that kind of response, so I was quite safe. Suddenly a
flicker of animation came from the eyelids and slowly he
squirmed into the foetal position and then looked at me with
one eye, 'What the fuck are you daein' here?' His words sent
a chill up the spine. He hadn't a clue what he had taken on. I
explained as well as I could, but he just lay back on the bed
moaning slightly now and again. 'No way,' he said. 'Look at
me.' It is true that at that moment he looked as if nothing less
than a month drying out at the Betty Ford clinic would help.
We had a couple of hours to play with, no more, no less. I began
by pleading with him. Then I began to sound like a spiv agent
in Elmore Leonard's *Be Cool*, in trying to convince him that here
was an opportunity to show off his wares, on a network stage,
at a time when he was rising in popularity, when his record
was selling brilliantly, and as a way of getting through to a

football audience there was no better show than *Football Focus* on *Grandstand*. I don't know how long I spent harping on that, until I saw some response. Something was stirring inside him.

'You promised faithfully you would do it,' I told him, without explaining that's how I had imaginatively interpreted his telephone grunts. He moved out of bed with the painstaking care of someone who had just been in traction. 'Wait for me downstairs,' he said. We did, but even so, I began to wonder what state he would be in by the time we got to Ibrox. When he did appear he looked presentable, but in that unkempt way which characterises him anyway. We piled into the car and drove to Ibrox, as he lay in the back, more sullen than normally he would be. We reached the interview position only five minutes before we went on the air. I was still worried about him. He looked dried-out but solemn. But as soon as I heard the handover from Frank Bough to Glasgow, Connolly came alive. He swept through an interview about his love of football, and especially Celtic, with the typical Connolly impromptu gusto that was making even the camera crew crack up. London saw it as a superb, colourful item. In thinking back to the carcass I had seen in the Drymen bed only two hours previously, you could only see it as a triumph of the human spirit. We concluded my most nervy New Year's Day ever by ending up near midnight in an Indian restaurant near Glasgow University with Billy, despite his team having been beaten 1–0 earlier in the day, leading a conga of customers around the restaurant, even through the kitchen, in a demonstration of his incredible powers of recovery from Hogmanay self-mutilation.

London was delighted. Although I was treading the narrow line between being a skivvy for them and a man who unashamedly wanted network recognition, I was willing to risk some legwork on their behalf. Another Scots comedian, having seen that, actually promoted himself to try to get on *Grandstand* as well – the late Chic Murray. Chic was unique, with one-liners which were stunningly simple and hilarious, all in the one: 'After I told my wife that black underwear turned me on, she didn't wash my Y-fronts for a month.' His deadpan delivery made it for him. The trouble was that he never turned it off. After he had asked me about suggesting him to *Grandstand*, which I realised was a non-starter, he invited himself to a birthday party in our house and stayed three days. We loved the man, but three days of eccentricity we eventually found hard to take. But we stuck with it, for after parting from his wife and stage partner Maidie, he became essentially a profoundly lonely man, constantly seeking company, and we would sometimes find him late at night, after one of our programmes, sitting alone in the BBC canteen in Glasgow, where he ended up being a companion to the all-night security men. It seemed to fit with the oddities of his life that his most promi-nent film role was to play the last American ambassador in Vietnam in a Hollywood film. His last contact with me was when he had left a note in my office with a question. I had used the phrase 'heinous offence' in one of my commentaries at Easter Road. It simply read, 'Heinous? As in "Heinous Beanzous"?'

Chic had not yet registered with the English the way Billy had, but the episode with the Big Yin had raised my profile among the decision-makers at the BBC in the south. We accepted it as if we were subjects of a colonial power, a broadcasting Raj, which countenanced no dissent. They would not budge, for instance, on the sacrosanct BBC news at nine o'clock, thus putting paid to any live coverage of Celtic's European tie with Milan on 19 April 1972, which cut across that news time. It did provoke some outrage amongst some of the Scottish public, with the inevitable reaction that, had it been an English club, they would have moved the news. In 2009 a Scottish League Cup penalty

Apparently by the age of 4, I had already realised that 'sitting on the fence' could actually imperil your health. The best option was to face one way or the other.

Aged 15, winning a school race, indicated a convenient fleetness of foot which helped in escaping critics in later years.

So there I am, decently educated (second row from back, centre) in late teens, at Coatbridge High School, but harbouring no more ambition than simply to chat up someone from the front row.

Left: Skilled photography camouflaged the fact that I was suffering a hangover of Hemingway proportions from a bachelor party the night before. Jess is propping me up, as she still does four decades later.

Right: Twelve joyful years in a classroom led to an eventual farewell from the profession in 1969 which was more like leaving for the trenches than 'Goodbye Mr Chips'.

They passed the champagne-filled European Cup-Winners trophy along the plane as we returned from Barcelona with Rangers in 1972. The faces of journalists Alan Heron of the *Sunday Mail*, Ken Robertson of the *Sunday Express* alongside me, and Ken Gallagher of the *Daily Record* behind us, indicate that we barely survived a night of suspense and trauma.

Germany 1974. Kenny Dalglish, Danny McGrain and Tom Hutcheson were part of the best side we ever sent to World Cup finals. These were the days when players would sit and talk with you without texting their agents for permission.

Billy McNeill, as co-commentator, with me in the Malaga Stadium in 1982. We didn't know whether to laugh or cry when Willie Miller and Alan Hansen put on their Laurel and Hardy imitation which effectively knocked Scotland out of the World Cup.

Travelling the world with Jock Stein, as Scotland manager, on 'spying' World Cup missions took us to the geyser park in Roturua, New Zealand, months before the World Cup finals of 1982. His cheeriness is deceptive-looking. He was by then a man tiring of the rodeo-like challenge of football management.

Sean isn't looking for his ball but reprimanding his wife Micheline for getting in the way of the monitor which is showing the interview he has just recorded with me during the World Cup in Spain in 1982. The disappointment is that Ursula Andress did not appear on cue from the Marbella sea behind.

Terry Wogan's birthday party in 1984 during the Olympic Games in LA led to a joint radio and television insert in which we both interviewed each other. The fact that we look like consenting adults is because we were sitting in a Jacuzzi in the back of a stretch-limo. Where else could that happen but in Sunset Boulevard, Hollywood...

The LAPD almost threw me out of the Dodgers Stadium during the Olympics of 1984 as I attempted to cover the demonstration sport, baseball. None other than Mickey Spillane's Mike Hammer was on hand to help out and prevent another 'LA Confidential'.

Charlie Nick and I about to introduce *Grandstand*'s coverage of West Germany v Scotland in Queretero, Mexico in 1986. 'Archie sleeps wi' Charlie' used to be sung by a certain element on the terracing. In truth, we never got round to that.

Jimmy Hill, Trevor Brooking and Sir Bobby Charlton in the background were all mates, even though a couple of hours later I did not weep with them in the Azteca Stadium at the Hand of God incident.

Outside the equestrian enclosure in Seoul at the 1988 Olympics. The Princess Royal's ex-husband Captain Mark Phillips is annoyed at me for poking a camera lens in his face without written permission. My lack of concern is that I had witnessed his living quarters in Buckingham Palace where his status was like that of a boarding schoolboy.

At the Jackie Stewart Celebrity Shoot at Gleneagles in the late 1980s. The Big Yin recalls the New Year's Day when, with a deadline looming, we broke the world speed-record for recovering from an all-night binge.

This was the Saturday night crew. *Sportscene* established and fostered me over the years because of these very professional people. The young lad kneeling at the front is the sole survivor of the team. Now, what WAS his name again?

The robes of the Rector of the University of Edinburgh sat easily on the shoulders of a Glaswegian for three years from 1983. This sober scene is in marked contrast to my involvement in another Edinburgh caper when my voice assisted in a scene of grand seduction by none other than Ewan McGregor.

Merry Christmas *Happy* *New Year*

All the very best through out this coming Year

To Archie & Family

Thank you for an enjoyable night. It was appreciated tremendously

Jimmy, Ben, Jimmy, Rab & Ian

Be of good cheer, say five murderers to me with their Jimmy Boyle-designed Christmas card, made in Barlinnie's Special Unit, in thanks for the talk I gave them one night about broadcasting. They put away a lot of victims between them. But after the visit I staunchly supported the penal experiment.

This was my last film for *Grandstand*. It is aboard Sir Peter Blake's Round the World winning boat *Steinlager* in Auckland Harbour during the Commonwealth Games in 1990, as he taught a young English gymnast, and me, how to steer. I was beginning to sense that for me the bow was pointing to an exit from the BBC.

Words do not necessarily flow from the mouths of great players like Bryan Robson, the former superb Manchester United and England captain. To try to get him to say anything as co-commentator during Eurosport's coverage of the Norway-Scotland World Cup match in Bordeaux in 1998 was like trying to extract elephant tusks using tweezers.

They have simulated a press-box at the Hampden museum. The silent dummy beside me is untypical. In truth a press-box is the sports equivalent of the old chattering 'steamie'.

It took a skilled plastic surgeon to extricate me from my indispensable broadcasting sheepskin which now resides in the Hampden Football Museum. It has worn well. Rather better than its owner.

Arthur Montford and I were closer than people imagined. And now we can boast together that, compared to the contemporary scene, we chronicled the Golden Age of Scottish football.

shoot-out semi-final between Celtic and Dundee United had to be switched from BBC1 over to 2, to accommodate the ten o'clock news. Nothing changes. These occasional incidents of imposing their will on us were met by a largely acquiescent BBC Scotland, who tugged the forelock and knew their station in life. However, it has to be said that any consequential debate about an independent Scottish BBC would have to take into account the fact that then, as I am persuaded occurs now, Scottish viewers do not, and did not, take kindly to being deprived of network programmes going out throughout the rest of the UK, when BBC Scotland decides on an opt-out.

But London, two years after that Celtic European tie, faced a problem. England did not qualify for the 1974 World Cup Finals. Scotland did. We were left wondering at first how London would play this. An early indication was given when Jonathan Martin, a stickler for being recognised as a representative of metropolitan power, came to Glasgow. He was to be overall editor of BBC's World Cup coverage, and whether we liked it or not, we would be dovetailing into their production team. The main purpose of the visit was to get at the Scottish team manager, Willie Ormond, who, although neat and dapper in appearance, always gave the impression that he would be overwhelmed by events; as he eventually was. We took him to lunch in the Ambassador Restaurant in Blythswood Square in Glasgow. Martin over a pre-lunch drink whispered to me that he would like to see me in the toilet. Knowing him to be a family man, I felt that was safe enough. Inside the loo he took out a fat, white (definitely not brown – the BBC are above that sort of thing) envelope which he stressed was stuffed with fivers and at some juncture in the meal I had to pass it under the table to Ormond. The Scottish manager must have been pre-warned, or else he thought I was trying to caress his thigh, but after an initial fumble, I was able to pass the cash to him, in a veil of secrecy John le Carré would have applauded. Ormond had been bought. In one sense, the secrecy was laughable. But it was done, not just to put a smile on Ormond's face, but to indicate to me who really was going to be in charge in this joint Scotland–England operation, and that they now had the Scottish manager under their thumb. Preposterous though it seemed at the time, I have to admit it did pay dividends, because of the chaos the Scottish players and officials eventually got themselves into on a World Cup trip, artfully described by journalist Hugh Taylor of the *Daily Record* as the Tour de Farce.

The press, and Willie Ormond and his players, went to war with each other. Ormond, mindful of his white envelope, treated the BBC representatives as if they were his blood brothers. The animosity really started before they left on their Belgian and Norwegian warm-up games, with what Ormond thought was unjustified criticism of him and his players, and the over-dramatisation in the press of the Jimmy Johnstone incident, when, breaking a team curfew, he took out a rowing boat just off Largs beach, and proceeded to lose his oars, after which the boat began to drift towards Arran and the Atlantic Ocean. He was saved eventually. But Ormond's lack of disciplinary control and the slack attitudes of the players were trashed in the press. So, off we embarked, on a plane towards Europe, first stop Belgium for a few days, then to Norway for a game, and then on to Germany itself. The tone was set on the first flight. By the time the plane had reached the first layer of cirrocumulus and was still at an angle, we each had been given a bottle of champagne. The players were not excluded. By the time we reached Bruges, so much booze had been consumed that there were few leaving the plane who did not see dull, flat Belgium as Judy suddenly saw technicolour Oz after the monochrome of Kansas. We were, in fact, heading for the World Cup like bus-trippers bound for Blackpool and a knees-up at the September weekend.

One scene encapsulates much of my distilled memory of that World Cup. It occurred in a hotel in Dortmund on the morning of Scotland's opening World Cup game against Zaire. I was sitting in company with Jock Stein, whom the BBC were using as an analyst, and his bookmaker friend Tony Queen. Into the lounge ambled the captain of Scotland, the late Billy Bremner, who, seeing us, sped in our direction and thumped himself down beside Stein, almost as if he had found a long-lost father, and without much ado began to pour his heart out to him. About what? About the shambles which more than adequately described the warm-up tour and the two inadequate games against Belgium and Norway. He was savage about the press, and indirectly about the team manager as well. What he did not tell Stein, although I had (Stein loved a gossip) was the performance of the players on and off the field. He did not tell him of the night in a Norwegian students' haunt with the beer flowing, and of how along with my commentating colleague from London, John Motson, I witnessed Bremner and Jimmy Johnstone, as merry as newts, coming to sit beside us to serenade us with melodies, with an aplomb only inebriated players can manage. And of how an enraged team doctor had been sent by the manager to prise them out of there, thus proving Ormond's lack of guts. Nothing was said of the farcical feud between players and press, which saw them banned from training, and the late John Mackenzie of the *Daily Express* obtusely banned from the official SFA flight, with the said journalist delighted that he could get a headline out of that, and make his colleagues jealous of his notoriety. Not a word about how the players ripped a sponsor's emblem from their boots because they weren't being paid enough. Nothing came from his mouth about all of that, but only about how hard done by the players all were.

Suddenly, with Bremner in full spate, Stein reached out a huge fist and placed it close to Bremner's face, a fist that had hewn coal in Lanarkshire years before, and, on his own admission, one that used to feed bread to the rats a thousand feet underground during his tea-break – a fist crafted in menace. Bremner stopped and paled. The Celtic manager lashed into him about how players should stop feeling sorry for themselves, stop blaming others and go out and prove themselves and how they were in a different league from the 'pygmies' from Zaire, as he put it, and should go out and crush them. This was a moment which was more than just putting down a whinger, but a turning point in the Scottish team's fortunes. From that moment Stein became the spiritual leader of the party, through his ministry with the team captain. Bremner had been shaken rigid by the venom of Stein's address, and the tough little man could not have avoided carrying Stein's writ into the dressing room. Other players afterwards throughout the tournament sought Stein's counsel, which he, extremely expeditiously, granted. Ormond still wore the tracksuit, but he was not the real driving authority. Bremner, through Stein, was that. But Ormond was still talking to us, the BBC, if not most of the press, or at least not with the degree of frankness he was delivering to us. That was the point. The white envelope had turned out to be our One Ring in this crazy Middle Earth of the World Cup.

It also seemed to add to the self-importance of the World Cup editor, Jonathan Martin, who had struck the deal. To say the least, he was not a man you warmed to. Some of his colleagues would have thrown themselves out of the window of a high building, just to avoid going down on the same elevator as him. His sustained imperious attitude gave the impression that an act of generosity or benevolence would have stained his prodigious work ethic. Not all within his purview were intimidated by him, notably David Coleman.

Coleman, it has to be said, was immediately approachable, but also imbued with a sense of invincibility. I never thought he had the same appreciation of the nuances of football as the man he replaced, Kenneth Wolstenholme, and I thought he was much more authoritative covering athletics. But he had a powerfully striking voice which commanded immediate attention, turning the humdrum into the effervescent, just by applying his vocal cords to the subject. In so doing he had become an untouchable. You felt that even the top executives were in awe of him. This he demonstrated one night in Frankfurt. It was late. Coleman, Stein, Queen, myself and producer Bob Abrahams, a pugnacious little bastard from London who was the self-proclaimed tough guy of the whole operation, were mulling over events so far, with glasses of German Hock, or orange juice in Stein's case, oiling the conversation. Martin appeared from nowhere. He was, indeed, one of these infuriating men who always seemed to appear from nowhere. Rudely and abruptly he butted into the conversation and asked Coleman if he could go to an editing suite and add his voice to some videotape they were cutting. The commentator put down his glass, calmly eyed the man and addressed him with the following words, coldly and clinically: 'Jonathan, there are big pricks, there are little pricks. But you are the biggest little prick in the business.' You could sense everybody round the table retreating into their personal shells. The thought that the man supposedly running the show was being addressed as if he were Manuel in *Fawlty Towers* was one to make you hold your breath.

Now, within the BBC a tape had been privately circulating for some time before then amongst its sport production staff, of Martin being abused from the studio floor by an irate Coleman, losing his temper and treating him with contempt. Obviously being accustomed to this treatment, Martin astonishingly hardly batted an eyelid and simply cautioned him with a meek, 'Now, now David.' And then turned on heel and left, like a waiter accused of serving the soup cold. Coleman was letting us know that, if he snapped his fingers, such people would come running after him. This might have been raw arrogance. But it was also an education to me, as a rookie, of the power of star quality. Is this what we all ought to aspire to? Do we feel broadcasting fulfilment will be attained only if we can tell our notional bosses to take a running jump? Was it not worth a damn being on television at all unless your ego could appear to have been created by Dr Frankenstein? Or was Coleman simply an egregious exception?

That scene, and those thoughts, lingered with me as I witnessed how a bunch of self-indulgent players had failed to comprehend the importance of preparing for and playing in a World Cup. They had followed up a 2–0 victory over Zaire with a creditable no-scoring draw against Brazil, including the infamous miss of Billy Bremner which almost stopped my heart in commentary, when his legs seemed to turn to jelly, only yards from goal, and the best of all the chances was missed. When the whistle sounded on the last game, a 1–1 draw with Yugoslavia, confirming that an unbeaten Scotland side was nevertheless now eliminated from the World Cup, I turned to my colleague Arthur Montford and said something to him. He didn't reply. He was inconsolable, wounded beyond speech. He seemed to epitomise, even more than myself, what the nation would undoubtedly be suffering. But when we returned home on the official flight, thousands turned out to greet us like all-conquering heroes. That day the seeds of self-delusion were being sown. The bitter harvest was to be reaped in South America four years later.

14

SURVIVAL RATES

The small detective with the large cigar protruding from his mouth apologised for the air-conditioning having broken down in the police station, which was now like a Turkish bath. Every now and again he would take an enormous gulp on his cigar and expel huge clouds of smoke, but when he spoke it was always stuck on the side of his mouth. He looked like Edward G. Robinson in *Double Indemnity*. 'All right,' he said, 'What is your statement?' and poised his fingers over the typewriter. I started.

'I came out of the hotel at about eleven o'clock this morning and walked straight across the road to the beach.'

'Which hotel?' he asked.

'The Meridien. Right at the end of Copacabana.'

He started to thump the typewriter with two fingers. 'So what happened?'

'I walked on to the beach. It was cloudy, as you know, and I was surprised that the beach was so empty. Hardly anybody there. I had been warned about pickpockets and the like, so I walked down to the water's edge, took off my tracksuit and then backed into the water until it came up to my neck, but all the time keeping my eye on the suit which had my wallet in it. My eyes never left it. I came out and sat beside it, to dry myself off. Then two small boys came along and started to kick a ball near me. They kicked it up in the air for me to head it, which I did.'

He took the cigar out of his mouth, turned and looked at me, with a smile suddenly spreading over his face, then added, almost wickedly, 'And then you started to play with them?'

I nodded. He turned to the typewriter, shaking his head, greatly amused, sniggering and continually repeating, 'You started to play with them,' words that rendered me a Rio de Janeiro buffoon. Then he said something in Portuguese to his couple of colleagues, who both bellowed with laughter. It was time to defend myself.

'I only kicked the ball about four or five times, then I sat down. They kept shouting "Zico, Zico". When I put on my tracksuit about ten minutes later, the wallet wasn't there. Gone.'

He thumped the typewriter almost in glee. 'How much?'

'Two hundred and fifty American dollars. I just don't know how they did it.'

This time, he paused and looked at me before giggling again and pounding his typewriter with obvious relish. He certainly knew how they had done it. Rio de Janeiro had stung me. Or two kids, about ten years of age, had. The visit to this police station just off the mazily tiled promenade leading to Ipanema, was an undignified formality. The kids' brilliance at skinning me in front of my very eyes was almost something the police were tacitly admiring. Though later I was to learn that police policy degenerated into hunting after these vagrant street-boys, and shooting them at random, to try to clean Rio up.

'When did you arrive here?' the officer asked.

'Yesterday. We're staying here for a few days on our way back to Europe. From Argentina. I was attending the World Cup.'

He suddenly put down his cigar and put his hands in his face, and began to moan, theatrically. The others suddenly became very animated, as if I had said something which disturbed them. I had. It was then I realised why I had heard nothing of the samba beat around the city since I had arrived. Brazil was in mourning. They had only finished in third place in the finals, behind their bitter rivals, the winners, Argentina. Third place equalled ignominy. The entire nation must have felt it was like being duped by two small boys on a beach at Copacabana. For those few moments we were united in mutual humiliation. I had come a long way to lose two hundred and fifty dollars on a South American beach. It was the premium that life was asking me to pay for a remarkable odyssey. It had been worth it.

The trail had begun a year before when, in 1977, we travelled to South America with the SFA party and players, in their efforts to acclimatise to the particular conditions of that continent, in preparation for the possibility of reaching the finals in Argentina. One of the three games was against Brazil. And just along the road from our hotel, on Leblon beach the day before that game, some of us saw Scottish team manager Ally MacLeod run into the waves like a kid on a school outing, and then disappear under a huge wave and not appear for some time, but then surface to wave back at us frantically as if he had found treasure from a sunken galleon. We waved back, as you do when kids are splashing around on a beach. He wasn't fooling around, though. He was drowning. It took us a few moments to realise that, so we waded in, to get near him. There was the great self-publicist barely able to speak, and looking humbled by the waves. We got him out, and thereafter when he had fully recovered, his power of rhetoric returned, and oddly, he seemed to want to leave no one in any doubt that he had had a near-death experience. This flirtation with eternity was but nothing, compared to what lay in store for him the following year.

Argentina, 1978, was wounding and stimulating at the same time. To watch a cheerful, personable, approachable guy undergoing an ordeal of which only a Torquemada would have approved was deeply unsettling. I had felt a personal stirring of unease, many months before, when I assisted him in a brewery-sponsored tour of the country to cities and towns, as he bathed in the glow of admiration which came from his ecstatic nation. I felt that if it didn't come off for him, the fall from grace would finish him. Failure, set against optimistic hysteria, could only mean a death warrant. When I watched him cuddle a dog on a hillside in Alta Gracia, the town we were all based in, after the defeat in the first game by Peru, 3–1, and heard him tell us that the animal was probably the only friend he had left in South America, you could tell he was slipping into self-perpetuating misery. After the game against Iran, who we assumed were the Glenbuck Cherrypickers of the tournament but which ended in a 1–1 draw, my colleagues in BBC television in London deliberately and maliciously edited pieces together with close-ups of Ally's contorted, tortured face on the bench which were the closest television has ever got to portraying Edvard Munch's *The Scream*. In a sporting setting, there really was no way back.

The win against the ultimate finalists, Holland, in Mendoza, 3–2, but which meant nothing in terms of qualification, was summed up beautifully from underneath a wide-brimmed hat in an airport lounge by a pissed-off looking Alan Sharp, the Scottish novelist, who had interrupted his screenwriting business in Hollywood to travel to the game, when he pronounced, 'We didn't win, we just discovered a new way of losing.'

Beat that, you felt. I saw Ally again, once, before he was sacked. It was at a function in Glasgow and in a sense I was slightly embarrassed when I talked to him because I knew what was going on behind his back, and Mr Jock Stein was involved.

I had been asked by the greatest gofer ever in the Scottish game, the journalist Jim Rodger, to phone Stein in England, where he was ensconced, miserably it has to be said, as Leeds United manager. When I did, Stein asked me if I wouldn't mind announcing on Harry Carpenter's *Sportsnight* that he might be interested in the Scottish job as a successor to Ally, but without attributing any comment from him. Stein was clearly setting the ball moving amongst the media to push him up front, and I had the best platform of all on network television. When I told my colleagues in London about that, they moved me into top spot on the programme, where I virtually demanded that the SFA immediately contact Stein, who would be willing to serve his country.

I think even a man of his status was beginning to feel he was being forgotten, and that some would have thought he was wholly unavailable, given that he had only been in his new post for several weeks. The following morning I heard a sports bulletin on radio which included an interview with Stein, who, when asked about my story on *Sportsnight*, replied by effectively saying that I was merely flying a kite. But the old fox had indirectly put his bid in, and as day follows night, so his cunning machinations got him the job. Frankly, I think he would have got it anyway, but he wanted out of the Leeds position as quickly as he could. I had helped hasten the inevitable.

So Ally was out of a job, and I was down by two hundred and fifty American dollars, although hoping that a family living in abject poverty in some shack in the shanty towns clinging to the hillsides around Rio would be eating more healthily than they would if I had not decided to take a dip off Copacabana beach. For all of us who had come through, and been close to that Argentina experience, there was a feeling that life would never be the same again. I can't exactly be sure when that mood lifted, and in any case I tend to think we could have been deceiving ourselves into believing that it deeply wounded the national psyche, when essentially it did not. People seemed to be going about their business as usual when we returned. We had been embarrassed, certainly. But it wasn't like the failure of the Darien Scheme exactly, although some seemed to try to make it so.

From out of the depths of the indignities suffered in South America came the new sense of proportion about our footballing abilities. The rabble, festooned in tartan, which spat at MacLeod after the Iran game and tried to effect a lynching party assault on the team bus afterwards, was to be replaced by a future generation of jolly realists called the Tartan Army, whose only capability of assault is on the ears, with their incredible, repeated rendition of a chorus from 'The Sound of Music' which has now baffled countless numbers of opponents trying to work out what those lyrics have to do with the land of Burns. The source of that transformation was Argentina.

As we were out there trying hard to make sense of it all, two men had emerged back home meantime, who you felt could take our minds off the wounds through their personal duels – John Greig and Billy McNeill. Both men had become managers of Rangers and Celtic respectively, during the World Cup Finals. Both of them threw themselves into their posts with relish, and the uplift you felt after visiting them was distinctly like having been in the presence of the harbingers of a new age. In a way you felt that they would be in their posts until the last ice in the Arctic melted. They were born for their positions. It wasn't to be like that, of course, because football politics, the bounce of the ball, injuries, personality clashes, money, can all conspire to make presumptions a hazardous exercise. Greig, a superbly witty man, who personified Rangers grit as a player, could not have been more amenable and helpful, until the bullets began to fly. 'He lost the dressing room,' one of Rangers' outstanding players,

Alex MacDonald was to tell me years later. That phrase can either be the most damning of verdicts in football or something almost poignant, as in this case. When I went to interview him before a Cup Final and filmed a training session during which one irate player, Ian Redford, told Greig to stick the ball up his arse, I knew all was not right. It all ran counter to the image of Greig, the tough guy. Indeed such was the pressure that it began to affect his health and on 28 October 1983 he resigned.

Billy McNeill, even in adversity, never appeared to be anything other than supremely confident in riding out storms. He was always articulate. Indeed, when he left Celtic as a player, I hired him to work for us at the BBC as a reporter and he suffered the indignity of being asked by his former manager Jock Stein to leave the vestibule at Celtic Park one day, when talking to some of his former colleagues, because he was now with the 'meeja'. Like Greig he had his successes as a manager, but he had to deal with one of the most pompous men I had ever encountered, the chairman Desmond White, who ran a tight ship, to say the least, and whose announcements on crowd attendances at Celtic Park could not have been bettered by Hans Christian Andersen. We always added on another ten thousand for the sake of reality. Davy Provan, now with Sky Television and the former Rangers-supporting boy who became a Celtic star, summed up Billy's fate for me. 'Billy's pressures stemmed from being squeezed between the demands of the players for more money and the obduracy of the board, completely dominated by Desmond White.' Billy left Celtic in June 1983, so I contacted him immediately for commentary work, and for years on and off we became professionally attached that way. So two legends had been sent packing, for different reasons of course, but which shook the earth for those who believed in natural selection. The traditional species, at that stage, looked to be dying out.

We wrongly assumed, though, that we would see less of one major figure, Willie Waddell, who had now pushed himself upstairs to an executive position with Rangers. He looms large in my memory as one of the most influential, if not terrifying, figures I had to deal with. About six months after the demise of Greig in 1983, I visited Ibrox for an interview with one of the players and sat at the bottom of the marble staircase which led up to the boardroom level. Sitting there you would have thought that a bull had been let loose above. I could hear the shouting and bawling floating down the stairs, as the distinct voices of Waddell and his new manager Jock Wallace indicated a major fall-out. We would learn that it wasn't unique. It was virtually a daily occurrence. Waddell, in his new executive position, was exerting his power in ways that would shock even the hardest observers. He had resorted to bullying, fuelled by recurring visits to the ever-handy drinks cabinet. Frank King, Rangers accountant for a period, actually had a nervous breakdown through it, and one morning crept under the bed in his house, refusing to come out, unable to face up to it any longer. But let us put this in context. Waddell saved Rangers. Had he not been around at the time of the Ibrox disaster and the riots in Barcelona, to provide a stern, but resolute and organised image of the club, they might have ended up as laughing stocks. He punished himself, though, in that process. Day and night he worked to salve the wounds of Barcelona, providing a degree of dignity in the aftermath of the sixty-six deaths on stairway 13 only eighteen months previously. His later behaviour tends to obscure his positive achievements, like the establishing of a modern stadium at Ibrox. He had never been a shrinking violet, and when I met him, during his *Scottish Daily Express* days, he could be gruff and distant, if you were not one of his buddies. But he was popular amongst the press. Then the incredible pressures took its toll of his nerve and his dour personality, and led him to the sad conclusion that he could drink himself out of the daily grind.

One day, accompanied by my London producer, Jim Reside, I went to Ibrox to ask for an interview with him about the opening of the first new stand in the reconstruction of the stadium. The little Rottweiler of a man at the foot of the stairs, called Bobby Moffat, who acted as his Swiss Guard, refused to let us mount to his office until he got the say-so. He kept us waiting for over an hour. When we eventually opened his office door, he was standing, trying to keep his balance by holding on to the seat behind his desk, and as we entered, he unleashed a volley of obscenities against us, the general drift being that we were 'bliddy' (his favourite adjective) arrogant to think we could expect an interview. He then almost fell into the chair, and tried to put his elbow on the edge of the desk, but only succeeded at the third attempt, before regaling us again with a string of curses, pointing his finger accusingly at me, but increasingly becoming drunkenly incoherent. Reside, who knew nothing of Waddell's reputation, turned on his heels and bolted. I wasn't far behind. This was proof of the rumours that by about eleven o'clock in the morning he was incapable of normal behaviour.

In Berne, one morning in 1983 after a Scotland international game there, I came down to breakfast very early and was told by a waiter that there was a man lying behind the bar. It was Waddell, a guest of the SFA, dishevelled and asleep, a crumpled mess of a man. Many of his detractors, those who had suffered under him, might have been delighted to witness such a degrading spectacle. To me it was a tragedy. As I stood over him, where he had apparently lain all night, I thought of the slightly crouched, dynamic winger who had cast a spell over the Ibrox support in the 1940s, with some of the most dramatic wing play in the history of the Scottish game; of Waddell as a manager with his hard-fought triumphs; the political figure

163

racing around Europe to hold the Rangers community together under intense pressure from all quarters in the 1970s; and his most enduring legacy, the magnificent new stadium he had bequeathed the club. It was just hard to work out. Football had built, then destroyed him.

I remember in later years Lawrie McMenemy informing me of the problem Brian Clough had with booze. He was drowning in it. His eccentricities multiplied through it. But Clough was by nature, it seems, an outward-going, socialising drunk, eliciting sympathy from those around him, who realised he needed help, not ridicule. Waddell had not been of that kind. He was a bitter and abrasive drunk, capable of losing total control. That ought not to have deprived him of help. But it was in short supply, as it has been, traditionally, for the compulsive drunk in our society. The helping hand usually has another drink in it. I recall Joe Aitchison, at the age of eighty, or thereabouts, telling me in a television interview about the man he had trained, the great Benny Lynch, who won the world flyweight title in 1935, but who died at the age of thirty-three, a shambling drunk, moving from one pub to another looking for handouts. Joe ascribed Benny's self-belief in the ring as 'moral courage', as he put it. There was an element of that in Waddell, in facing up to the huge problems his club had, after the disaster and the riot, and sustaining, personally, much of the pressure mounted on the club. Thereafter, like Lynch, he degenerated. He did not end up destitute, like Lynch, but certainly lonely and friendless, both victims of the classless scourge of booze.

Not that that was confined to managers and players. Virtually all of us in the trade drank. Some more than others. Stein used to sit deliberately, late into the night, as the classic insomniac and renowned teetotaller that he was, in a corner of some foreign hotel, waiting for the media to trundle in at all hours, so that he could wittily and/or scathingly rip into us, for our aberrant social habits, as he saw it. The image of the pressman filing his copy, the phone in one hand, a drink in the other is hard to eradicate from the public mind. Films and literature have amplified that. So, I suppose, has reality. I not only witnessed heavy drinking but indulged in it myself, thoroughly enjoyably, it has to be said. One of the ways of relaxing the night before a live broadcast was to have a dram or two with others of a like mind. In that culture, total abstinence could be considered a crippling frailty. As a result, it was interpreted that some colleagues could not last the course. Indeed, at the funeral of my good friend Alan Davidson of the Glasgow *Evening Times*, a superb and sometimes underrated writer, Jimmy Reid, the political commentator and Clydeside union leader of the past, and a close friend of his, delivered one of the eulogies, in which he took the opportunity to lecture many of the media present on the culture of booze, which he suggested was responsible for too many mishaps in the profession, and that essentially they should clean up their act. This was based on some remarks that had been printed in some parts suggesting Alan was the victim of drink. I found that a slur. As I pointed out in my own eulogy, he had simply opted for a lifestyle which gave him great satisfaction and both of us had spent hours sitting over our drinks, putting the world's wrongs to right, from which we derived more benefit than attending editorial meetings. In my eulogy, I emphasised that the pressure of journalism and meeting deadlines made access to the bar that bit more tempting and that, in any case, Alan had exercised the greatest of all freedoms, to live a life as he chose it. It just so happened that it did not embrace muesli and Pilates. He did drink a lot. But then so did I. He was the unlucky one. We did note that that same evening, in the restaurant to which we had all repaired, Jimmy Reid was seen downing large whiskies. Drinking both enlivened and soured the professional world we inhabited.

Waddell and Stein, though, shaped and honed my political instincts, by my being caught up in their jet-stream. They laid the foundations for me to be able to face up to the unpredictable nature of this business and how to try to ride or parry metaphorical punches. After them I thought I could face up to anything. Then an episode in my life occurred in which I learned that the cuts and bruises in the scraps with these two men had prepared me for the entry of another gladiator into the arena, intent on taking on all-comers.

Alex Ferguson and I developed a healthy, early relationship in the 1980s. We would sit in the boot-room at Pittodrie, Aberdeen and gossip, like two old women at the steamie. Gossip about anything. Footballers, managers, women, politics, religion. He would often broach the subject of how Rangers tempted him to become their manager, illegally I suppose, but that their non-signing of Catholics at that period would be too much for him to abide. Like Stein he was fond of a blether and of revealing his fangs against those he didn't like. And those he didn't like were denounced with a venom which could stun you just listening to him.

He unexpectedly invited me to an Aberdeen Supporters' Rally in 1984, where a surprise presentation was made to me of a glass bowl. It was all his doing, for what he considered was my positive attitude to his club, which he considered was never properly appreciated by the majority in the Old-Firm-inclined media. I wasn't pro-Aberdeen. I was pro-Fergie. I just took to his breeziness and his irreverence, when he would talk, perhaps out of turn from time to time, but with refreshing candour. This support for him was never more forthcoming than when we went to Mexico, in 1986, for the World Cup Finals, when he was manager of the national side. One of the most interesting fringe activities was his festering feud with the SFA secretary Ernie Walker. It was over all sorts of matters and at one stage

Walker excluded the media from any contact with the Scottish players and manager, and even our BBC cameras were banned from entering the camp. Fergie, nevertheless, flouted that ban, by coming outside to talk to us (he had received no white envelope, by the way). I took his side on this, and as the tournament progressed, virtually willed him on to success, as others around me questioned some of his team selections, including the dropping of Graeme Souness for the final game against Uruguay, in the slum suburb of the city called the Neza, even though Souness had no legs left on him after the searing heat of Queretaro when West Germany beat Scotland 2–1.

I also appreciated that at the end of that tournament Fergie had done as well as any manager could have, under the circumstances, and had Stevie Nicol of Liverpool not missed a staggeringly easy chance to score early on in that game which turned out to be goalless, Fergie would have qualified us and been smothered in hallelujahs. I tried to emphasise that fact, of which he was appreciative. Earlier, on that damp, chilly, but glorious night for Aberdeen in Gothenburg in 1983, when they lifted the European Cup Winners' Cup, he rushed off the pitch to meet me on the sideline, ready to interview him, and grabbed me in an exultant bear-hug that betokened not just joy, but an abiding friendship. However, three years later, when I commentated on a game in Dublin, in 1986, between Scotland and the Republic of Ireland, I criticised the Scotland and Aberdeen goalkeeper Jim Leighton for coming out of his goal, flapping weakly at crosses. Later that week, I went to Easter Road to cover one of Fergie's last games, shortly before he left for Old Trafford, and as I walked into the vestibule at the ground, he spotted me, and suddenly started to scream abuse, including the now well-used phrase for rubbishing the media, 'What do you know about football?' Enough, I would have thought, for him to have encouraged the presentation of a gift from supporters two years previously. However, it was not the occasion for sophisticated point-scoring like that. It was time, after all the escapades with Stein and Waddell, to stand square and retaliate. The spume from our saliva struck each other like consenting adults, as nostril to nostril we hurled as much obscenity at each other as we could muster. The group around us were silenced and gaped – even that hard nut, his assistant manager Archie Knox, seemed to go pale. Suddenly from amidst the throng a tall police super-intendent appeared and sternly intervened with, 'Gentlemen, if you don't stop this immediately I will have to take some action.' We turned away from each other. Fergie into the dressing room, me down the tunnel to the ground itself, fuming.

I have pondered that scene often. If it was meant to rupture what I had always imagined to be a solid relationship, then I had got the message. But, after all, Cathy Morrison, to whom I used to pass love notes continually under the desk, walked out on me as well, at primary school, when I was ten, but I got over that and lived to tell the tale. No, I concluded that my meeting with the two wee boys on Copacabana beach had been much more significant. The rules of engagement, on that stretch of sand, were now much clearer than those for dealing with a football manager.

15

STRANGE ALTERNATIVES

Big Peter they called him, and big he certainly was. He wore swanky suits, and his lush, greying hair and his erect walk lent him the look of some Charlotte Square banker from Edinburgh. Banker he was not, and Charlotte Square he probably had never been near, unless on a Rangers supporters' bus which had lost its way en route to Easter Road. He had been born and brought up in Brigton, as he pronounced it, had played the big drum in an Orange band and now looked incurably rich. He was the man who carried me to Liverpool for the famous Wales–Scotland showdown in 1977, in his chauffeur-driven Rolls Royce. And lest I am giving the impression I was feeling like royalty throughout that trip, it has to be recorded that on the return journey, Glen Daly, the famous Glasgow comedian and Celtic fan who wrote their famous signature anthem, 'It's A Grand Old Team To Play For', was badly hung over and vomited all over me. I took it as placidly as one can, vomit being a not unusual Glasgow acknowledgement of a good night out.

The passionate Proddy and the tireless Tim together might have appeared to some to be a strange combination, except for the fact that they were from Glasgow, where bonds are struck over the divide with an alacrity which defies the outsider's view of the city, and that they were both successful. Peter ran a carpet factory in Maryhill. Glen ran a comedy store at the Ashfield Club. And they were fans. They loved football. I was invited to front a presentation at Peter's carpet showroom once, for a considerable wad of fivers, and from then on Peter regarded me as a pal. He would lead me, eventually, into another culture. For one day he said to me, sincerely, but at the same time casually, like an after-thought, 'By the way, Arch. If you ever have any trouble with anybody, let me know. I could soon have it sorted out.'

Broadcasting brought people like Peter into my life. Being on the screen and attracting people to you, for whatever reason, led you into a supermarket of unintended relationships. Some extremely brief, others enduring. Enriching life would probably be too strong an expression to use, but in all kinds of ways it was stimulating. Many of the public were attracted to so-called television personalities, like proverbial moths to the flame, crossing paths with me only because I was the regular face of a Saturday evening, nothing more than that. It wasn't as if I was preaching any dogma in introducing sports programmes, it wasn't as if I was trying create a cult following. It was just because I was there, saying things, sometimes deliberately provocative things to a specialist football audience, but nothing that would suggest I was reaching down into the soul of the community and commanding respect for profound thinking. I, therefore, simply attracted disciples of the 'weel-kent face'. Superficial though that might have been, it did take me, at times, away from the confined rigours of broadcasting to meet people and ways of life that would have been beyond my ken otherwise. I loved that part of my business, being known, having doors opened to you, which ought not to have, but did; of meandering down the byways of life which would have been unknown territory otherwise. I was particularly fascinated by Glasgow men like Peter.

STRANGE ALTERNATIVES

As his phrase 'sorted out' had occasionally slipped over the lips of such as Lucky Luciano, I tried to retain a neutral response to it, as if I knew, possibly, what he really was suggesting, and at the same time didn't want him to think I was an ingénu who hadn't an inkling about the ways of hard men. Was he serious? I didn't pursue the matter. I just nodded acknowledgement. To be perfectly frank, there were people in the media I would like to have seen with their feet in a concrete base and dropped over the edge of the Dalmarnock Bridge into the Clyde. I reacted publicly to criticism as if I hadn't a care in the world. Privately, I endured it like a ferret eating its way up the large intestine. I fantasised about revenge in ways that would not even have passed through the mind of a CIA operative. I felt it was therapeutic to imagine the most horrendous retributions. Such was the reaction to criticism of my first live commentary.

It was at Hampden Park, on a wet night, in May 1969. The mud was eradicating the numbers of both the slithering Scottish and Northern Irish players and making them almost indistinguishable from one another. I commentated from low down in the soaking south enclosure of the stadium, on a night when driving rain caused the lowest crowd for a Hampden international (7,483). Jacques Cousteau would have been more appropriate for the job. I received criticism in the *Sunday Mail* which I thought would lend a premature ending to my career. Pol Pot would have received better reviews than this one, which effectively dismissed my efforts as a waste of time. They used one of my own favourite Scottish words from the commentary to describe the performance, 'dreich' (meaning unendurably drab). The long pregnant silences which were interspersed throughout the commentary were not to heighten the dramatic tone of the one-all draw. It was because I couldn't see, most of the time, what was occurring on the other side of the pitch.

To his credit, Peter Thomson, the editor, understood the peculiarities of that evening and told me that if I was going to survive I had to develop a thick skin. I never did really, although I pretended to. This was my first real experience of being keel-hauled publicly. Thereafter, there was no hiding place. You were under scrutiny, perpetually. That came with the job, of course, but I think that helped generate feelings of suspicion of everybody in the business, even people close to you. Were they for or against you? Whether it had anything to do with my own nature, or whether it was the natural outcome of the sustained public pressures which could make you feel that at any time you might fall off the edge of a cliff, it is difficult to say. A clue, though, was given me by that excellent commentator, and old friend, the late Brian Moore, in his autobiography. In it he admits he became almost paranoid in thinking that various people were plotting against him in different ways at ITV. It was difficult to believe that of Brian, whom I always regarded as a confident, well-grounded, nerveless man.

Nevertheless, I did get harder with the people around me. I did occasionally blow a fuse. I did want to get my own way, not sometimes, but all the time. One of the young producers I got on well with, and with whom I spent many a great social evening, actually said to my face once that within the department I had developed the manipulative skills of a J.R. of *Dallas* fame. Thankfully, he was not a Shakespearean scholar, or else he might have conjured up Iago as well. Thus it seemed to me that anyone wishing to develop a resilience in this trade would be well advised to study Machiavelli, interspersed with the lighter, recreational reading of Edgar Allan Poe.

But here in his flashy suit, encased in his Rolls Royce, was Peter, successful Glasgow businessman, suggesting the unthinkable. I put it to the back of my mind, until one day he phoned me and asked me if I would do him a particular favour. Tommy

172

Burns was to have a presentation made to him by a local Celtic supporters' branch, and would I act as chairman for the night? It was to be held in the Blackhill Tavern. Those who do not know the name Blackhill should be informed that, at that time, it was considered safe to visit only under the protection of a counter-insurgency unit. This I am sure was a gross insult to many decent people who lived there. But everybody knew how the notorious Glasgow hardman Arthur Thompson, of whom tales of gangsterism and his connections as a hit man with the Krays were now circulating around Glasgow as if he had a Robin Hood appeal to him, had had his car blown up, just outside his house in that neighbourhood. His enemies were after him and blew up his car with gelignite placed underneath it in August 1966. Thompson survived but his mother-in-law, who was also in the car, did not. This tavern was only a couple of hundred yards away from Thompson's house. So when, at first, I declined, I recall Peter saying vividly to me, 'The invite is from Arthur. He would be very pleased if you could make it.' Meaning, of course, that he wouldn't be too chuffed if I didn't. I was intrigued, and admittedly also slightly uneasy.

The evening proceeded smoothly and I was royally entertained with a 'guard' put over my car outside. Then I was told Arthur wanted to see me. He was sitting quietly in a corner. 'Hello, pal,' he said simply and handed over an envelope which was obviously for my stewardship of the evening. As I took it, I certainly wondered if that was all that would be involved. It wasn't. Again I received another invitation to chair a charity dinner in a hotel in Glasgow, after which the transport arranged for me and my wife was in a huge limousine, which I discovered had Arthur and his wife sitting in the back. The car stopped off at his place and we were invited in and offered stovies which he had cooked himself. At two o'clock in the morning I am not normally disposed to stovies, but in Arthur's house I discovered I was finding it difficult to refuse. At the same time I was hoping that the chauffeur outside had taken the trouble to check underneath the car for any suspicious objects. All that flashed through my mind as I battered my constitution with greasy stovies.

All these invites, given in the name of various charity events, which suddenly flooded in from big Peter and Arthur's sources, were, I believe, attempts at establishing some form of respectability. Pick up weel-kent faces and you form a social bridge of sorts. For instance, I was to deliver a speech at another function, and then afterwards I was told I would be sitting beside David Hodge, the Lord Provost of Glasgow, no less, at a table which included Arthur, Peter and a coterie of their friends, including a sharp-suited contingent from London, who were quite clearly not members of the Carlton Club. But the Provost, noticeably, and to the open disgust of the table, didn't show up. Probably some of his officers had warned him off, and pointed out who he would be sharing the prawn cocktails with. I began to question my own relationship with the group, suspecting that I was becoming a kind of surrogate PR for some of the hardest men in the city.

I had to work out a diplomatic way to say 'No', emphatically and finally. They didn't make it easy for me when Peter said that, for all my help, Arthur was going to gift us something for our new house in Bothwell, just outside Glasgow. 'A skull as a paperweight?' suggested one friend of mine when I mentioned that. There wasn't much to do about that. He appeared at our house one day with a measuring tape and proceeded to take the dimensions of the new fireplace we were installing. Without saying too much, and indeed he was a man of few words, he left. A week later Peter invited me out for lunch and on the way took me to a workshop where we saw Arthur hunched over a long slab of mahogany, carving it with a lethal-looking tool, and sandpapering and scalloping the edges of the wood with great finesse. He was making our wooden mantelpiece. When eventually it was installed, my wife and I would sit and look at it wondering what other artistic carvings had been made by that same hand, on more animate objects. It felt as if we were under the sway of an alternative culture.

It all ended abruptly, though, when one night at the tail-end of a BBC ball in Glasgow, an aspiring hardman began to get fresh with my wife and a friend of hers by trying to push his hand down both of their cleavages as he stood behind their couch. A fracas developed, in which after much pushing and shoving he was ejected from the hotel. He turned up the next day with bruises on his face (no punches had been thrown that night, just a lot of mild wrestling – so what was with the bruises?), a bouquet of flowers, a bottle of champagne and an abject, almost snivelling apology. Later that same night Peter phoned to ask me if I was enjoying the champagne and to tell me that the matter had been dealt with. That was it. Enough. This was definitely scary. Time to make the break.

When I think of it, I actually found myself going to ground. I avoided calls, I lied about alternative commitments, I made up that I was in London a lot of the time. Gradually, I think the message got through and months later I took a call from Peter, who said that it had been noted that I was making myself scarce. He actually sounded hurt. I don't know whether that was a threat or not but I laughed it off, and never saw him again. About three years later he came to a sad end. He was found, hanged, in his garage. It was said he had taken his own life. But differing rumours persisted that he had been under serious threat, that he had tax problems, that he had an incurable disease. I never found out the truth. It had all been a phase in my life which, frankly, I had found irresistible, fascinating, tempted by the adulation they heaped on me, their hospitality, their cash for services rendered as an after-dinner speaker, their sometimes witty streetwise banter, their ersatz glamour. I actually ended up boasting, deliberately, to some of the prudish faint-hearts in the BBC that not only had I known one of Scotland's most notorious men but that he had spooned me up stovies as well. I could tell they felt I was descending into moral turpitude. I had succumbed, not because of who I was, but of what I was.

However, after that I approached invitations with due diligence, and when the minister of a Carstairs parish implored me to attend a sports day and present prizes in his parish I gave it much thought. For it was to be held in the State Mental Hospital there, whose inmates included some of the most dangerous killers in the land, never to be released. It is still Scotland's Broadmoor. After much consideration I agreed, after ascertaining that there would be neither a javelin-throwing nor a pole vault event. The minister liked the tone I was adopting, although I was still tentative about it. However, what my wife and I discovered after we had gone through the security checks were events which would have graced a Sunday School trip, such as the three-legged race, the egg and spoon, and gentle bowls.

No, the real shock was that everybody looked so damned normal. Here we were amidst some of the most appalling psychiatric patients who had committed some of the most dastardly crimes, and yet you could not tell the difference between them and the warders. My next-door neighbour at that time looked more psychopathic (he had told me over the garden hedge that he didn't like my criticism of Motherwell). The inmates were pleasant, polite, helpful; in all honesty they brought to mind Beatrix Potter rather than Sigmund Freud.

The little man, Ian Simpson, who conversed pleasantly with my wife at the edge of the bowling green as I presented prizes, we were later told was a murderer three times over. The head nurse at the time, Tom Oswald, was trying to let the outside world see that these patients, despite their horrendous records, could be controlled, and live within an ostensibly civilised community. We were so completely won over that I agreed to become a patron of a group which would instigate more visits from the outside to break down the mistrust of such an institution. For the next few months I tried to recruit other personalities to join me in building the bridge between the general community and the patients, to lessen the prejudices against mental illness.

But it suddenly fell apart. Two of the men who took part in that sports day were Robert Mone and Thomas McCulloch. Since I spoke to many of the patients that day, I must have met them. Several months after we had been there, on 30 November, that same pair broke out of the hospital. Ian Simpson, no less, tried to stop them and was brutally assaulted with an axe and was scalped, his ears sliced off for trophies. They went on to kill a policeman, and savagely axed three others, before eventually being arrested. So much for the liberalisation of the system. I was accused of naivety by even close friends, against whom I mounted little argument.

So when they heard that I had accepted an offer to give a talk at the Barlinnie Prison Special Unit in early 1977, which housed half a dozen notorious murderers, all undergoing special attention within the system with the distant possibility of being reformed and passed back into society, they thought I was now an over-indulgent do-gooder. But I went. And met Jimmy Boyle, the former razor slasher, thug and hit man, who, in showing me his wonderful paintings and sculptures in his cell, and speaking of his ambitions to make a living as an artist and no longer being a threat to society, utterly convinced me. When I told a crime reporter about that afterwards, he sneered at me for being taken in and graphically described to me that one of the alleged ploys of Boyle was to cut off his victim's penis and stick it back in the person's mouth. I defended my presence at the Special Unit, though, extolled its virtues, and again spoke up, as often as I could, for this degree of penal reform. My only reward was a Christmas card that year from the eight convicted murderers, thanking me for having made the effort. Then I heard that tragedy, as at Carstairs, had come in my wake, when Larry Winters, one of the men who had spoken to me, like a big softie, in his cell that night, had died of an overdose of drugs, within what was supposed to be the 'clean' environment of the Special Unit. It was clear that my presence was not adding to the credibility of penal institutions.

When I stood for the Rectorship of the University of Edinburgh against Margo MacDonald and Teddy Taylor MP in 1985, I did try to stress my interest in looking at social ills of one sort or another and championed the cause of the Special Unit and Jimmy Boyle in particular. I went softly on Arthur Thompson, admittedly, as I felt that even within the historically liberal student body of the university, they might regard that as beyond the pale. The only real 'social' issue raised personally against me, by Margo's supporters, was the rumour that I had once been a member of the Orange Lodge. I at least had enough experience of that nonsense to know that no matter what you said, if people developed thoughts like that in their heads, not even frontal lobotomy could remove it. However, that piece of deliberate malice did not pay off, as I won the election and spent three significant years chairing the University Court.

So the Spaghetti Junction of diverse social routes, centred purely on the face which appeared every Saturday night on the box, led me in all kinds of directions. Some I recall with affection, others still make the skin creep. None, though, would I have missed. They are now indelibly part of me. At that time

I was becoming increasingly involved in broadcasting in London, because the year before my investiture at the university I had cemented myself firmly into the network team after my work at the Olympics in Los Angeles. In their rather superior way of looking at somebody from the provinces, which they considered Scotland to be, they gave the impression, ever after, that I went out to Los Angeles as a boy, and came back a man.

16

THE BIG EVENTS

For someone born only a hundred yards away from a cinema, thus regarding it as a second home, and where I proved that illicitly watching the screen for hours at a time would not lead inevitably to corneal transplants, Hollywood meant more to me than, for example, Bethlehem. *Angels With Dirty Faces*, starring James Cagney, stirred me more than Luke 2 chapters 1–38. That's just the way it was. I can hardly deny it now. I simply preferred one fantasy to the other. By that reckoning, I thought that when I would first set eyes on the large HOLLYWOOD sign, clinging to that hill above LA, I would feel some kind of elation that I had come home, as it were, or had reached some spiritual destination. The fact of the matter, though, is that I was stuck on an LA freeway when I first saw it, heading for another freeway, then eventually to join another bloody freeway, to get us to the Rose Bowl in Pasadena, to do commentary on an Olympic Games football quarter-final match.

The expected crowd of almost 100,000 all seemed to be trying to get there at the same time, and were obviously experts in fending off deep frustration. Mine was deeper than most, because I was being paid to be on time, and it seemed that I was losing the battle. This definitely was 'suburbia of the soul', as John

Mortimer had described these famous acres. We sat it out patiently, and did get there to watch Brazil destroy the opposition and to observe a chattering American crowd, plug-ignorant of the rituals of watching a football match, munch their way to obesity with hot-dogs, popcorn and Coke. But the day was a reminder that LA stopped for nothing. There might be an Olympic Games in town, but they had the Oscars every year, did they not, which made them inured to special occasions, and the inhabitants existed in a metropolis that seemed to stretch into infinity.

So the Games would just have to wait their turn to gain attention in this self-indulgent city. And you didn't really know there was an Olympics under way until you reached a Games venue. The other cities I was to attend, for other Olympics, all seemed drenched in a visible Games presence of posters and flags. This was a commercially minimalist games, pared down to the bone after the financial excesses still suffered to this day by the citizens of Montreal and their Olympics in 1976. For me, it was a test of how to try to make some sort of mark in a huge team of commentators, some of whom were greatly influential, like David Coleman, Ron Pickering, Stuart Storey, Barry Davies and Terry Wogan – the *crème de la crème*.

The day the BBC videoed Terry and myself interviewing each other on his birthday, sitting in a Jacuzzi, sited astonishingly in the back of a lengthy open-topped limousine, under a blistering sun, in a courtyard inside a surprisingly smog-free Columbia Pictures Studios just off Sunset Boulevard, illustrated, in just one image, the bewildering nature of the Olympic Games of 1984. There were many images which still cling, but that is always the introductory one, opening the gates to a profusion of others, in the best of all possible Games for me.

I was to go eventually to Calgary in the winter for the Games there in February 1988, and in the summer of that year to Seoul for the Games in Korea, as a roaming reporter and commentator. Had LA gone badly for me I would not have made the other venues. I had been earmarked to go to Moscow for the previous Games, but because of the political situation and the decision by the USA to boycott the Games, I was sacrificed. The US boycott was in objection to the war being waged by the Soviets in Afghanistan and in support of the mujahidin, who years later turned out to be so kindly disposed to us for our principled backing that they perfected the roadside bomb for our troops. So for Moscow, the BBC savagely reduced the size of their projected team, and like many other broadcasters I missed being present when Scotland's Alan Wells won the 100 metres. Instead I travelled to Australia to film a documentary on his preparation for the event and consoled myself with that. It was a minor consolation, but any indignation I felt about being waylaid in 1980 was swept out of my head as soon as I realised that I could not possibly lie back, starry-eyed about the setting of our hotel on Wilshire Boulevard, and the broadcasting giants around, and simply wait for things to happen. Long before I reached the Wogan-in-a-Jacuzzi stage I had decided to try to make some sort of mark. Better that than languishing round the hotel pool for days before the official opening, waiting to be asked to do something.

I recalled an American I had met and interviewed at Gleneagles, the year before, about foreign golf visitors. He had given me his card and told me to phone him, if ever I got to LA. His name was Jack Hennessy. He had given me a souvenir tournament badge which had the prominent and famous nose of Bob Hope, the American comedian and film-star, on it. Hennessy Cognac sponsored the Bob Hope Desert Classic at Palm Springs, as it so happened. It set me on a train of thought that perhaps, just perhaps, there might be a connection I could make. Jack came down to see me, only a couple of hours after phoning him, and took me to the famous Lakeside County Club in his sparkling white Cadillac and lived up to his word about hospitality by standing me lunch, and more importantly introducing me to some of the denizens of the bar, including the animator who had established *Looney Tunes* and had devised Woody the Woodpecker. He was simply called Norm, and he proceeded to give me a rigorous lowdown on this renowned bar, which had provided sustenance to Humphrey Bogart, Peter Lorre, Sydney Greenstreet and Mary Astor, every single day, when they were filming the great *Maltese Falcon*. When I asked him about one of my childhood heroes, Humphrey Bogart, he didn't hold back. 'Why, the most unpopular man in the club was Bogart. What a misfit he was. Nobody wanted to go on the course with him. People thought he cheated, kicked the ball in the rough and all that, and when he'd been on his binges he'd come down here with a hangover the size of Santa Monica pier and be the most miserable sonofabitch in the ENTIRE country. One day a guy in the industry was told he'd been drawn in a foursome with Bogey. He pulled out! Almost unheard of. When he was asked for his official explanation, he just told the committee, "If I want to play with a prick, I'll play with my own!"'

My slight disillusionment on hearing that was soon forgotten when Jack told me that he would try to get in touch with Bob Hope. He went to a phone and after a few words, signalled me over and handed it to me. 'Say hello!' I said, 'Hi, Bob', as one does to someone you've known, but, equally never known, for the whole of your life. Within a few sentences he agreed to be interviewed prior to the opening of the Games. I slightly panicked on hearing that, because, at that stage I had no authority to decide where cameras should go. At the same time Hope's name was the insurance policy. After I had let our office know about the interview, there was first an astonished silence, then pandemonium broke out, in seeking to re-arrange recording schedules to accommodate what they now saw as a major promotion for their Olympic coverage.

The following day we rolled up in time to discover Hope was away having an Olympic uniform specially measured for him. When he did appear, eventually, he walked through the French windows from the lounge, swinging a six-iron he had in his hand, and immediately walked back in again after our cameraman informed him his shirt was too dazzlingly white for his lens. He did that without a murmur, although I could have quietly thrown a poisoned dart at the cameraman for risking being told to shove off. But, trouper that he was, Hope calmly changed into a multi-coloured shirt and not only proceeded to talk humorously about the Games, but actually, when I asked him tentatively, did a promo for *Grandstand* straight to camera. I thought an agent would jump out from behind a bush demanding some exorbitant fee for this. The only scare was in editing it in time, and properly, after it had been originally hacked to bits by a producer who didn't like working late hours. Re-edited, Des Lynam squeezed the promo into the programme just before *Grandstand* went off the air, and for me it set the ball rolling. Especially when I showed the office the Olympic cap which Hope had given me as a souvenir. It had a buttoned-down brim which when you snapped it open revealed the words, 'Fuck Russia'.

From then on I could have done what I liked. They gave me a camera unit to roam LA at will. We did a sequence in the LA Dodgers stadium on baseball, a new sport to the Games, and three times were ejected by an officious big-mouthed security woman, midway through my interview with the former actor (now TV baseball reporter) who had played Mike Hammer in Mickey Spillane's detective series. Three times we were ejected from this so-called prohibited area, and three times we sneaked back in to allow him to finish his Bronx 'de boids and de bees' accented explanation of his favourite sport. Then, when she got the police to us, a woman in the crowd stood up and defended us with a statement which Franklin Delano Roosevelt would have applauded: 'These guys are our guests. They're Brits. They fought alongside us during the war! Have you bums ever heard of the London Blitz? These people suffered for our freedom and now they'll go back home thinking America's a dictatorship! You should be ashamed of yourselves, you bums!'

Duly fortified with this sentiment, I finished my piece to camera in the middle of the crowd, rammed a baseball hat on my head, lifted a huge popcorn bag, dipped into it and finished with that piece of American pragmatic hokum, 'If you can't beat 'em . . . join 'em.' The crowd applauded my conversion. This jollity carried over into the utterly meaningless piece of nonsense with Terry Wogan, in our limousine Jacuzzi, talking about ourselves mainly, ostensibly celebrating his birthday, for which the Jacuzzi session was a birthday present from his colleagues. It was something you might have called pure Tinseltown; he, sending the interview out live on Radio 2; me, recording the piece for television simultaneously. It was self-indulgence of a kind not unknown around the Hollywood hills.

That was the mix I embarked on. Helping create a kaleido-scopic view of the city, even to the extent of eating three typical American breakfasts, in the space of twenty minutes, at a famous diner there, until they had reshot it to the producer's satisfaction. I'm now left with a lifelong aversion to pancakes with maple syrup. I spent more time with a camera crew, roaming the city, than at a stadium with a microphone.

Working at any Olympic Games is like being part of an invading, occupying army, come to impose ridiculous ideals on populations who absorb them, by and large, as merely tran-sient entertainment. The same feeling existed in Seoul and

Calgary when I was there. But not nearly as acutely as in LA. There were many of us who felt uneasy about the American free-market culture which had permeated these Games. The only nation not to see the torch entering the stadium on television at the opening ceremony was the USA. They were on a commercial at the time. The torch relay was also sponsored around the differing states, like it was a travelling vaudeville act. Now nobody goes around quoting Baron de Coubertin, like itinerant evangelists, and the pomposity of Olympic ideology is usually restricted to opening and closing ceremonies, no matter which city you are in. And we all knew that the Games were probably awash with performance-enhancing drugs anyway, so there was no spouting Billy Graham of Olympic scripture amongst us. There was unease, though. You wondered where this behemoth was heading, its exponential growth like one of those unstoppable plants in a science-fiction movie. Four years later provided some of the answers.

The 1988 Winter Olympics in Calgary was historically significant as the last Games of the Cold War era. We had thought that the new science applied to drug testing had made the system foolproof and produced a relatively 'clean' games. I actually had to film an item trying to explain the extensive efforts gone into to catch cheats, who would be exposed by gruesome tests involving high-resolution gas chromatography, high-performance liquid chromatography, gas chromatography/mass spectrometry, fluorescence polarisation immunoassay, and radioimmunoassay. Try saying that in one sentence. It took ten takes in front of a camera to get that right. Enough science there to have detected a steroid-tainted flea.

Whether cheating was becoming equally sophisticated or not, we had a relatively 'clean' Games. But we had a debacle of another sort one that caused you to re-evaluate your own ideas of what passes as athletic achievement, and how there can only be the thinnest of lines drawn between admiration and ridicule. It came in the form of the myopic 'Eddie the Eagle' Edwards, the Gloucestershire plasterer who suddenly emerged as Britain's sole ski-jumper.

He saved the Games from mediocrity and became its shining star. The response to him was unique. You cringed, you laughed, you hyperventilated, all in one. When I saw his first practice jump I thought a spectator had surreptitiously got on to the slope at the top, and as a dare had made this effort, a kind of winter equivalent of streaking. What, apart from his own audacity, put the spotlight on him, was the fact that the Games turned out to be so bland. First, the snow disappeared. When we arrived there was plenty, the temperature at 12 degrees below. Then the remarkable, warming Chinook wind blew in from the Pacific over the Rockies and the prairie turned from white to brown. When you stood at the top of the ski-slope and looked down, what you saw was a thin ribbon of snow which had been imported from the Rockies, set against the brown monotone of Alberta. By the cunning use of cameras, the producers were able to make it appear that winter had not been usurped.

Around the city not much was catching the eye, until Eddie Edwards appeared. He was engulfed in a media hysteria which was born of a need to find Games heroes. No matter that the myopic little man finished fifty-eighth and last in the 70 metres jump, and fifty-fifth and last in the 90 metres. He had pluck, and people watched, perhaps not admitting to themselves that they were waiting for a catastrophic end to it all. But when I interviewed him, you could never tell whether he was taking himself seriously, or whether this was some big send-up of Olympic competitive standards. Then, when we all heard that a Las Vegas showman was claiming he could make him a cabaret star, even the greatest Olympian present was about to be eclipsed.

Almost the entire Games media travelled out to a nightclub to talk to him, to watch him on the stage with dancing girls. This turned out to be the biggest media scrum I have ever been in. Cameramen and reporters were exchanging punches with each other as they tried to corner him for interview. You could see in their wild, demented eyes, a need to get something out of a little man about whom all media were now saying, 'Thank God for Eddie, rescuing us from the luge and ice-dancing.' It was also sad to see him on the stage, hopelessly ill-advised by the people around him, and even one of the Las Vegas people admitted to me that all this was fraudulent and sad, and that nothing would come of it. It was all to do with publicising the nightclub we were in, which had had poor public response during the Games. Eddie was being used, and we, in return, were using him to colour the drabness. Thankfully, he did exploit his derring-do, commercially, in later life. Then, with our guards lowered, and thinking that scientific vigilance had rooted out the cheats, thus introducing an era of purity, came Seoul, in the summer.

In the middle of the night in our vast hotel in Seoul in 1988, I took a call from my BBC editor to inform me that Ben Johnson, the winner a couple of days earlier of the 100 metres gold medal, had failed a drugs test, and would I make my way down to the Olympic Village to see what was afoot in the aftermath. The aftermath was as though a massacre had taken place down there, as the place was now besieged by marauding camera crews, not knowing what to do, except take shots of themselves marauding around, for Ben Johnson had flown the coop. He was away already, out of the site and heading out of the country. From that moment the Seoul Olympics was irreparably tainted.

Whom could you now trust, if a Blue Riband event had been won by stealth? This feeling was amplified by the man rooming next to me in the hotel, the athletics commentator Ron Pickering.

He was physically a large, powerful man, with a sharp, bright intellect of a kind superior to most of his colleagues around him. I had become close to him in LA, talking over our largely shared, leftish political views, and his distaste for the dumbing-down Americanisation of practically anything, the only exception to which was his admiration for their high academic standards that his own son was then enjoying at Stanford University. He was fond of malt whisky. Since I am not averse to it myself we would enjoy a dram or two, solving the world's problems together. He was also a wonderfully fluent and insightful athletics commentator, who had to put up with the Coleman ego, as Jack had to with the Giant in his beanstalk days. Indeed, when they sat beside each other in the commentary booth, at one stage in their joint careers, they had a microphone each, but this caused the voices to clash from time to time. So their Scottish producer, Jim Reside, who was charmingly nicknamed the Snake by his colleagues, decided they would have to share the one mic. As Ron himself said, to get his share of the mic and wrest it from Coleman's grasp for his turn, he had to take on the techniques of a Sumo wrestler. I never listened again to them without envisaging that the transfer of one voice to the other came as a result of a furious bout of arm wrestling. Shortly after the Johnson revelation, he knocked on my door and the words remain etched. 'Come in and have a drink. You'll need a stiff one, after what I have to tell you.'

In there he poured a large one and then said, 'Say nothing about this at the moment but I heard a British athlete has been tested positive. I think it's Linford.' Down the hatch went a considerable amount of the gold stuff, for as Ron knew the British sprinter Linford Christie well, I could tell this private information had traumatised him, and that he needed somebody to talk to. It was staggering, especially as I had organised an interview with Christie the day before, in which he had impressively talked about the shame that Johnson had heaped on the whole of athletics, especially the sprinting world, adding that the result would mean that nobody would even trust the likes of him, Linford Christie, any longer. The irony of that was not lost on the pair of us. Frankly, I met few people who liked Christie, who treated the press in an aloof, casual way, denoting thinly disguised contempt. Several days later the news did emerge that he had indeed failed a test, and you felt as though you were witnessing the collapse of any decent standards, and that probably the concierge at the front desk might be selling the Johnson steroid, Stanozolol, under the counter as well. Who next, for God's sake?

Pickering, who continually complained to me of this 'damned hiatus hernia I have' and who never ate anything late at night as a result, nevertheless emptied his malt whisky bottle with me in the next few days, as the conjecture continued. I remember, as we savoured our elixir, Ron reminding me that the very first athlete ever to have been disqualified in the Olympics was in the Mexico Games of 1968. A Norwegian modern pentathlete called Hans-Gunnar Liljenwall had tested positive for excessive alcohol in his blood. As we downed our malts we could afford a chuckle about that. Now we were into a more devious subterranean world. Christie, it has to be emphasised, was later exonerated and it was shown that he had been taking ginseng products which had led the testers down the wrong trail. However, that announcement cleared nothing. It wasn't science which predominated, it was mistrust. The doubts simply didn't clear.

Seoul is a mixture of the modern and ancient Orient. The two elements of the city coexist happily in a successful dovetailing of progress with tangible retention of the past. Skyscrapers dominate the skyline, but the surrounds are like going back to the rickshaw environment of the opium trade. I should know. Because after the Johnson and Christie shocks, the BBC dropped all other options for me and set me on the trail of potential drug stories. Again I had control over a camera unit, but not in the same sense as in LA, which was based on providing dabs of colour to the output. This was the pursuit of the hitherto unexamined dark side of the Olympic soul. It was a pointless task, but the editorial team were leaving nothing to chance. They dared not miss another drugs-test failure. But it was a fruitless task.

It had all started out as a promising Games, in a personal sense, when the editor asked me to run a section of the torch relay, and record the event for an item in their *Olympic Grandstand* preview. Des Lynam, who arrived in South Korea the day after that decision, tried to get me replaced by himself for that run, but to his credit John Philips, the overall editor, refused to do so and stuck by me. So, in the tiny provincial town of Chongju, I received the torch from the incoming runner and ran the one kilometre to pass it on to another runner, on its way to the capital itself. Thousands were out, lining the streets, cheering us on, as our cameras captured the scene. When I delivered my feelings, breathlessly, to the camera, just after I handed the torch over, the editor thought how natural and emotional I had sounded and looked, with tears streaming down my face. What I did not tell him was that the tears had been generated by the amount of smoke that was filtering into my eyes from the torch itself, which as the run progressed felt like a ton weight, filled with oil as it was, and got lower and lower, as the arm became cramped. Anything else I suppose would have been an anti-climax after that experience. But the Johnson affair was the pivotal moment. The Olympic movement seemed thereafter in disarray, the ideals scattered to the winds and nobody really trusting anybody. I never did get even another sniff of a drugs story after that, but we all started to believe, rightly or wrongly, that this now overblown event was riddled with cheats.

Nothing of that idiosyncratic nature ever emerged in football's World Cup Finals. There had been some poor individual performers and some appallingly weak sides in those competitions, but they never represented a radical break from the norm, like Eddie. On the other hand a World Cup could provide crowd enthusiasm which Olympic Games never matched, and could distinctly reflect other kinds of social problems outside of drug-taking. The sight of a line of men, feet spread, hands against the wall, being held at gunpoint outside the stadium in Cordoba in 1978 for more than two hours during Scotland's game there against Peru, told us that we were visitors to a ruthless dictatorship.

The sight of young girls, no older than primary school age, in the slum area of the Neza, in Mexico City, in 1986, trying to sell their bodies to passing supporters, told us that this country was appallingly, cripplingly poor and that sheer chicanery, by the then Brazilian president of FIFA, João Havelange, in association with television companies, had taken the final to a country that did not need it and would not prosper from it.

The pitched battle between English fans and French police along the streets of Marseilles in 1998, after their 2-0 victory over Tunisia, reminded us that this global sport would forever be regimented and that even the innocents would be herded like cattle at times, in the name of security. But, in Spain in 1982, we experienced scenes that seemed to reflect Burns's belief in the brotherhood of man, when Brazil met Scotland in Seville on 18 June. We witnessed the longest dancing conga line ever seen on the planet, comprising men and women from such as Auchterarder and São Paulo, places of great cultural similarity, swinging its way through the city centre like a multicoloured thread in search of a tapestry. It was the night I commentated on a thunderous goal by Davy Narey, which my colleague Jimmy Hill described as a 'toe-poke'. But that downgrading of the shot, and Scotland's ultimate annihilation by four goals to one, was much less important than crowd scenes which denied the global trend of hooliganism. We seemed to have cleansed the sour diet of Argentina out of our system.

Straddling World Cup Finals and Olympic Games was made easier by the brilliance of the men surrounding me, the technicians, the producers, the reporters, the commentators, all of whom worked with a professional ease that hopefully rubbed off. It looked like it was paying off for me when more offers of work flooded in from the south which, to the annoyance of BBC Scotland's Head of Programmes, gave him the impression I was regarding work north of the border with less care. That was nonsense, but emanated from a man who simply did not like being argued with, as I had certainly done on occasion. I could tell he was particularly aggrieved at my being taken even further out of his ken when I received an invitation to consider something that was couched initially, and without any prior explanation, in a simple telephone question: 'Do you object all that much to getting up very early in the morning?' The questioner was meaning an entirely new BBC project. They were calling it Breakfast Television.

17

THE BREAKFAST MENU

Working in early morning television is a bit like feeling you are taking a bath, fully clothed, like Tony Curtis in *Some Like It Hot*. You are dressed as normal, but it still feels as if you are in the wrong place at the wrong time and the feelings about the experience are decidedly mixed. The alarm-call in the ungodly hour bites at you, the world is dark and still. You travel through London as if it had been hit by a neutron bomb, devoid of humanity. London without traffic is a blessing in one sense and a vision of the end of the world in another. You then have to walk into the contrasting brilliance of the studio lights, which hit you with the impact that Tam O'Shanter must have felt when Kirk Alloway 'seemed in a bleeze'. On the one hand, you feel at the centre of things, at the hub of broadcasting standards which command respect throughout the world. On the other, you know that either you, or the whole experimental project, could be axed overnight. In fact the whole of the media world in the late 1980s was in the middle of the Thatcherite revolution, and on the other side of London, at that very time, ferocious battles were being fought between police and the print unions to settle News International's move from Fleet Street to Canary Wharf and the disembowelling of the unions.

During that period I meet Andrew Neil, then editor of the *Sunday Times* and with whom I had worked at BBC Scotland, coming off the shuttle at Glasgow Airport from London. We're at the head of the throng disembarking. He suddenly grabs me by the elbow and leads me behind a pillar in the terminal building. 'Wait till they pass,' he says. 'Some of the union men are there. They've given me a hard time. I can do without that now.' We stay there until he feels the coast is clear. The editor of a famous newspaper, in hiding in an airport, perhaps epitomises the almost pathological tensions which permeated the media world then, and the residue of which persists to this day. I interviewed Neil and the late Sir John Junor in a television programme called *Three's Company* in which these two media giants of the political right made it clear that they hated each other with a venom, and when Andrew Neil told me that he had received death threats, Junor said witheringly, 'Who would want to go to the bother of trying to kill you?' Ego can cause fractures in apparent political unity. They were united, though, in their distaste for the public service ethic of the licence-fee-supported BBC.

Inside the vast half-moon shaped building of Television Centre, men and women have been awake all night, assembling the news for a breakfast programme which, as a broadcasting concept, is passing through its embryonic test period, the sort of programme the likes of Neil and Junor would have decried as a needless extravagance. It is the first few years of early morning television, contesting, as it has to, the dominance of breakfast radio. The night-shift journalists at their computer screens don't look like pioneers. At that hour they simply look as if they are in rehab for insomniacs. No clacking typewriters, just an eerie hum, occasionally punctuated by an oath or two. On their screens they might be handling news of an impending nuclear war, or another football managerial sacking. But it is all the same to them. They have made it through the night and the mood is one of solemn triumph. The sight of the presenters coming through the door is like a whiff of reality seeping in to remind them that shortly, by 9am, it will be all over.

Jill Dando floats swiftly through the room towards an editorial desk, thick script in hand, her blondness, newly coiffed, like a stimulating beacon amidst the artefacts of drudgery. She seems then, and even more in retrospect now, unassailably the English rose. On and off screen she is a purveyor of gentle charm. On and off screen Paxman is witty, acerbic, matey or pugnacious whenever it suits him. He is moody. Together they combine to make you feel you are blessed to be part of a class act. This, though, seems the peak on Darien for me, from which I can see a vast new ocean of possibilities.

But basically that experience was all about how to live with discomfort, and appear to be normal at the same time. What I did, initially, in joining that strange environment, was to marvel at the ones who had established themselves by doing exactly all of that – the real pioneers. Frank Bough, whom I had known through the years as the main presenter of *Grandstand* and so many other varied programmes, was at the top of his profession, the kind of broadcaster who could have swung from a chandelier, one-handed, and still talked to camera like it was a cuddly toy. He had that technique of assertive intimacy, and such a well-recognised personality that the BBC in 1983 decided he was the very man to convince the world to turn off their radios of a morning and watch the box instead. It was always going to be a difficult task to take on the bleariness of the world at that time. And everybody knew that there was great dissension within the BBC itself about this project, as many authoritative voices thought it would fail miserably.

Selina Scott was beside him on the couch on my first morning. They were cheery and welcoming to somebody who was actually feeling like a rookie, on that first outing. I knew, even from the outset, that the sports slot was simply a breather for them both. The editor would give me about five minutes of air time in which to make some impact. Fitting in beside two really seasoned studio performers, I felt I was in competition with them. I was also aware that the entire news production team would use the sports segment as a useful interval for them to tidy up what they had already transmitted, and get ready for the next dollop of the serious stuff.

Fred Friendly, who produced all the programmes for the great Ed Murrow, took the trouble to write in his book, *Due To Circumstances Beyond Our Control*, about their years together at CBS in the States, that the sports element in news had to be more than a mere announcement, like the PA at the ballpark, and not like a game of sticking the tail on the donkey. It had to exist, if at all, as a meaningful, integral part of the presentation. Well, you could tell within seconds of being in the building that this was a sticking-the-tail-on-the-donkey environment and that I was going to be put to the test. At times I felt, in the early days, they weren't listening all that much to what I was saying, which is what prompted me to tear up the prepared scripts and write my own material. In fact, this was to become a contentious issue with some of the editors.

Although Selina had lent the programme that necessary initial charm, it was a fellow Scot who made me feel even more at home, Mary Marquis. She would be brought in occasionally to give Selina some rest. It was certainly trying for both ladies to get up in the middle of the night, though by their first appearance at 6am they would look as if they had just stepped out of the pages of a glossy magazine. Every time I see that mysterious lady in the Scottish Widows commercial I am reminded somehow of Mary's darkly seductive appeal on the screen, as she slipped into place of a morning. She was a success in London and it was always gratifying to know that somebody could make it like that south of the border. You couldn't have any ambition in broadcasting in Scotland without hoping that you could eventually make an impact on the UK network. So the sight of her in the morning always heartened me.

However, as I was to discover, television can be brutally transient even for a well-established performer. A couple of years after I had started there I received a phone call from Mary, a tentative, almost nervy call, which was surprising coming from one normally so cool. It was clear that she was trying to sound me out about what was happening in the south, and did I have a new contract and how was the programme shaping – all in all a strangely probing call. Even as she spoke I suddenly realised that I hadn't seen her in London for some time, and I knew then what it was about. She was out of it, and didn't know which way to turn. She had been dropped. I know not in what terms. Abruptly? Elusively? 'Don't call us, we'll call you' sort of manner? Whatever, here was a delightful presenter who desperately desired the network exposure and added elegance to it, but one way or another had been shown the door. I think she called me because, by now, I was well established and she had heard through the grapevine that I was on a new contract. In broadcasting terms it was like a call to the Samaritans. Simply talking would help. She never appeared again on the programme. You do not allow yourself to succumb to the inevitability that the same fate will befall you at some time. It's not worth dwelling on closure. But sometimes, as in Mary Marquis's case, you are suddenly drawn up short, and take pause, and look through the glass darkly.

But the bigger shock was to come. How do you face up to a mate, someone you can talk to in manly terms, who has a massive professional reputation, who looks and sounds like a regular guy, and you have just woken up one morning to discover that he is splashed all over the *News of the World*, with stories of sexual escapades which would have made George Best seem like John the Baptist? That's how we had to react about Frank Bough, a man for whom we had the greatest professional respect and genuinely liked as a man's man. We had known he was no Trappist Monk. And we lived and worked in a milieu of professional people whose morals were not exactly attuned to those of the Pilgrim Fathers. Even so, we were stunned that he had been caught in a brothel, performing scenes more akin to Crufts dog show. Perhaps we were principally shocked by the stupidity of it all. How could he have laid himself so open to exposure? How could he have got caught, for heaven's sake? To be honest, hardly anybody I spoke to around him expressed moral outrage, just incredulity at his naivety. Silly ass, yes. Moral reprobate? That was a debating issue amongst us.

I remember having a discussion about that the Monday morning after the lurid revelations with fellow Scot Francis Wilson, the weather man who later went to Sky and who always gave me the impression he did not give a damn about management. Outrageously, after the initial shock, we just thought it was hilarious. To envisage Frank, in lingerie, being led round a room like a dog on a leash, dented nothing but our funny bones. As Francis said, with the same kind of wistful expression he has announcing low pressure about to hit the west of Scotland, 'It's like hearing Cinderella was Miss Whiplash!'

Did Frank make for the first flight out of the country? Not a bit of it. When I talked to him in the Kensington Hilton Hotel at a farewell function that was held for him, when he was on his way out, he was remarkably sanguine and, without delving further into the details, did bring up the news exposure, since we got on well together. I remember his plaintive remark, 'What man doesn't have some failings!' It was a line which not even

Andy Capp would have tried. Frank was doomed. I think he did believe he could somehow survive this, initially, but then came the revelation which did for him. He had been taking cocaine. Again I was informed, by the producer who worked closely with him, that he had admitted the drug habit to the tabloids in a deal which would guarantee closure of the episode, and prevent them from further breathtaking disclosures. His ending came in that strangely unique BBC way. He was invited to meet with an executive in a hotel in London. When he arrived he was shown to a suite, where drinks and snacks had been laid out on a table, as if they were expecting a whole group to be in for an afternoon of reminiscing over old times. But in fact only a single executive turned up to inform him that he was being sacked. The meeting lasted only a few minutes. Bough simply turned and left, leaving a table full of goodies and an illustrious BBC career behind.

I missed him and did feel sorry for him and still do, as I know he had to have a liver transplant in 2001 when cancer was discovered. Ought we all to be held to account for our behaviour in private life? Did appearing regularly before the public lend any of the media a warrant to know everything that goes on in your life? We debated that amongst ourselves during that episode, knowing full well that the executive case against Bough was that the BBC as part arbiter of taste in society had to avoid offending sensibilities, at almost any cost. When you think that a couple of decades later Max Mosley, the boss of Formula One's governing body, won the right to privacy for even the most garish of sexual escapades, then you could perhaps wonder whether Bough could not have shown more bravado, and toughed it out, using the same process. But it was a different age then. He was on the box, constantly, and every appearance would thereafter trigger some reaction by a public which had been influenced to some degree by Mary Whitehouse and her

National Viewers' and Listeners' Association. He had little chance of survival. It gave me no satisfaction to learn that it was another Scot, Gerry Brown, a man born in the Gorbals, who had sharpened his teeth in investigative journalism with the *Scottish Daily Record* and had pursued Frank slavishly to the brothel antics, and who, thereafter, as Eliza Doolittle said, 'Done him in.'

Then came Jeremy Paxman. He coincided with the disappearance, not only of Frank, but of the family-orientated couch in studio. The desk was now the podium, as the programme was turning to a harder news style and called *Breakfast News*. He always arrived ahead of me every morning by at least a couple of hours. He would roll past my desk with more than a hint of a limp, and barely a glance at first, as I pummelled the computer keys to put my script straight into autocue down in the studio. This was at a time long before he created that persona which is now commonly known in the media as Paxmanesque. But there is little doubt that even without knowing him personally in the slightest, before this, he did convey utter self-confidence and not a little hauteur in the way he looked at you.

At first there was nothing we found to say to each other outside of perfunctory greetings, and having been so familiar with Frank for so many years I did find this awkward. Then in a curious way we found a link, and so began a very warm relationship. We were in the make-up room together, sitting side by side. I joked that the girl in the smock was actually using Polyfilla on my face. He smiled wanly. Then I happened to remark that since starting the early morning programme I could not get a decent sleep, worrying about missing the alarm call at 4.30 every morning. Since his alarm call was even earlier than mine, he did admit that he had major problems with sleep and had tried everything to get a few decent hours of it. Since nothing had worked outside of voodoo, he had decided to go to a hypnotherapist for treatment. That didn't work either, even after hours of expensive consultation. One day the therapist told him he should just stop worrying about not sleeping. It was the worry about it that was causing the loss of sleep. 'I spent all that bloody money, and then I was told just not to worry about it,' he said. Then added, 'Tell you what, the advice worked. So save yourself some cash. Just don't worry about it.' It obviously helped him, and I did try to stop worrying about it, but worrying about being unable to stop worrying about it seemed to get me in a bit of a fankle. However, knowing that there were others who had the same problem did eventually calm me down. But in all the three years I was there I was lucky to get four hours of sleep a night. However, Paxman and I had found that tenuous bond.

He had not the slightest interest in sport, other than angling, which was a passion for him. As angling was not one of our priorities you could tell he would introduce me as if I was about to emit in Swahili. The relationship was purely formal and mechanical. Then one morning I put some lines into the script which made him guffaw, and I think startled him to a degree. The next day I could tell he was up for something that was warmer, less stuffy. I think the reason was that the other sports presenters stuck to the glue of formal presentation. I was attempting to inject a bit of fun. He responded. On the air we began a series of banters which caused occasional apoplexy in the production gallery, where they were slaves of the stop-watch and immaculate timing. None of this had to do with sport. It was about us. It was about little quips which seemed mutually insulting. He loved it and so did I. It was at the time when *nouvelle cuisine* had raised its ugly head and we plundered that subject between us. I might have had only five minutes to deliver a sports bulletin, but in the links between us we seemed to have enough time to berate the tyranny of the new minute portions you got in fancy restaurants. And wine snobs. And fancy clothes. And traffic noise. And alarm clocks. And freebies. And the mini-skirt (which got us some stick internally for cultivating male chauvinism). And virtually anything that had nothing whatever to do with sport. For his part he liked to ridicule my passion for football. For mine I would suggest he was something of a snob.

When I handed back to him one morning I said something which was to cling to him, at least among the sports people around me, 'And now back to the BBC's resident yuppie.' All this for just a few seconds of banter between items on screen. It was a pleasant ding-dong, and quite the opposite of the current image of the man, who is now seen as somebody who could fry an egg just by looking at it. But the early signs of aggression and lack of respect for politicians were already brewing and I savoured it especially one morning.

You began to feel that increasing recognition of the Breakfast programme was reflected in the wide variety of people escorted into the make-up room before programmes. You never knew which personality would sit beside you next. And the chat would begin, whether they knew you or not. It reminded me of the women in the old Shettleston 'steamie' blethering blithely on regardless. There was one particular morning when John Gummer, the Minister for Agriculture, passed me on his way to the studio as I was coming back in for a freshening. He stopped, deliberately, looked me through the spectacles on his little weasel face and this man, who introduced us to the Norwegian language by having once been described by one of their ministers as a 'drittsekk' (shitbag), pronounced, 'I cannot believe you can be so enthusiastic over sport. How can you get so worked up about it? I cannot believe it.' And, smirking, he was led towards the studio. You can say I sat back, feet up, with renewed interest in this political pipsqueak, hoping that a studio light would come tumbling down at the right place, thus incurring a by-election at a sensitive time for the government. We had no need for that. Another fate was approaching. With aplomb Paxman turned him inside out. You could tell that he had a distaste for the man, and while that may not be the measure of how you judge political interviews, I felt like applauding.

Our friendly jousts on screen continued, to such an extent that we were actually preparing our so-called spontaneous quips, until some editor in the upper echelons decided that enough was enough and that we were going over the top, too often. They felt this repartee was getting in the way of simply transmitting the news. We had to cut it down. You felt that censorship was being applied. Paxman's contempt for that view was contained behind the scenes, whereas now you would not dare to contemplate what would leave his rebellious lips in front of camera.

During that spell he would lead a gang of us to a wine bar on the edge of Shepherd's Bush Green, where the traffic jam was invented, at about 9.30 every Friday morning, and we would go through this unearthly early-morning ritual of drinking several bottles of champagne, completely guilt-free in watching the rest of the world set off to work just as we had ended ours, taking stock of our odd broadcasting situation and berating those bastards who tried to dictate to us from above. One morning he told me in no uncertain manner that I should get the hell out of Scotland and make a career in London and that he would try to help me in any way he could. I thought that might have been the Bollinger talking. We staggered out that morning into the clogged traffic as he kept harping on about it and I was almost getting embarrassed by his enthusiasm. Almost, but not quite. Anybody punting you like that is not to be sniffed at, especially as you are beginning to think that you are merely on a treadmill, going nowhere.

But true to his word, a week later I got a call from a journalist at *Time Out*, which was truly forging new ground in London Town's coverage. She had been contacted by Paxman to sound me out about ambitions and she stressed how much he enjoyed my contributions. Flattering? Of course. And the piece duly appeared, making it seem that my future lay in the capital city, although I had taken care to go easy on expressing such an ambition. At the same time I carried the feeling that it wasn't on. Enjoy this experience while you can, because it's not going to last – that more or less is the thought that kept me going. I tried hard to convey to family, friends and other colleagues that there was a huge distinction between the quality of the work you were presented with on network, and the quality of life in London itself.

At first, during the time I was travelling between London and Glasgow every week because of the contractual commitments on both sides of the border, they would put me up in the Kensington Hilton Hotel, which for a while had the appeal of comparatively sumptuous living. But, eventually, even a five-star hotel, in its very impersonal relationship with you, can develop the appeal of a Colditz, as I was again to find out later in Paris. After a contractual change which put the emphasis on my London engagements I rented the property agent Donald Storrie's flat on the edge of St John's Wood for the rest of my stay in the capital. Even that did not help me come to terms with London living. I was torn between my obvious aim to make an impact on network television and the peace of mind I always felt in getting the hell out of the capital, every weekend, back to Lanarkshire, where the folk around me seem to live like lords compared with the congested, cramped, choked, Londoners whose metropolitan belief was that there was no lifestyle to touch theirs. I let them wallow in their own stifling parochialism. However, Lanarkshire would not provide me with the opportunity to have a film unit at my behest to meet people and go to places I would never have dreamed possible.

I would, for example, sit in the Long Room at Lords and interview the great cricketer Denis Compton, who was a boyhood hero of mine, and who talked to me as if he had known me all my life. I could sit in a pub in the East End and chat to Frank Bruno before one of his big fights, and put on the gloves with him in the ring for a camera shot. I would stand like an upper-class twit on the banks of the Thames, blazer and all, sipping a Pimms and sounding as if I did know something about the Bertie Woosters of this world who inhabited the Henley Regatta. I would be shown firing some rifle or other on the range at Bisley. I would stand in the mudflats of the Thames Estuary talking about oysters and trying to link them (yes, it does sound improbable) with the upcoming university boat race. I would take cameras to Wembley for all sorts of previews, including one evening when an old man with a very bad limp approached and with great difficulty tried to speak, obviously recognising me from the box. He had clearly suffered a stroke at some time. Somebody beside me said it was Tommy Lawton, the great English striker who used to put the fear of death into me when I was a kid, listening to his name mentioned on radio when he played against Scotland, and who was rightly nick-named Hammer of the Scots, a man I had wished, many years ago, to be struck down by lightning. When I recounted these days to him, he started to weep, tears rolling down his cheeks, as a recollection of his majestic self was too much for him to bear. Putting a comforting arm round the Hammer of the Scots then, the man who had once scared me as much as Boris Karloff in *Frankenstein*, was like an act of mutual reconciliation.

But, in the wide range of stories which one could cover and which were much more varied than anything that could be offered in Scotland, I simply preferred it when we could get outside London itself. I found myself standing, on one occasion, on the deck of the great yacht *Steinlager*, with its captain, and eventual winner, Sir Peter Blake, at the start of the Round the World race in 1989, and several months later was invited to take the steering wheel and part guide it around Auckland Bay, when I was there for the Commonwealth Games on the basis of a *Breakfast Time* interview. So, once I had been seen on the deck of a boat, other ideas came to producers' minds, like sending me to reflect on Cowes Regatta – especially when I told them I had met and interviewed the Duke of Edinburgh twice before, and he was about to take a prominent part in the Solent. They assumed I might have a way of gaining another interview. I let them assume that to give me a couple of days soaking in the briny down on the south coast. I knew there was little chance, based on my two other encounters.

The first was when I approached his office to arrange an interview in Aberdeen University, in the mid-1970s, where he was about to make a speech on 'shamateurism' in the Olympic Games. The office agreed, but I had to submit questions in advance. I sent them off for their perusal but had not heard 'yea' or 'nay' on them before setting off for Aberdeen four days later for the interview. They did have my home phone number. It was Ronald Allison, the ex-BBC man who was then the Palace press officer, who confirmed with me what subsequently happened. They did want to contact me to OK it. One of his men phoned my home. I had gone, my wife was teaching, and left in the house by herself was a delightful, but blunt-spoken, cleaning lady from Baillieston in Lanarkshire, where, when occasion demands, they call a spade a spade. She had been constantly warned about the crank calls you could be subject to because of public prominence. When she answered the phone and asked the gent who was calling she got the bland reply, 'Buckingham Palace'. I was told by a decidedly amused Allison later that our lady, putting two and two together on the basis of our warnings, retorted with, 'Stick it up your arse,' and then slammed the phone down.

It didn't stop the interview, although throughout the rather innocuous replies I could barely rid myself of the image of the Palace anatomically intruding on the royal personage. This whimsical image counteracted the aloofness and coldness he exhibited that evening, just as he did on the second occasion when, in 1986, as Rector of Edinburgh University, I had lunch with him and the Principal and he hogged the whole conversation talking about the values of monastic life in Greece until we felt brain-dead. So accepting the almost impossible task of getting him on the sloping deck of a yacht was not only a subterfuge on my part to get free of London for a few days, but was also a means of savouring a new environment, since my sailing experience had been limited to pushing out model boats from the banks of Hogganfield Loch, just down the road from Barlinnie Prison.

I felt I was prepared for any kind of cultural leap, after having experienced Glorious Goodwood just before, where I had had the unpleasant task of interviewing perhaps the rudest man in Christendom, the clerk of the course, who would have made Gummer seem a charmer, and who could not hide his distaste for this Scot who talked mostly about football. He did not talk down his nose to me, he slalomed down it. Now I did meet some English Hooray Henries who would have driven me to form another Jacobite rebellion, if it wasn't for the fact that I thought perhaps even less of fundamentalist Scottish Nationalism. Toffs you could take, especially if they were buying the drinks, and I tried my best to merge as seamlessly as I could on those occasions when I went out on the prowl with a film unit. It would have been nice to have followed in the footsteps of Fyfe Robertson, the bearded Scottish broadcaster who became such a popular figure in the 1960s and 70s, with his idiosyncratic reports from around the UK. Indeed, I think I copied some of his approaches to subjects. At the same time I had to admit to myself that I, the Scot, was being found wholly acceptable and more warmly inserted into programmes than an English equivalent would have been broadcasting north of the border.

So, off I went, in what I knew would be the fruitless pursuit of the Duke. There was no chance of any such interview, even though from the shore we filmed him as he guided his crowded yacht in and out of the traffic in the Solent. How could we fill the vacuum of an anticipated royal interview? It fell into our laps, almost literally, when someone who had heard we were looking for a freebie (our budget for the trip wouldn't have purchased us a rowboat) offered us a boat to present the programme from the quayside. We got up early the following morning and set up the cameras on the deck of this large speed-boat, when suddenly, from behind a cabin door emerged four nubile ladies clad in bikinis of such scantiness they would not have made up a single table napkin between them. The owner of the vessel then made it clear that he wanted them in camera shot, one way or the other, with a hint that if they were not included, the deal was off. We had half an hour to go to trans-mission. He was demanding not so much his pound of flesh for the arrangement, but more his acres of flesh. He then added, 'You can have them topless, if you want.'

Even my young producer, who had started slavering at first (I wasn't exactly immune to their charms either), began to blanch. He knew as well as I that the men who ran *Breakfast Time* were hard-nosed news types who could be as solemn as those men in their black gowns who sent the Witches of Salem to their fates. Hedonism was out. Kate Adie, and that ilk, were definitely in. The harder news image had to prevail. Bikinis on *Breakfast Time* at that juncture would have been like finding a page three girl in the *War Cry*. Sod it. Let's have a go. That unspoken thought then took over, between my producer and me. Not topless, that was agreed.

When they handed over to me live, all they saw was a close-up of my face and as we pulled back, all was revealed. The four ladies grouped themselves around me as if I needed protection from the elements. That other Scot Sean Connery could not have been surrounded by as much pulchritude in his heyday. They didn't get the Duke, they got flesh instead, as I hammered home the point that somebody had to do the tough jobs in this programme. From the other end in London there was silence. No comment, which is sometimes worse than any sort of comment. They wouldn't have been jumping up and down in glee. Indeed, my style was now beginning to jar on some at editorial level. I could sense that. It wasn't until a good month or so later that anything was said about the *Men Only* ethos I had inserted. I was to discover what the man in the speedboat had been planning all along. One of the editors of the programme walked up to me with a magazine, laid it down on my desk and said, 'You're in *Playboy*.' And added, rather coldly, 'Congratulations. Quite an achievement.' There I was, in a photograph of the scene on the speedboat, ladies and all, with the BBC logo on the camera, clearly identifying us, obviously taken by someone set up to snap us. *Breakfast Time* in *Playboy*! What next? *Blue Peter* in *Men Only*?

This had been the *Playboy* boat for the whole regatta. I had taken the programme to places of dubious commerce they never thought, or hoped, it would reach. It was certainly no proof of the emergence of a broadcasting Renaissance Man, but simply of somebody trying to break the stiff-backed domination of hard news. Then the Breakfast experience took on another complexion when Paxman told me one morning that he was leaving.

18

FATEFUL DECISIONS

Paxman's decision to leave was a turning point, more psychologically than anything else, for I was now established as a network broadcaster and was getting invitations to appear in other programmes. I turned many of them down, including an invitation to appear, and be trashed probably, in Noel Edmonds' Saturday night extravaganza. I just didn't fancy Edmonds or his show. Of course I was wrong. I should have been milking every opportunity. While insecurity is endemic among television performers, there are times when you can easily delude yourself about how permanent you are. Because of the healthy relationship we had, Paxman's moving off to *Newsnight* was like watching a relative leave for a distant country, but at the same time another reminder that we based our existence then on shifting sands. After his departure, several announcers passed through the studio and then one in particular settled in, changing the whole atmosphere surrounding the studio presentation.

Nicholas Witchell's introduction of me, on air, on his first morning, was so rigidly formal it was like being spoken to by that voice in an airport which tells you that you are coming to the end of the moving walkway. There was nothing wrong with it, it was coherent, but it definitely sounded as if he had had a gun held to his head to force him to include sport at all. But he had come with a health warning. His nickname around the office was 'The Poisoned Carrot', with reference obviously to his gingery hair and other less charming characteristics. I had no personal animosity towards the man. He was always perfectly civil to me. Indeed, he was, and is, an excellent broadcaster. But I cannot disguise the fact that he was disliked more than any other man I had come across in that area. He had come with a reputation for being cool under fire, and when the BBC news studio had been invaded in 1984 by militant gays protesting about Clause 28, he took it upon himself to struggle with the invaders and quell them, while his colleague Sue Lawley read on unperturbed. He thus achieved the classic *Daily Mirror* head-line, 'Beeb Man Sits On Lesbian'. As headlines go it could only have been exceeded by 'Freddie Starr Ate My Hamster' in *The Sun*, but not by much.

You would have thought he might have been able to play off that, in a very human way. But, by contrast, he seemed to prefer to go the android way with other people. Perhaps they were being unkind to him. I saw him, distinctly, as a loner. Generally, loners don't really care much what people think of them. For when my wife and I took off to Guernsey for a short break one week, in walked Nicholas to the same hotel. He saw us, introduced himself formally, wished us a good break and then for the next week completely ignored us, walking past us in the corridor as if we were statuettes, and sat on a deckchair, or lay in the sun completely on his own, talking to no one. He did rise in my estimation when I heard that the Prince of Wales had mounted an attack on him at Klosters, saying, 'I can't bear that man. I mean, he's so awful, he really is.' How could the ceaselessly pontificating Prince know? Other than listening to tittle-tattle. And I was equally glad to hear that some of Witchell's colleagues, from other channels, came to his defence. He had no repartee in the studio. It would have been like bouncing off an iceberg. His presence coincided with my own unease at feeling that I was going nowhere myself. Rudderless, drifting, making money alright, and feeling I had no fixed address. There were still bright spots which simply perked you up. Like my first visit to the Palace.

Prior to the Seoul Olympics in 1988 we did many previews of sports men and women in preparation for the Games. In so doing we had caught the attention of someone at the Palace press office, who was looking for as much publicity as possible for Princess Anne's efforts to raise money for the Olympic effort in her capacity as President of the British Olympic Committee. We received an invitation to visit her in her office in Buckingham Palace, so that she could hammer home the points she wished to make. It is an offer you don't turn down, innocuous in news terms though it might be. We duly turned up at the front gates of the Palace and were directed by a policeman to a side entrance on the Hyde Park end of the building. We had a three-man BBC crew, the producer, and most surprisingly of all, in addition, the producer's girlfriend, a German lady who had flown over especially for this visit. Nice way to impress a lady. 'Like to meet the Princess Royal? Yes, that's right, Buckingham Palace!' How could a girl resist? She apparently was listed as an assistant producer. The producer merely thought this deception was a bit of a jape. What lengths men have to go, to get what they want from women, I had to think. Let us just say she was no Marlene Dietrich. She was in fact an impostor.

Once through the gate at the Palace railings we made our way, unchallenged, to this open door, which led us upwards towards her apartment. I stress the words 'unchallenged' and 'open door'. For we were able to walk in there with only one flunkey at the top of the stairs to show us the way to her office. Not one piece of authentication was asked for. It recalled, for me, the occasion when we took a BBC Scotland film crew into the parliament building in Edmonton, just before the opening of the Commonwealth Games there in 1978. We had wandered straight in, without any security check and wandered into the empty debating chamber and around the corridors, trying to find the office of the Premier, whom we had arranged to interview. Eventually we bumped into an ancient retainer who directed us to his office. It was empty. We waited a full half-hour until his charming secretary arrived and welcomed us. When the Premier entered I did express surprise at the lack of security, and told him such laxity would never be allowed in the UK. He looked at me, and with a certain amount of pride in his voice said, 'We don't need that sort of thing in this town. This is Alberta.' The following day, the jilted lover of that secretary walked into that office, unannounced, and shot her dead.

And here was a German who could have been a member of the Baader-Meinhof gang, for all that anybody knew, waltzing into the seat of royalty without so much as flourishing a pass. This, coming only six years after Michael Fagan had managed to enter the Palace and enter the Queen's bedroom, and after the scare of 1974 when the Princess Royal's car had been stopped and an attempt had been made to kidnap her. But, there we were, about to face the lady who had barked at the man ordering her out of the car at gunpoint during that attempt, 'Not bloody likely!' We thought it would not be prudent to bring up the subject of the surprising laxity and absence of any real security, since she did have a reputation for being testy at times.

She wasn't then. She knew when to turn on the charm and she did. She is much more fine-featured, and indeed, more attractive than any of her photographs reveal. We were in her surprisingly compact office which also doubled as a private dining room and led through to the single bedroom of her then husband Mark Phillips, known as Foggy, by all and sundry. We were surprised to see that it was like a cell, spartan and small, with a wash-hand basin – not so much a room, more like solitary for the recidivist. She settled in a large chair, and when she emitted a small cough, our producer, emboldened by his obvious attempts to improve Anglo-German relationships, dipped into his pocket and produced a grubby, soiled, crinkled packet of Polo Mints, which looked as if it had been found on the pavement in the Mall and which you wouldn't have offered to an emaciated mongrel. He then prised one into the half-released angle, as one does with Polo Mints, and held it out in front of her face, with fingers which looked as if they had spent some time working on the sump of a car. 'Can I offer you this Ma'am? It might help the throat,' he said.

Let me just record that the interview, when it took place, was articulate and straightforward. It was but nothing, though, compared with the experience of witnessing how royalty deals with second-hand Polo Mints. Her face became one of refined shock, tempered by wry disdain, and the good breeding of knowing when to be polite, whilst at the same time glancing at me with a look which was eloquently suggesting, 'Who is this bloody idiot? We don't do other people's Polo Mints! Not from the dustbin, we don't!' Thank God, I thought, he is desisting from an, 'Oh, go on!' But I was then having lurid thoughts that the Baader-Meinhoff lady (I know she wasn't, but I began to picture her as such) was about to burst forth with 'Down with the monarchy and capitalism!'

When Prince Andrew burst in just before the interview, expressing the hope that his sister wouldn't talk a load of rubbish, and was told by her to push off in no uncertain manner, the afternoon was becoming less predictable than we had expected. A cat can look at a king, and a princess can be offered a Polo Mint certainly, but as in all things, timing is of the essence. When we returned to the office I wondered what our editors would have thought about the possibility that the Queen's daughter could have been poisoned by someone posing as a BBC producer, who had cyanide tablets which looked like Polo Mints, and which if that was not to work, had an accomplice, brought in from Germany, who despite her bland appearance knew how to handle a Luger pistol, handed down from her father's time as an SS officer. Fanciful? To be sure. But these are exactly the scenarios which go through the minds of the security services nowadays. It might have been amateurish in the extreme but it reminds you, almost nostalgically, of an age, not all that long ago, when innocence prevailed, and trust was natural, and X-ray cameras were for your lungs, not your luggage.

I certainly had little respect for this particular producer, and if I had, with justification, reported this bizarre situation, it would have got him the sack. However, nothing untoward had happened and the general rule of thumb at the BBC then, and probably still is, don't rock the boat. For the BBC themselves would have been taken to task for the disregard of protocol. But I did make my feelings clear to him privately, and although he was organising sports output for the programme, I virtually ignored him thereafter. The distaste was mutual because he did not like the way I still interfered with scripts, and I knew he was prompting the younger elements at the assistant producer level to try to resist this. They did try, but got nowhere with me.

I was edging then towards that egotistical state when you feel you can do no wrong, and that everybody is out of step but yourself. I think that feeling was created as well by the growing public recognition which suggests you are of some significance. For instance, on the Monday after the Hillsborough disaster of 15 April 1989, in which ninety-six people died, Graham Kelly, the Chief Executive of the Football Association,

217

came into the studio to be interviewed. Not surprisingly, he was on edge, and being a very substantial figure, you got the impression that there was a considerable chunk of flab shivering underneath his clothes, like jelly. But I didn't realise just how much of a blue funk he was in till after the programme, when he walked with me towards the vestibule of Television Centre. As he got to the door, he turned and asked, 'What do you think we should do now?' Asking me? Was he about to travel back to Lancaster Gate, the FA headquarters, with some advice from me ringing in his ears? My self-belief did not extend to feeling I was the sage of law and order. Indeed, I had the opposite reaction. His credibility suddenly collapsed in front of my very eyes. He was utterly bereft of any positive thought on this. Frankly, I mumbled some platitude about not panicking. He fled. I thought of him later that midweek when I went to interview fans at Watford, before one of their games. I was astonished at the hostility they expressed about Liverpool supporters, and some of them said they would find it difficult to support the minute's silence which had been arranged for the match. They cited many examples of the kind of rowdy conduct they had had to endure when Liverpool visited town. In May of that year when I was at the FA Cup Final between Liverpool and Everton, despite the catastrophe that had struck Merseyside, I watched hundreds of ticketless Liverpool supporters risking life and limb, clambering over BBC outside broadcast vans to reach the rone pipes at one end of Wembley, so they could climb up and get into the stadium. Apparently, few lessons had been learned.

The lesson I certainly had been learning was that Paxman had been right. I had to make a choice between London and Glasgow. One or the other. I was clocking up more air miles than an astronaut. The crews got so familiar with me that I would get invites to sit with them in the cockpit for some of the landings. I, who, if truth be told, never liked flying. Then the decision was taken for me, by a gentleman at BBC Scotland who certainly did not like me as much as my English colleagues. I saw him as an arrogant bully, who treated the sports staff as if he was a plantation owner in the Deep South.

During this time I travelled to Italy for the World Cup Finals. Scotland were playing Costa Rica in their opening game and were generally speaking being given the runaround. I said so in commentary. You can't kid the public. Some people obviously thought you could, including Jim Hunter, Head of Programmes at BBC Scotland, who sent a message demanding that I lend a more supportive voice to my country. I sent a message back inquiring if he wished me to sing 'Flower of Scotland' during the commentary. It was a message of defiance, couched the way it was to reflect the utter stupidity of his intervention. It was also a suicide note. I knew he was not the sort of man to countenance acts of irreverence against his august self. When we eventually met, after the World Cup, and he told me that I would only be used sparingly from then on, and that in effect I would have to concentrate on my work in London, I left his office and with an immense sense of relief asked my agency Bagenal Harvey in London to send in a letter releasing me from my BBC Scotland contract. I regretted leaving so many great colleagues with whom I had learned my trade. But I felt as if released from a tyranny.

The sense of relief in not having to race between two contracts every week was counterbalanced by the need to find one particular strand of work which I could concentrate on. I was now a Londoner in effect, but without the clear-cut identity which football in Scotland had provided, and I knew despite my appreciation of being on network, occasionally in *Grandstand* and *Sportsnight*, as well as *Breakfast Time*, that I would miss the Scottish game badly. I did some network commentary for *Match of the*

Day but it was limited. I knew this would be difficult to break into, with Motty and others like Barry Davies and Tony Gubba rightly valued for their work. What is more, although you need an agent to get on anywhere in London, it does not follow that work will flow prolifically from that. The Bagenal Harvey agency which I had joined handled many personalities, including David Coleman and a host of others. Their needs and desires had greater priority than this comparative newcomer to the network scene. I was well down the pecking order. So I had to start to fend for myself, and at a function at a club in Soho I met a Scot who asked me if I could come up with any ideas for his film company in the way of commercials or corporate videos. He asked me to come to his office one day when I told him I did have contacts in the Scotch whisky industry, and that perhaps some of them might be interested in corporate videos. I turned up and realised that I was about to go to work for Andrew Lloyd Webber. I was in the offices of the Really Useful Films company, an offshoot of Webber's theatre group.

Here, then, came a spell in which I spent much time with my new-found friend, this former cameraman, in and around the famous, or notorious Groucho Club, which attracted media and showbiz personalities like iron-filings to a magnet. It was the place to be seen and heard, so I was told. All I did, mainly, was drink, and talk about video ideas and listen to my friend admit that to watch Andrew Lloyd Webber in a temper was like watching Krakatoa erupt again, and again, and again. He was certainly in awe of the great man, with the suggestion that Lloyd Webber was the Genghis Khan of showbiz and he was simply terrified of him. I wasn't at all surprised by that revelation, since I had come across a hint of it when we had taken our cameras to Manchester, on an earlier occasion, to interview the theatrical impresario Bob Scott, now knighted, who was then leading the bid for the Olympics for the city in the mid and late 1980s. He told us that when Lloyd Webber arrived for the Manchester opening of *Evita* in his theatre, he went to his hotel room, then came down again to take the limousine to the show, and immediately went into a tantrum. He phoned Scott, who was waiting at the theatre, and complained that the car wasn't at the front door of the hotel for him. When Scott then contacted the hotel management, he was informed that the car was no more than ten yards from the entrance. When he got back on the phone to the composer, and explained that the car was within toddler's distance from the front door, he was blasted with a string of obscenities over the phone, ending up with him refusing to walk the ten yards to the car, and with the concluding reason, 'Don't you know what happened to John Lennon?' They reversed the car to the door. According to Scott, Lloyd Webber then ran out of the hotel door and threw himself into the back seat, as if he had been in the sights of an Armalite.

From such men terror can flow, and I knew that my friend's job was on line, so I tried desperately to help him out, by making contacts with people with various business interests who might be interested in corporate video, but discovered that I was in a fiercely competitive market. There was one prospect I pursued with confidence and developed the interest right down to the level of getting a presentation all beautifully packaged up, which was watched by a representative of the firm we were chasing, who looked as if she was no more than eighteen. She decided against us, chose another film company and shortly after that my friend was sacked by Lloyd Webber. No more Groucho Club. No more dipping into the freelance film market. The BBC seemed like a haven of security compared with London's independent film environment. And, hearteningly, I was surrounded by people who were sympathetic, after hearing I had severed my connections with BBC Scotland. One such was Jill Dando.

221

The first time I met her was, not surprisingly, in the make-up room. Before she walked in, I had been sitting there trying to identify the lady lying back in the seat beside me, who had just had her hair shampooed. She was black, tiny and wrinkled. An old lady, brought in to talk about pensioners' rights perhaps? Then, when she was offered a coffee and said simply, 'Thank you, so much,' to the make-up girl, in a low purr, it was unmistakeable who she was. Eartha Kitt. The woman once described by Orson Welles as the most exciting woman in the world looked frighteningly old. It was perhaps a heartless reaction, but women like that carry the burden of men's expectation around with them, as they do their own vanity bags. Disillusioned? By a good degree. Now by a curious coincidence, about a couple of months after that, the BBC asked me to present a six-week series of Friday night chat shows on Radio 2. This was to follow the series which the now famous television gardening presenter Alan Titchmarsh had just completed. I had to chat with guests and play an assortment of music. And one of the guests they had booked was Eartha Kitt. The image I had in my mind was of the old granny, which now distinctly blotted out anything of her memorable classic pose in a shapely, sequined gown standing at a microphone breathing sensuously about the 'old fashioned millionaire'. We did a two-way chat, she in London, myself in Glasgow. Here, I have to pause and take a deep breath in recollection of a comment she made, and which caused me great ridicule amongst my colleagues for some time thereafter. As she purred away at me, and I mumbled at her about her career and the men in her life, she suddenly interjected with words which might have stopped the nation in its tracks: 'Has anyone ever told you, you have a very sexy voice?' In that moment of bafflement and confusion I can't really recall whether I informed her that 'No,' nobody actually had. I defended myself against the ribbing, nay, dog's abuse, I was dished out by my friends by insisting that Eartha was, without dispute, an arbiter of all things sexy, as Armani was with men's clothes, and who amongst them could contest what she had to say on these matters? It did not cut the mustard. Indeed, it had a curious effect on me. I honestly did find myself, for some days after, talking in a lower octave, especially to ladies when I met them, to see if they would weaken at the knees. I left most of them thinking I was probably in the early stages of pleurisy.

So, that morning, with Eartha Kitt's looks being salvaged in the make-up room, Jill Dando walked in. She suited the screen. It enhanced her. I am not suggesting she was not attractive off-screen. But she was one of the few people I met who quite definitely seemed to blossom on screen, rather than the screen doing them no justice at all, which is so often the case. We knew in the first few weeks she appeared in studio that she would be destined for higher realms of broadcasting. What was also so startlingly contradictory were the scurrilous rumours which surrounded her. The virginal, Botticelli-like *Primavera* image she wafted around the studios and office, which made her seem so agreeable and pleasant to talk to and work with, contrasted with the rumours of boyfriends and affairs. In the studio she definitely had the capacity to make it sound as if the sports item was what the world was waiting to hear, despite war and plagues abounding.

Her position amongst us seemed to fit the pattern of the pressure which attractive women had to endure in the hard-nosed journalistic world, where lust could spawn the most lurid imaginings. But that is what, in fact, bubbled around her in whispered and not-so-whispered conversations. Whether she knew anything about that I could not tell, but regardless of what her private life was like she certainly didn't deserve this insidious chat. Sadly, this affected even me. Because about ten years later,

223

on the morning I heard she had been murdered, it was to these rumours that my mind leapt. It is scary, even now, to admit that, but that is what went through my mind, as I could not come to terms with how such a lovely woman could be gunned down on her own doorstep, other than through a *crime passionnel*. As the case developed, other more credible possibilities made mockery of these thoughts. But if not Barry George, then who did do it? Her character remains unblemished, as far as I'm concerned, but I certainly would not be at all surprised if those pedlars of rumours are regurgitating them and trying to put two and two together in a fanciful way.

There was an assembly line of women moving into the studio to introduce my items, one of whom was a lady I knew would get to the top, regardless of who would get in her way. Kirsty Wark. One evening, at a large-scale Variety Club dinner in Glasgow that I was compering, some months before her first appearance down south, she suddenly rose to her feet beside me and grabbed the mic from my hand and proceeded to belt out some message to the audience, with the implication that I was slouching around too much, and that she wanted to take over proceedings. I put it down to the fact that she might have been going a little bit heavy on the plonk they gave us that night. Arm-wrestling a microphone with her was not conducive to a productive relationship, so I tended to steer out of her way after that, until we met up in the studio in London, upon which you could easily conclude that here was a Jeremy Paxman in skirts. A different specimen from the fragrant Jill Dando, who was still around, charmingly introducing my items, when my career in network television came to a sudden and abrupt end.

The climax came in an office in BBC Portland Place, where once, years before, I had had the opportunity to launch a new career but turned it down. Here was where it was going to end. I was in preparation for a radio programme. Cliff Morgan, the eloquent Welshman who had just been moved from his post at BBC Head of Programmes, had now effectively retired from mainstream television broadcasting and was presenting this pleasant Saturday morning radio programme, which dealt with off-beat minority sports. I was replacing him for three weeks while he went on holiday. I remember the time of day well. Four-thirty on a Friday. The phone rang. It was my agent from Bagenal Harvey. He told me in no uncertain manner that an ultimatum had been delivered, through him, to me. I had only half an hour to make up my mind about it. I was being accused of a serious breach of contract.

Three weeks prior to that call, I had received a request from the Head of Programmes at Scottish Television, David Scott, to front a new sports discussion programme which was going to be called *Sport in Question*. I was desperately keen to do this and received a clearance from the editor of *Breakfast Time*, who effectively said that what I did in Scotland would not affect anything I was producing in the south for his programme. On the back of a fanfare of publicity about the new programme, and the fact that they were going to hire me to present it, Radio Clyde's Paul Cooney contacted me and asked if I would be available on Saturdays for football commentary. Once again I cleared that with my London editor. Once again it was widely publicised. It was all set up, and I was prepared, much more happily it has to be said, for the trek back and forward, on the shuttle, between London and Glasgow. After the BBC Scotland experience, it was good to be wanted again. But then came the call on that Friday afternoon. In essence the agent had been contacted by the head of BBC contracts in London, to point out that the agreements to work for Scottish Television and Radio Clyde were a glaring breach of my existing BBC contract with *Breakfast Time*. The ordinance came with a strict threat that if I didn't cancel my agreements by five o'clock (half an hour later) then I would be in breach of contract and dismissed summarily. A call to them to accept their interpretation of the contract would suffice. My agent was in no doubt that somebody at BBC Scotland had meddled in this, and that in London nobody would have been concerned about my cross-border arrangement. I tried to get hold of the editor of *Breakfast Time* to confirm that he had consented to the arrangements I had made in Scotland. It was impossible at that time of the day. He was gone for the weekend. I could make no case without him. But then what hit me forcibly, sitting there pondering, was that I was in fact in exile, just marking time. The homing instinct pulled it off for me. That is not to say I did not consider the harsh practicality that, if I had to renounce my agreements with Scott and Cooney, I would be dead and buried for all time in Scotland. I phoned the agent at ten to five to let him know I was not going back on the commitments I had now made in Scotland. He was disappointed, and perhaps with good reason. Anybody with any interest in broadcasting in London aspired to get into one of the major channels one way or another. My decision to kill off my BBC London contract he and many others would have viewed as an act of professional suicide. My wife and I packed our bags and flew home the following day.

19

HOME BREW

I walked into a buoyant building. Radio Clyde was thriving. But you wouldn't have thought so listening to some people. I was asked to speak at a charity dinner shortly after I returned. The chairman for the evening, long-winded, as many of them are on these occasions, gave me an introduction which seemed more detailed than the Book of Job, and in conclusion, he uttered words which caused great amusement, when he said, 'Broadcaster from *Sportscene, Grandstand, Sportsnight, Breakfast Time* and now . . . ' Pause for effect. '. . . Radio Clyde!' They laughed, as if on cue, as the chairman seemed to be suggesting, no doubt to comical effect only, that I had fallen from grace. I was fully aware of the effect he was wanting to convey, in contrasting local radio with the Olympian heights of network broadcasting. But you only had to be in their new building at Clydebank, within sight of the still remaining traces of the area's great shipbuilding era, to sense that this station had soared in self-confidence, from its generally perceived upstart status as the first commercial station outside London to taking on the BBC, and was now festooned with awards for different varieties of broadcasting. They had also significantly usurped the BBC in the West of Scotland as the genuine platform for public discussion of football.

Richard Park, who went on to radio fame in London, had started the sports output. Stein used to call him 'Ibrox Park', suggesting an illicit allegiance. By the time I arrived, Paul Cooney had been established, and he and his team were masterly at capturing the sometimes bitter rivalry which existed in the city between the Old Firm supporters. And none more so than James Sanderson, or Solly as he was known, who, although a newspaper man, had taken to radio like a kid to a toffee apple. He just relished it. In fact I think the secret of his success was not just his ability to be provocative, irrepressible and outrageous at times, but the fact that he seemed to forget, at times, he was actually on radio, and let fly without inhibition. This he did on that famous occasion in Montevideo in 1967, just after Celtic had lost a highly controversial and wild game against Racing Club, in the World Club Championship play-off. In the airport departure lounge, Peter Lorenzo, a prominent London journalist, made a disparaging remark about Scottish football. Solly, a tiny man compared with the bulky Englishman, promptly left-hooked him and left him flat on his back. Sadly, Solly had died by the time I arrived at Radio Clyde. But his legacy remained.

Somehow his successors could never quite retain his cocky irreverence, which could anger and amuse almost in the same sentence. But Clyde could slug it out solidly nevertheless, and the programmes they put on roared along in a manner that made the BBC equivalent seem quite staid. The other remarkable fact was that when I was just starting out and first walked into a radio station, I was told with absolute certainty that radio had had its day. With television growing in popularity, Peter Thomson said that radio would not see out the decade, and, even if it did, it would only be catering for minority tastes ranging from gardening to stamp-collecting. These were his very words. They seemed prophetic. Who could argue with that, as television was beginning to threaten to turn us into troglodytes, hunched around the box, day in, day out?

Thirty years later radio was thriving, and still does. It is doing so by offering the public immediate accessibility and inter-action, which television finds clumsy to emulate. The radio style which I had been schooled in at the BBC had an audience all right. But you were never aware of it. You would go into a studio and recite your pieces and feel you had done nothing more than closet yourself with fellow professionals in a cosy relationship from which the rest of the world was excluded. That's how it felt. We didn't seem to exploit a relationship with the public, other than replying to letters which came to the BBC mostly from middle-class listeners who knew how to punctuate and use adjectival clauses. In the main it was all so proper. Indeed, Archie Hendry, the announcer who broke me in to BBC ways, told me that he had been offered advice once, by a senior executive in London, on how to treat those who corresponded with the Corporation. 'Be polite. But regard everyone who does so as a bloody idiot!' That, in a nutshell, was the divide that existed. Serve, but for God's sake, don't be servile.

That is not to say there was a lack of professionalism. Great broadcasting took place there. Bill McLaren, that superb rugby commentator, sharpened his teeth first of all on radio, and the first radio football commentaries laid the template for others to follow. But there was one incident I recall which demon-strated, in its own small way, the cultural gap that existed between Clyde and the Beeb of the early days.

There was a golf tournament in the north of Scotland which went by the name of the Buchan Firkin Trophy. Try saying that several times to yourself. As tongue-twisters go, it is a gin-trap, with horrendous possibilities in store for the live broadcaster. One afternoon, the result of the tournament was passed to a sports announcer by the name of Andy Cowan Martin, a man with the body of a Toulouse-Lautrec but with a magnificent baritone voice which belied his unfortunate physique. He looked at the words Buchan Firkin, and took cold feet. He passed the paper to his companion, who looked at it with the expression of a man who has been passed a note saying there was a bomb under the table, and passed it back. Andy simply threw it on the floor, instinctively feeling that it was odds on, that afternoon, for one of the classic spoonerisms of all time. The result was never announced.

Clyde would not have thrown it on the floor. They would have exploited its pitfalls all afternoon. They could seize on weaknesses and idiosyncrasies to catch people's ears. Their appeal seemed to be not just the provocation they might arouse with their views, but in being able to seem to head off at a tangent so often, and yet make it sound relevant. Buchan Firkin would have resounded around the land and they would have made it a byword in linguistic temptation. That is why their phone-in for the public which they established jolted the norms of radio broadcasting, ranging as it did from the sublime to the ridiculous. As my granny would have put it, it was like enjoying the gossip in the 'steamie'. In a way Glasgow and the West of Scotland was speaking to itself for the first time. This interaction was energised particularly by Solly Sanderson. 'Were you at the game, caller?' – his riposte to a cheeky bugger at the other end of the phone line has entered the vernacular as the ultimate put-down of the armchair critic.

We at the BBC looked down on this. Uncouth voices and opinions were being unleashed on us. Glottal stops were tarnishing the air. Stupidity was being revealed. The great unwashed should be hidden from sight and not given platforms to air incoherent opinions. And how did we form those views? Because we were listening. Against what we thought were our better instincts, we were actually drawn to it. Or at least I was. It was catching on. Like wild fire. It took the BBC a generation to wake up to this, and hence the entrance of the popular and provocative Tam Cowan, a brilliantly funny man, in company with the anchorman Stuart Cosgrove, whose weekly irreverent programme, which can go right to the edge at times, stemmed from the new populist culture which had risen from the ashes of Reithian traditions and was all the more remarkable for that. But by the time I arrived, Clyde was winning the battle of the ratings by significant amounts in the early 1990s in the West of Scotland. I knew that fitting in was going to be difficult, regardless of the experience I had clocked up. Radio commentary on football is the life and soul of the game. You, alone, are the game. You can make it what it is, or make it what it isn't. The game is your voice, your attitude. Television commentary is like escorting someone through a picture gallery, in the hope that you say the right things about the right pictures, and are not going to be tossed out of the place for talking too much. You can do both, but the facility to cope only comes through practice and, since I hadn't been near radio for years, it took me a while to get into the rhythm and pace of the game. But Clyde continued to thrive, not because I had joined them, but because they tapped heavily into the major controversy of the time, the future of Celtic.

Walter Smith's Rangers team was churning out victories with almost bland regularity, as they ploughed on to try and beat Stein's nine-in-a-row achievement. Celtic were in turmoil. They seemed incapable of stemming Rangers' progress. The board of directors at Parkhead were not only being criticised, they were being lampooned. 'The Silence of the Bams' was one of the kinder tags pinned on them. Liam Brady was there when I arrived, and in one of the first games I covered at the old Broomfield, Airdrie, I noticed that as the players prepared to go into extra time, in a League Cup game, Brady simply walked around the group, hands in pockets, hardly speaking to them. It might have been a case of acting cool. If it was, it didn't work, because Celtic lost. But coolness has never been a preferred option of Celtic managers in situations like that. Fire and brimstone has. With one exception, outside of Brady.

Whatever David Hay did in private, in public, win, lose or draw, this delightful and civilised man looked as if he was utterly disaster-proof – taking press conferences, puffing away on his tiny cheroot as if he hadn't a care in the world. He too bit the dust, as Rangers ploughed on. And so had Billy McNeill, who seemed destined to remain at Celtic Park for the rest of his life. Rangers had the grip of a vice on them all. Clyde oiled the wheels of supporter resentment. The phone lines lit up their switchboard every Saturday afternoon, as if the end of the world was nigh. And, indeed, there were many who thought exactly that, as they began to mourn and complain bitterly about what looked like the passing of a great club. If anybody had any doubts about how seriously this was being taken, these would have been dispelled by witnessing one of the most uproarious scenes I had ever seen, which took place not on the field, but in the centre stand at Celtic Park on 1 January 1994.

Hugh Keevins, then of the *Scotsman*, and now firmly ensconced with the *Daily Record* and broadcasting regularly with Clyde, was by my elbow in the commentary position when, after thirty minutes, Rangers were three goals up. It was then, amid the clamour, that Hugh pointed out that some of the patrons in the centre stand were not taking this lying down. Indeed, they were on their feet, throwing punches at each other, and grappling in fine Cumberland-wrestling style as the game raged on. These were the high-flyers in the Celtic support, far removed from the more humble patrons, crowded on the far side of the ground. If that element was so aroused as to take up arms in rebellion, what chance did this club have for survival? The fact that Rangers were to win 4–2 was immaterial. What we had witnessed was not reaction to a defeat in itself but the acute awareness that Celtic were in a deep crisis. Hugh Keevins took the brunt of the calls that late afternoon, as if he was manning the line at the American Embassy as escapees tried to book the last helicopter before the Vietcong arrived. Frantic and desperate punters are what you need to boost ratings . . .

It is that crisis that made Scottish Television's *Sport in Question* so successful. As the title implied, it was meant to cover a variety of sports. But you simply could not avoid Celtic. Their possible demise kept cropping up, and I spent much of my time trying to widen the scope, but our studio audience was frequented by the disgruntled and, according to them, disenfranchised followers of the club, who felt that this television programme was some healthy off-shoot of our democratic system, and that on this hustings they could let fly. They did. One evening we had Liam Brady on the panel, and even though he looked like a failing manager, he was treated with respect. He merely talked about footballing issues to a live studio audience who were not inclined to drag him into the gutsier issues. It was the members of the club's board they were after. I doubt if Brady had listened to such venom before. And I didn't realise how shocked he had been as members of the audience, well up on the facts and figures, spelt out the financial peril facing the club. He lived close to me in Lanarkshire and I drove him home that night. When I dropped him off at his house, I was about to drive away when he tapped the window and asked me simply and gravely, 'Do you honestly think Celtic could just go under and disappear?' That the current Celtic manager could even ask such a question hinted that either he had been kept out of the loop and knew nothing of what was going on, or that he was reflecting on how bad he knew things really were inside Parkhead. I pooh-poohed the idea of

Celtic folding, although in truth, having met the eloquent businessman Brian Dempsey, the board's most vociferous critic, on several occasions, including the evening he was on the *Sport in Question* panel, I guessed that this club could actually be on the brink of folding. When the board eventually accepted our invitation to appear on the programme, the obvious happened. They were verbally trounced.

I had to admire the fact that the former Lord Provost of Glasgow, Michael Kelly, the board's main protagonist, didn't shirk this, because he was regarded then by the Celtic support as about as useful to the club's survival as a gaping hole in a parachute. Michael and I went back some years together. In my early days in broadcasting he had made up his mind that I was the embodiment of bias, and nothing, not even frontal lobotomy would have rid him of that notion. In our fair city of Glasgow, that is how the identity issue occurs: you are tagged and that's that. He demonstrated that in May 1986 when Celtic, against the odds, won the league at Love Street when they beat St Mirren 5–0, at the same time as the favourites Hearts lost their last game 2–0 at Dundee. In covering the latter game I expressed some sympathy for the Edinburgh supporters, some of whom were seen weeping on the terracing, having their long-sought glory snatched away from them so dramatically. It was like watching a family wake. You had to show a little humanity. Michael, the following week on a live radio broadcast, accused me of departing from journalistic objectivity in revealing my disappointment at Celtic winning the league title, and said the BBC should censure me. He was like that. One day he could sound like the lecturer he was, eloquent, forcible in debate and with obvious social concerns. Another day he could sound like a punter with a bile problem.

That night he gamely stood his corner, but you felt that he and the others had entered the end-game with their detractors.

One of these was Gerry McNee, the sportswriter and broad-caster. Gerry would never beat about the bush. He aimed, he shot. In his sights were Michael Kelly and the others, of whom his general contention was 'sic a parcel o' rogues'. On one of the evenings (there were so many Celtic debates it is difficult to pin down this particular date) Gerry appeared in the audi-ence and after having delivered the expected fusillade, drew out of his pocket a medal. He revealed that it was given him by Jimmy McGrory, the famous player and previous manager of Celtic, who had presented him with it. It was a Scottish Cup winner's medal. It had a quite stunning effect. For here was a strident critic, showing an affection for the club and its supporters at a time when his criticisms might have forced an alienation between them. In effect it was saying, you had better sort out who the real enemies of this club are. And of course there were many, all enjoying these spectacles on *Sport in Question* and boosting the viewing figures which even exceeded, at times, the main programme *Scotsport.*

Then there hove into view at Celtic Park one day, walking towards our Clyde commentary position, the little man who was to revolutionise Parkhead. I didn't know who he was. Hugh Keevins, though, had been expecting him. Fergus McCann. He was bald and with a slight eye-squint which reminded me of the silent film comic, Ben Turpin. But his strong, assured voice, with the broad transatlantic accent, swept away that image. What he had to say about his remedy for the club's financial situation did seem at that time quite fanciful. He ignored me and spoke only to Hugh. The next time he appeared at the stadium, Celtic banned him from speaking inside the ground and they had to move outside to the car park, to the Clyde outside broadcast van, to make the interview. It was now devel-oping into a farce, from which Ben Turpin would not have been far removed. Four months after the Celtic representatives had appeared on our discussion programme, they were ousted. We could have claimed, with justification, that we had hastened their departure by providing the most visible platform on which their follies were more universally exposed. The producers of the programme might even have regretted that Celtic had been saved at all, and that the crisis was over. For the programme was never the same again. It had its moments, of course, but after the Celtic controversies, bungee-jumping would have seemed boring. But much more importantly, I felt the programme, when it was taken over by Caledonian Television, and partly organised by the man who had previously been my lawyer, Jock Brown, was running out of steam. Clyde most certainly wasn't. Indeed, in the line of duty for them, steam was about to erupt around me as from an unexpected fissure opening under my very feet.

It happened at Motherwell, inside Fir Park. When the crowds have gone after a game, and you are left in the dark of the stand, only lit by the needle lights of the commentating equipment, the silence and the gloom can provoke thoughts that it is a place where 'ghaists and bogles' might appear. Little did we know it then, but one was definitely about to. The afternoon match between Motherwell and Falkirk had largely been uneventful. Except for one incident. During the game there had been a clash between Falkirk's Crawford Baptie and Motherwell's Nick Cusack. I had accurately described Cusack forcibly applying his elbow to Baptie's face, knocking him on his back. I thought nothing of that, and the game ended. About half an hour after the match my co-commentator Davy Provan and I were standing in the chill, at the back of the stand, engaged in the Clyde phone-in with the public. We then noticed a dark shape emerging from one of the stand tunnels. The voice calling up to us, to find out if we were finished, revealed the shape to be Tommy McLean, the Motherwell manager. It sounded casual and reasonable. He stood there for a full half hour, leaning against a barrier, until he heard we were finished and then proceeded to mount the steps towards us. As he neared us his speed increased and he barked, 'Did you say that ma player deliberately elbowed Baptie in the face?' His unleashed venom took us aback at first. What had happened, after all, had been plain to see, except by the referee, who had missed the sudden incident. The only way he could have known anything about what I had said must have been from a third party, since he was, of course, down in the technical area throughout. However, there seemed nothing to it. I replied that I had indeed said that. He suddenly leaped up the stairs at me and threw a punch. He missed by a country mile. Now, here I have to append the names of other managers with whom, at one time or another, I had altercations in which it seemed as if blood would flow: Stein, Symon, Waddell, Ferguson, Jim McLean. Everything, though, was verbal. But, here in the dark, with the wee 'bogle', this was historic. This was the first time a punch had ever been thrown at me. It was epochal. The incandescence of his rage failed to light up the stand, so I had only a small shape to aim at, as I retaliated and threw a right hook. To do so, and to have a fair chance of success with the blow, taking into account Tommy's size, I had to bend at the knees at the same time. It failed. Because stepping in between us was the gallant figure of Davy Provan, who, no weakling, was able to grapple the two of us apart. A caterwauling of mutual obscenities then rent the air, and ultimately the small figure, hardly placated, hurtled back down the stairs. Oh, how distant then seemed the Long Room at Lords, the croquet of the Hurlingham Club, the Pimms of Henley and the glittering yachts and curves of Cowes!

The consequences were intriguing. I knew that Bill Dickie, the very personable director of Motherwell, was a member of the SFA's committee which was to scrutinise terracing behaviour in the campaign against hooliganism. I wrote a letter to the Motherwell chairman, pointing out the stark contrast, and perhaps their hypocrisy over terracing violence in light of their manager's behaviour. But in the letter I had made a mistake. Referring to the incident which caused the row, there was a slip. I referred to 'Neil' Cusack, not 'Nick'. Back came a letter which must have been written under cute legal instructions. It was only a couple of sentences long, stating that there was no such player as 'Neil' Cusack at the club. End of story as far as I was concerned. I simply wanted to get on with life. But Tommy and Motherwell had different ideas. Not only was I banned from the ground, but Radio Clyde was entirely banned too. Now, without discrediting Motherwell in the slightest, I could have lived with that. Being banned from Celtic Park, or Ibrox, would have been like being emasculated. But Paul Cooney, very properly, did not want his station to be banned from any ground and asked me to offer the apology for my comment about Cusack which Motherwell were demanding to rescind the ban. I refused. It would have been like condoning managerial violence, it seemed to me. The affair dragged on. Fir Park was now a no-go area for Clyde, and I knew eventually something had to give because I did not want to embarrass Paul Cooney, who had done so much to bring me into the programme. So, many weeks later, I told him I would issue a statement about this, and to alert Motherwell to that.

I was at Pittodrie. I was there for the commentary. At the top of the programme, Paul handed over to me, to make this so-called statement, which I knew would not have the same staying power as the Gettysburg Address and its significance for the democratic process, but would simply get us our damned seats back at Fir Park. I couched it in such ambiguous terms, such convoluted prose, such long-winded terminology, such use of

metaphor, that it could either have been interpreted as a grov-
elling apology or a criticism of the Saudi royal family. It probably confused them at Fir Park, or they had been bored out of
their minds listening to it. The affair petered out. In later years
Tommy and I became professional colleagues, and he was to
travel as my co-commentator around Europe for Scottish
Television. We had some entertaining nights out together, and
not once was the episode mentioned. Football, thankfully, does
not adhere, generally speaking, to that old Bourbon tag, 'They
learn nothing, and forget nothing.' Then, when least expected,
came an offer, not long after that Motherwell incident, which
was so mysteriously couched it was irresistible. It came from
Paris.

20

I'LL ALWAYS HAVE PARIS

You might think it would be impossible to find a wilderness in the heart of Paris, given that you can walk around it contentedly until your feet call for mercy, with your eyes glazed by the sweep of its boulevards and the vitality and sophistication of pavement life. But I found one. It was called Eurosport. It has a mammoth output now. It didn't then, in the early 1990s. This new European television satellite station had been set up on the left bank of the Seine at Le Pont d'Alma, immediately across the river from where Princess Di and Dodi met their fate. For lunch we would often stroll across that bridge and sit at a bistro where you could see right through the underpass where the accident had taken place. The building we were housed in, on the other side, could have been built when Napoleon was courting Josephine, for all I know, as it looked venerable and splendid on the outside, but inside would have been turned down by the Addams Family. The main corridor was the Champs Elysées of the Parisian cockroach population. The studios and broadcasting booths emitted a faint odour that pre-empted the need to visit the famous Paris sewers. I had been told that it had been Gestapo headquarters during the Occupation and perhaps there was a residual need to let it decay. The cafeteria-restaurant, you would not be surprised to hear, was immaculate and bountiful. They do get their priorities right in Paris. Outside our office window you could virtually reach out and touch the Eiffel Tower. Eventually you almost forgot it was there. The wilderness analogy extended further than just the dilapidation, and the obvious inability to hire an adequate cleaning firm, but to its staff and production values. They were French in the main, which would not be too surprising, given where we were, but most of them were young, inexperienced, wildly ambitious, and with no idea of the basic standards of programme preparation.

So why end up there? It came through a call made to me by a man they were eventually to call 'Statto'. Angus Loughran, the son of the former conductor of both the BBC Scottish Symphony Orchestra and the Hallé, was a freelance broadcaster who did get around a bit and, for reasons that are admittedly obscure, found his way to Paris, where he had been attracted by a new station badly in need of experienced broadcasters. There was a lot more to it than a simple telephone call from him, though. Having travelled so much previously, I had the feeling of being bogged down, and my London exposure to different levels of broadcasting meant that the mention of a new broadcasting station in Paris intrigued me. I was still broadcasting with Clyde and Scottish Television, but this seemed a useful, not to say bizarre, supplement. Angus was a little-known man in those days, but later he was to don a gown and candle and become 'Statto' of the Frank Skinner and David Baddiel late-night comedy show. God knows how he clinched that, but suddenly he had been catapulted into something of celebrity status. He had long sought something like that.

Some of the tales Angus spun had touches of the Baron Munchausen about them. But he was a most generous man who principally aimed to please. And he had helped find me a new outlet. It was also timely. Paul Cooney had been away from Clyde for a spell, which had allowed me both to present the show and commentate at matches. It was a big task – and an even bigger one was dealing with the mastermind at Clyde, Alex Dickson, the Programme Manager, a man with a tireless brain which seemed to run in several directions at once, and whose relentless issuing of memos to me was like being zapped by every starling in the city of Glasgow. Remorseless and sapping he certainly was. Enough of this already, I kept telling myself, without actually disliking the Saturday broadcasting. Indeed, that part of it was a joy. First aid was needed, and it came. Paul Cooney returned to the station and it was clear that he would take over the presenter's seat I had kept warm for him, leaving me with commentary. He did, and the Tolstoy of memo-writing promptly halved my fee. No real gripe from me, as the work-load was hugely reduced. And during Paul's absence, in 1992, I had been awarded a Sony Gold for being British Radio Commentator of the year. The fact that Andrew Neil, for whom I used to write columns in the *Sunday Times* when he was editor, was on the short-leet for that award as well, does suggest it was a new and perhaps odd category, but I can only suppose that the award was related to the overall presentation of the programmes I had been involved in. I wasn't one to argue about categories and took the award gratefully at a function in London. That award could have been for pibroch-playing, for all the French knew and cared. They gave the impression that you would be qualified to work there if you were able to tie your own shoelaces.

Paris took on a shadowier complexion when they showed me where I would make my first broadcast for them. It was deep in the bowels of the building, in a small, claustrophobic cubicle of the type which the North Koreans used to convert prisoners, where you went in as yourself and came out as the Manchurian Candidate of the film. In this case, you went in as a broadcaster from the old school and came out the other end as Eurosport Man; the man prepared to flirt with absurd conditions for vicarious thrills, mostly because you got free trips to Paris. The difference was astounding. It did really feel as if the world was being left behind, as they shut the door behind you and left you in semi-darkness. And there was the sudden eerie silence, so intense, when not even the munching of the cockroaches could be heard. They were obviously good at insulation if nothing else.

The object of the exercise was to commentate on highlights of a football match. This was the particular signature of Eurosport. All Eurosport commentaries at that stage were done in cubicles in their Paris studios. Constantly imprisoned in these booths, as we were, Eurosport was the Bastille of European broadcasting.

The man who had been in the cubicle before me, and who came out looking ghastly pale, had been commentating for a solid two hours. Little wonder. He was their truck-pulling correspondent. He could salivate at the sight of a Leyland truck. And at a huge big Merc? We are probably talking orgasm here. If truth be known, the station would have taken donkey-wrestling from the Carpathians just to fill the many hours of screen-time to which they had committed themselves. Early on, I was on the verge of suggesting, purely in jest, that they should consider welly-boot throwing. But I realised they were so desperate for material that they would have thought this worthy of pursuing, and without doubt they would have put their researchers on to tracing the offices of the World Welly-Boot Throwing Association. They had to feed themselves on sporting activities which the terrestrial stations would not have touched with a barge-pole, or left-overs which had been broadcast days before by other stations around Europe. They were the hand-me-down channel.

Left in the booth, I was to commentate on highlights of the game between Universitatea Craiova from Romania and the Bulgarian side, Lokomotiv Plovdiv, two teams I had never seen before. This kind of anonymous fixture could cause brain seizure. There are moments when you would rather cover Nude Darts, and this was one of them. I looked down at the list of names they had given me. Many of them looked like terms you would find in Black's Medical Dictionary. I looked at the black and white screen. The players resembled midges dancing against a bright flame. So, clicking my heels, I set off down this yellow-brick road. I was now in a fantasy world.

To this day, I know not whether this was a friendly or a European tie. It is not that I hadn't done booth-commentary before. I had commentated on Olympic football in LA in 1984. We did these in a booth, just off Sunset Boulevard in the old Columbia Pictures Studio while the early games were being played in the Rose Bowl in Pasadena. I repeated that in the Seoul Olympics of 1988, for football and other events. But in Paris this seemed to be like wearing a blindfold and being asked by an optician to read the bottom line of a chart. After about twenty minutes I realised something had gone very badly wrong. As badly wrong as you can get. I discovered that when the name of the first scorer, and a score-caption, came up on the screen which indicated that Plovdiv had scored. According to me it was Universitatea. And had been for all those twenty minutes, as I had waffled on about their passing abilities and discipline. They had transposed the names of the teams in the list of players they had handed me before the game. Rage was futile. I was trapped. I looked through the glass pane of the booth at the young French producer who had armed me with this gin-trap, and vehemently mouthed 'Bampot!' at him. He smiled back, to prove that the sound insulation was perfect, and that lip-reading the Glasgow vernacular was not included in French Baccalauréat studies. Without breaking stride, I turned one team back, instantly, into the other (was there any other way?) and floundered on, counting my blessings that, at that time, the viewing audience in the UK for Eurosport would not have filled a single-decker Glasgow bus.

Misidentifying a player is something we try to avoid, as the most obvious of all holes in the road. But to actually get the identity of two teams wrong is like falling into the Grand Canyon. I came out of the booth like I had been in a tumble drier. When I searched out the young producer afterwards, with the *entente cordiale* a now frayed concept, and wishing to do him some sort of harm, I was met with a beaming smile and 'Bon, bon!' and an outstretched hand, which threw me, since at the same time he was cheerily hailing the commentators from the other languages, caught up in the same catastrophe, and emerging from their booths like survivors of a blitzkrieg, to tell them that we should all repair to a café, at the corner of Avenue George V, across the Alma bridge from the studios, and have some drinks. His apparent lack of concern at what had gone on, and his buoyant cheeriness, took the wind out of our sails. So the potential lynching party was exposed to that unbelievably infectious French charm, which can camouflage so many of their inadequacies and would leave me to think, so many times, that they had no sense of how to grasp realities.

This was Parisian *politesse*, that which can strangle at birth even the most genuine complaint, with a mix of feigned innocence and charm, and the use of the most potent weapon of all, Paris. For an odd feeling was developing. As we sat nursing our wounds, we at least had a glass of Côtes du Rhône in our hands, and we were looking down the stretch of the glittering Seine where the dining boats, the Bateaux Mouches, were plying their trade. Nearby, people were heading for the Crazy Horse

245

nightclub a few paces away, and elegant women clipped by, heading, you thought, for some clandestine meeting which would be more than *tête-à-tête*, and loud Frenchmen, smoking themselves to death, downed their *pastis* beside you, most of them looking and sounding like Jacques Chirac; and the wine was not plonk but something that seemed good for the soul. We had been forewarned that Eurosport at that stage was as organised as a finger-painting session in a kindergarten, and it had just dished us up a tiny taste of what we might be letting ourselves in for. But where we were sitting at that moment made Shepherd's Bush Green in London and the Cowcaddens in Glasgow seem like the Gulag Archipelago. The famous line of Henry IV of France came to mind, when, against his very nature, but to ensure he gained the throne, he converted to a new religion, with the comment 'Paris is worth a Mass.' For me, it was worth a try.

More practically, I figured that there was huge potential in a station whose footprint stretched, even then, from Macgillicuddy's Reeks in the south-west of Ireland, right through to the Urals in Russia and southwards to the Mediterranean rim, and into parts of the Middle East. There was also the fact that just a week spent in the City of Light was enough to convince me that the French lifestyle was the life for me. Compared with hectic, dog-eat-dog, Thatcherite London, this environment seemed to provide an easy balance between work and play. Their thirty-five-hour week, and the general impression that nobody ever got sacked in France and that you had to die to lose a job, or take the incredibly early pension, might have been the legislative basis of it all. But, over and above that, they knew how to treat work as simply a means of creating time and money to seek out enjoyment. It was more genetic than legal. So I decided to dig in for a long haul, if they would have me. They did. Within a few months, we moved out of the old

Gestapo headquarters to a custom-built set of offices, further up river, and near to the ultra-modern studios of the most powerful French television channel, TF1, which was part of the parent company which now owned Eurosport.

Most of our work was done late at night, which meant I found myself being turned into a perpetual tourist. I wandered the city at will during the day. I began to know the left and right banks of the Seine as well as some of my French colleagues. There wasn't a museum I hadn't been in after about six months, commuting back and forth from Glasgow, as I did every week. One day I found myself saying to my wife, who was there on a visit, 'I want to show you the bullet holes in the Crillon Hotel which was a target for the Resistance just before the Liberation,' and suddenly realised that I was now so beguiled by the city that I was now virtually a tourist guide, and had to be careful that the seductive nature of Paris would not lull me into a complacent life while this new station was still trying to find its feet and placing broadcasters into occasional jeopardy.

The commentating booths became steadily better. They were no longer torture chambers, but were bright and spacious. But the challenge was just the same. You could never tell if the information handed to you about any game or event was strictly correct. When we covered the Copa America, in Ecuador, for instance, in the early 1990s, we had to rely on faxes sent to us before these games from local correspondents out there with team names and numbers. But since my commentary was being used as a guide for the stations in the Far East, I had to get up early in the morning to do these games live, so that when the game was recorded, a tape would then be whisked to Charles de Gaulle airport and it would be put on a flight for Hong Kong.

One morning Brazil were to play Peru. A fax certainly arrived with names of players on them. But no numbers. As Brazil never really take the Copa America as seriously as some of their continental challengers, and since many of their players then were based in European club football, Brazil would field second-string players, of whom relatively little was known. They did so that day. I could recognise none of them. Peru's anonymity went further. They had no numbers on their jerseys. It was going to be difficult to walk out on this, as with some justification I could have done. But I knew Eurosport had a commercially viable agreement with stations in the Far East. I knew that a motorcyclist was waiting outside, engine revving, waiting for me to finish so he could speed down the dreaded *périphérique* motorway with the tape to catch the flight. I took a deep breath and launched into this. The tape did get to Hong Kong in time. I don't know where it is now, but it would be a collector's item. It may, in fact, be the only football commentary ever made without a player's name ever being mentioned. No names, no pack drill, as they say. How is that possible? Anything is possible, if circumstances have turned you into an Indiana Jones of broadcasting, surviving incredible perils. One thing definitely helped. There was no scoring. So I didn't need to identify a scorer. I just talked over the pictures as if I was lecturing on the ethos of South American football. Waffle, with lots of mention of my time strolling down Copacabana beach, helped pass the time.

These were the risks you simply had signed up for. But then you would mix with the different nationalities, the Dutch, the Germans, the Belgians, the French and you felt you were bonding in the certain knowledge that although chaos frequently reigned within this fledgling station, we could just survive its zaniness, for there was no pain that could not be cured by a saunter down the boulevards and a glass or two of Bordeaux. The Dutch had a 'guid conceit' of themselves. They were the loudest, most argumentative and conspiratorial. Nothing passed under their radar. Jolly and funny they could be, even when they were back-stabbing with the alacrity of hired assassins. Compared with the Germans they were the gypsies of the group. They certainly liked to decry the Germans as much as they could. That latent mistrust of the Germans reminded me of the remark Jock Stein had made to me in Germany in 1974, when he was analysing why the superior Dutch side lost to Germany in that final. 'The Dutch will never forget the war. That's what affected them. They didn't just want to win, they wanted to rub it in. They should never have allowed the Germans back into that game.'

The only real reservations we had about the Germans were about those broadcasters who had emerged from the old GDR, behind the Wall. Anybody who had any professional status there must have been connected to the Stasi, it was thought. They didn't seem any different from those from the West of the country, but the Dutch encouraged us to think, for instance, that the dapper German dealing competently with an athletics commentary might in fact have been an informer for the dreaded secret police. But I found all the Germans to be straight and direct, and whilst I had many enjoyable evenings with Dutch colleagues, none of them ever seemed to rush to pick up the tab. Then there were the French.

Much as I would laud their cosmopolitanism and the finesse with which they applied their social skills in entertaining themselves and others, in business they were bewildering. They changed their minds so often, on so many issues, that you felt like hiring a clairvoyant to second-guess them. From what you began to learn from reading newspapers, and speaking to other foreigners who did business with them, Eurosport was far from unique, but mirrored much of the ethic of commerce in that country. 'Don't bloody trust them,' a businessman told me on a flight into Paris once. He was French-Canadian, with all his relatives still flourishing in Paris, and his affection for the old country might have tempered his views. Not evidently so. 'As a working principle,' he went on, 'assume that somewhere along the line they will lie to you.'

This sort of view was echoed several times in conversations with a range of Europeans. It was not a horrible den of iniquity I had entered, of course. I was, in fact, inside a highly polished culture of indifference to facts. An example of that, on a minor scale, but pointing to more general issues of trust, was the case of a French colleague, a delightful man and extremely popular with all the languages, who came round us all looking for money, with which he would guarantee each one of us a press ticket for the season to all games at the Parc des Princes – press tickets being difficult to obtain. We all duly forked out. We never saw the tickets, nor did the money find its way back to us. For all we know he might have used it as a down payment on a *pied à terre* in Montmartre. It was fraud, in any language. He still circulated amongst us, though, and far from being expelled from the company, he was promoted. His status had actually soared. It then became clear that no Frenchman would be accused of any mistakes, however egregious they might be. And there were plenty.

So we would line up together in our different cubicles to broadcast in those various languages. Editing for a variety of languages could lead to spectacular mishaps. Celtic were playing Sporting Lisbon in the UEFA Cup in the 1993/94 season. They had won 1–0 in the first leg at Celtic Park. We gained the rights to cover the second leg in Lisbon. Now, commentators varied in how to approach recorded highlights. Some of the less assured would actually watch the whole game live, coming into the station before entering the booth, so that they were replete with the information required. But to try to make it sound as spontaneous as possible, I preferred to stay in my hotel room until only a few minutes before I was required, then I would slip into the booth, and with the properly checked team-lists, I would then treat the highlights as if they were live. The gung-ho way. I simply did not want to know the score in advance. But that night, when I had successfully eluded everybody and was about to settle into the booth, a passing Dutchman happened to blurt out that Celtic had been eliminated. I was annoyed that he had revealed that. But at least he hadn't given the score. I could, therefore, reflect that spontaneously. We started. Midway through the first half, Sporting scored, to make the aggregate score 1–1. Since the footage so far still indicated an aggregate score of 1–1 – and yet I had been made aware of Celtic's elimination – I built up the prospect of extra time dramatically. At what appeared to be the final whistle being blown at ninety minutes, with the score the same, I launched into the prospects of how Celtic would cope with that, but noticed at the same time the Portuguese players leaping up and down in jubilation, as if extra time was a preferred stimulant in that country. Something was wrong . . . again. Very wrong. For the programme then ended with me still rabbiting on about extra time. Somebody had messed up the pre-commentary editing, cutting out Sporting's decisive winning goal which came in the 62nd minute.

Around Europe, the many who now listened to the English language version were poised on the edge of their seats, nervously waiting for an extra time that never existed. There was only one thing to do – I said 'Goodnight!' and dived out of the cubicle to find out if my colleagues were any the wiser. They were. They had all seen the game live before the recording, and knew what had happened. There was obviously an Inspector Clouseau loose in the building. We discovered, in fact, that the mangled editing was from the hand of a young girl, who, applying the French logic which prevailed when she was running out of editing time, felt the goal had to go. She made it disappear. That was definitive Eurosport. On my way back into

Glasgow I bumped into Scottish comedian Andy Cameron at the airport, who ruefully asked me, 'When's extra time being played?' It was a reminder to me, if nothing else, that more and more people were tuning into this station, and that I was running incredible risks in trying to treat it as if I was with an overseas BBC, instead of the anarchic station it was.

At the same time, though, you could feel the growth of this channel. Simon Reed, the brother of Oliver, the actor, had appeared and assumed the mantle of English-language commentators' organiser. He selected them for a variety of jobs, and of course was in the position to appoint himself to any commentating role he wanted, but specialised in tennis and ice-skating. From his own involvement in trying to improve the quality of broadcasting, and with many more languages coming on board, including Spanish, Italian and Portuguese, there was a feeling that, despite the occasional gaffes, its credibility was inching upwards, if not exactly soaring.

I received a phone call one day from a sports paper in Tel Aviv, asking me if their correspondent could come to interview me in Paris. I had no idea why. When he eventually arrived he pointed out that Eurosport was big in Israel, and around the Middle East, and I should be aware of the effect I was having on the football population. Like increasing attendances at the Wailing Wall? He didn't quite get the point of my question, but he did promise to send me a copy of the paper with my interview in it. He did. There it was on the front page – a large photograph of myself with a banner headline. But it was all in Hebrew. Nobody could translate it. The local Rabbi was unavailable. They ran a competition in the office for a guess as to what it said. It was won by, 'WANTED. FOR THE MANGLING OF THE ENGLISH LANGUAGE.'

For me, it was a warning not to take any broadcast for granted. Based in Paris you were devoid of the normal cut-and-thrust of press or public reaction which could tend to keep you focused. This was the big danger, lapsing into being less aware of a widespread audience out there. Then the tyranny of the cubicle began to be relaxed. We began to be sent to games. We did a lot within the Parc des Princes for Paris St Germain, French international and Cup Final games. I travelled with Trevor Steven, the former Everton and Glasgow Rangers player, to Madrid to cover the final of the Copa del Rey, and then to Switzerland and Norway with Mark Lawrenson, now of BBC fame, for UEFA cup games. The feeling of getting out and about seemed unreal at first, as if you were on day release from an open prison. But we were not entirely free. One Friday evening I took a call from the Eurosport offices informing me that they had won the rights to a World Cup play-off and could I do the commentary? The problem was, the game was the following morning and the match was between Australia and Iran in the MCG cricket ground in Melbourne. Easy. I had my own broadcasting equipment, with its special BT line, already set up for emergencies. I brought Trevor Steven down from wherever he lived at that time and we both sat in my living room in Bothwell, Lanarkshire, following the Eurosport transmission on our television set and commentated throughout Europe on this rather dramatic game which saw Australia shunted out of the World Cup.

When I eventually heard a recording of that match we really did sound as if we were sitting in Melbourne. The proof that we got away with it was that about an hour after the programme I met a friend of mine in the supermarket and he almost dropped his free-range eggs when he saw me, utterly convinced that I would have been enjoying a post-match barbie by then.

The negative side of it was that Eurosport began to think of saving money by not bringing me to Paris but using that same domestic technique for a whole variety of broadcasts from curling to athletics to bowls and, of course, football. I was now into cottage industry, sitting at home doing it. But then a confluence of two events jolted me out of a growing complacency. One was a World Cup. The other was a heart operation.

21

THE RETURN

Sean Connery and Alex Salmond walked regally down the broad Parisian staircase, so close together you felt Moses would have had more difficulty parting them than he did the Red Sea. The greatest living Scotsman and the tubby politician were greeted like royalty by a throng of Scots businessmen and showbiz personalities in the Buddha Club, the vast nightclub adjacent to the Crillon Hotel, on the eve of Scotland's World Cup opening match with Brazil in June 1998. The World Cup had come to France, and for the first time you felt that Eurosport, the incarcerated station, could flex its scrawny muscles, and try to show that it had something to offer outside of being, as Budd Schulberg once wrote contemptuously of someone, 'a pimple on the arse of progress'. We were all there that evening, to commune with the notion that Scotland could beat Brazil, and the fact that we were still twenty-four hours from putting that preposterous idea to the test meant that the booze flowed and the nationalistic sentiments gushed.

Sean, sitting beside me at a large round table, asked me profound questions about Scotland's chances, and I gave him the usual wildly optimistic analyses. I have been with Sean several times and can never get beyond being tempted to ask him the first meaningful question that hovers around my lips, 'What was it like watching Ursula Andress walk out of the sea in *Dr No*?' but never actually have. It was no time to be frivolous, we were into deep patriotism, a kind of solemnity was called for. Sean was looking appropriately dour. I had encountered that guarded dourness several times before when our paths had crossed. This was most notably in Toni Dalli's restaurant just outside Malaga during the World Cup of 1982, when we took cameras to interview him about his love of team and country. For there I discovered he was distinctly touchy. As we were ploughing through a huge plate of pasta, with Billy McNeill the great Lisbon Lion, mulling over stories about Celtic with him, his wife Micheline kept twittering on, almost ceaselessly, about the tiny dog she had with her, until Sean could stand it no longer. He put down his fork and spoon, looked her in the eye and hissed at her, 'Would you please shut your effing mouth!'

So, no. That evening in the Buddha Club in Paris was not the time for chirpy anecdotes. We talked instead about exile. He enjoyed his affluently. I did it sparingly, out of decent enough hotels, but seemed to exist continually out of a suitcase. But I did indicate to him that, thankfully, this might be coming to an end. For the unfortunate illness of a colleague had changed prospects. I was contacted by Sandy Ross, one of STV's most prominent producers, and asked if I could fill in the vacancy left by Gerry McNee, their commentator then, who was in need of heart surgery and would not be able to commit to the remaining games of the Scottish league season. As this did not conflict with anything I was doing for Eurosport, I accepted eagerly. But the World Cup was looming a couple of months hence, and Ross did posit the possibility that although he hoped Gerry would be fit in time for that, he might have to ask me if I could consider that as well. So, to the surprise of many, I popped up for the first time in almost ten years on Scottish screens, to commentate on two live television matches.

For even with thoughts of the imminent World Cup forming in the mind and making preparations for the games I would cover for Eurosport, I had to concentrate on one of the tensest finishes in the league's history. Rangers were only three games away from beating Jock Stein's famous nine-in-a-row title record. Celtic were striving to stop that happening, as if their very heritage was at stake. The fans were discovering nerve-endings they never thought they had. Conspiracy was afoot. Nobody believed that anybody was beyond scrutiny, in who might be involved in helping one or the other achieve that feat. Even ball boys taking their time rolling the match balls into play were suspected as co-conspirators. And I knew I would get it in the neck as well. I did, after my first game back, when with Charlie Nicholas at my side as co-commentator, I opined that the sending off of Amoruso of Rangers in their match at Pittodrie against Aberdeen, which was to be drawn 1–1, thus costing Rangers a valuable two points, was unjust. No death threats exactly, but enough scorn was heaped on me, from various quarters, to confirm my view that Paris was definitely worth its broadcasting risks. At Dunfermline, for the second match, Celtic scored first and then, affected by nerves, conceded the home side's equaliser to end the game 1–1. Charlie, I thought, was excellent at my side. He didn't allow his obvious affection for his old club to cloud his judgement. Indeed, I was to discover he would anger some of the Celtic support for his candid remarks. It merely underlined how far he might go in this trade, for the syco-phants, with one or two major exceptions, never last the pace. The pedants, of course, would point occasionally, as they do with other ex-players, to a less than avid respect for strict gram-matical correctness. But this is much less important than the authenticity of their views. Charlie was now far removed from the young lad I had interviewed for the first time, years before, in his house in Maryhill, even though I knew at that time that he was destined to make a big impact on Scottish football. Indeed, such was my unstinted admiration for his play that, in my time at the BBC, the Rangers supporters had cottoned on to that fact, and whenever they spied me on the television gantry at matches, set up the chant, 'Archie sleeps wi' Charlie', in a lilting, and, at least, non-sectarian chant.

In the short time available to me in covering three games back in Scotland I was never to meet Wim Jansen, the Dutch manager of Celtic who helped stop the Rangers juggernaut. But I had done a radio commentary for Clyde, the day Henrik Larsson made his debut from the subs bench at Easter Road in August 1997, as Celtic went down to defeat, and heard my broadcasting colleagues denouncing Jansen, with the prediction that he would not last a month in the job. And that Celtic had bought a real bummer in the guy who had come off the bench and given the ball away for a Hibs goal, namely Henrik Larsson.

Jansen would obviously have been worth getting to know. But I knew most of the other major participants well. Jock Brown, Celtic's Chief Executive, had been my lawyer, of course, and from the chat I listened to, I could tell he was becoming increasingly unpopular amongst the Celtic support. I had learned of his appointment walking down the Champs Elysées one Sunday morning, reading the *Sunday Times*, and I thought there had been a misprint, and that they really should have been referring to his brother Craig. I couldn't fathom this. I knew of his deep dislike for Rangers and that he had once told me that going to Ibrox revolted him at times. That is about as much as I could link to a relationship with Celtic, although a very tenuous one.

Then there were Walter Smith and David Murray. Together they had made a mistake of historic proportions in Smith's last season by announcing, well in advance, that the manager would be leaving at the end of it. It was wholly negative, and, as the season wore on, the players conveyed none of the dynamism needed to get that tenth successive win. They simply ground out results. Smith and Murray had gone a year too far. Somebody new should have come in. What Rangers had needed at the start of that season was reinvigoration. It was a club which had gone to sleep whilst on sentry duty.

Three games done, I returned to Paris, with the news that Gerry McNee had recovered, thankfully, from his heart operation and would be fit enough to fulfil his World Cup duties, and, at the same time, to hear from Eurosport that they had decided to splash out some money and bring in two former English managers as assistant commentators. First to be hired was Bryan Robson, former Manchester United player, who had been one of the finest midfield players in the world. A modern box-to-box player, the scorer of some great goals, he had still to earn his spurs as a manager with Middlesbrough at the time. Then there was 'The Turnip', Graham Taylor, former England manager.

On hearing of these appointments, I felt that at last some people somewhere would begin to take Eurosport seriously. However, we didn't know what we had let ourselves in for with Robson. I didn't meet up with him until about half an hour before the Norway–Scotland game kicked off in Bordeaux. He came on to the commentary platform in an almost breathless state, and I began to wonder if his legendary capacity for sinking pints, along with his great mate and wonderful defender Gordon McQueen, who was out in France with him, was taking its toll. Not so. His opening remarks to me were as follows: 'Bloody hell. A Scottish supporter tried to pickpocket me outside the ground there. I grabbed his wrist and was about to banjo him when he recognised who it was and said, "Oh, it's you

259

Bryan! Gie's yer autograph." I could only laugh. You gotta hand it to the Scots.' I wasn't exactly sure what his last remark meant, although an unfair mind might have thought he was denouncing us all as pickpockets.

But, sadly, that was virtually his longest contribution of the afternoon. It was immediately clear that either he didn't want to be there at all or that he was incapable of stringing two consecutive thoughts together. At times during the commentary I had to check that he hadn't gone off to the loo. He sat there impassively, unmoved by events on the park, and when I tried to elicit anything from him, he responded in that deep, solemn voice of his that would have been more in keeping with covering Remembrance Day at the Cenotaph. I had no idea what they were paying him, but a man with his pedigree wouldn't have crossed the Channel unless it was going to help towards a Porsche. The fact that it wasn't pennies was borne out to me the following morning, when I was phoned by Simon Reed, the organiser of commentators, who no doubt had been party to hiring him, and who angered me by implying that I wasn't doing enough to 'bring out the best in Bryan'. A ventriloquist wouldn't have brought the best out of him.

I hoped the circumstances would be different when we travelled to St Etienne for the infamous Argentina–England game, where I expected him to be as chirpy as a blackbird, since, after all, he had captained England sixty-five times. In one of the most dramatic games ever between the two countries, Michael Owen scoring a remarkable opening goal and David Beckham lashing out at an opponent and being sent off, Robson responded as if he was being asked to explain the complications of VAT invoices. So I just ignored him and got on with it.

Now it was in the early 1970s that assistant commentators began to appear. Normally they were ex-pros. This soon became the norm. Commentators were no longer soloists in live broadcasts. Jock Stein was the first major name to sit beside me. He spoke frugally, but with sharp insights, and I remember his words muttered in my ear, off mic, when we sat high above the Anfield pitch in 1977, the night Scotland played Wales in the deciding game for qualification for Argentina. He was looking down at the massive, vociferous and aggressive Scottish support. 'I hope to God we win tonight,' he said. 'If we don't, they might take this town apart.' He clearly sensed that the mood of triumphalism could be tipped in exactly the opposite way.

Alex Ferguson by my side, at Wembley in 1981, watching Scotland win 1–0, had the same kind of approach as Stein. Concise and meaningful, with tasty acerbic comments about particular English players. Alan Rough was like listening to a companion at a match with you, to cheer you up. He certainly did that for me at the Scottish Cup Final of 1984 between Aberdeen and Celtic, which went into extra time. Before they went into that period I felt my bladder was about to burst. I had to pay a call. We were broadcasting live. I had to signal to Alan, using body language, that nature was calling. He looked puzzled at first, then, still talking through my mic to the public I simulated the peeing action to Alan until he realised where I was heading. I put down the mic and left him to it. I knew the risk I was taking, for Alan was a total novice to broadcasting in these days, but nothing could deter me from easing the torture I was experiencing. So I left him to take on the millions listening in, and leapt up the stairs from the commentary position, only to discover there was a queue at the loo, congested, of course, by the men of the fourth estate, who indubitably had been at the sauce at lunchtime. I made few friends as I wrestled my way to the front of the queue and recklessly and with abandon relieved myself, and then rushed down again, hoping that Roughie had not flaked out through the pressure. But he was enjoying himself, joshing around as if he had been at it all his days. I could claim I had inadvertently acted as midwife to Alan Rough emerging as the broadcasting pro he now is.

Then Billy McNeill did so many commentaries with me that for a spell we became a recognised double act. You name the competition, we did it together. Billy was simply articulate, and wasn't there just because of his footballing pedigree. He only let me down once and that was in Malaga in Spain in 1982 for the last fateful international between Scotland and the USSR. As Scotland's hopes sank, after a ludicrously conceded goal when Alan Hansen and Willie Miller contrived a Laurel and Hardy act when trying to go for the same ball, a Russian official sitting in front of me had kept raising his arms and blotting out my view throughout the entire match. I had asked him several times to desist. After they had scored that awful goal, he did the same again, and I lost the plot. I punched him solidly on the back and shouted on him to stop it. He rose to his feet. He was at least 6 foot 10 and looked like a Siberian version of King Kong, with huge fists, one of which at that moment was beginning to bunch ominously. I smiled, weakly I suppose, and slid slightly under my desk, in the hope that my noble colleague beside me would sort this man out. But Billy, being the astute man he is, was half under his desk as well. It only proved that Russians are susceptible to that well-proven Glasgow facial expression that conveys the message, 'It wisnae me!' Confounded, the Russian sat down.

When I used Ray Clemence – the English goalkeeper adored by the Scots for allowing a trundling Kenny Dalglish shot to go through his legs for a winning goal at Hampden in 1976 – for the World Cup in the USA in 1994, we invented feuds to arouse interest. For we were incarcerated again in a Eurosport booth in Paris for that entire tournament, which led us to the kinds of frustration only ever experienced in France before by the Count of Monte Cristo in his dungeon. Unlike the Count, we had no means of escape, so we decided that we had to avoid at all costs the tedious custom of commentator and sidekick agreeing with one another all the time. I think we were going to extremes when we would come to verbal blows, arguing about whose throw-in it was in a match. But it worked. People listening liked the abrasive relationship, little realising that it was manufactured by two men almost pleading to be listened to.

Alan McInally, of Celtic and Bayern and now with Sky Sports, Davy Provan of Celtic and Scotland and now prominent co-commentator with Sky Sports, Andy Walker of Celtic, Derek Johnstone and Fraser Wishart of Rangers, they all worked in tandem with me and, indeed, propped me up on more than one occasion in terms of identification problems, and in helping to convey the sense of urgency that you always knew under-pinned any meaningful commentary. They all had that. Robson had not, and I felt I was floundering beside him, and would have despaired had it not been for his compatriot, the much-maligned Graham Taylor, whom the tabloids had savaged with as much vitriol as they would have a paedophile. Tragically, in life now we are affected by such publicity, whether we like it or not, and although I had striven to keep an open mind about him, the image of the turnip superimposed around his face which *The Sun* used effectively after England's 2–1 defeat by Sweden in the 1992 European Championships quarter-final, with the heading 'Swedes 2, Turnips 1', was difficult to erase. Furthermore, I had been warned by Lawrie McMenemy, who had been Graham's assistant manager with England, that his former colleague did have a bit of an ego, and the fact that he allowed Channel 4's *Cutting Edge* programme to make a fly-on-the-wall documentary on him, during his last season, was proof of that. Indeed it was the sort of documentary which consolidated my belief that anyone permitting those sorts of portrayals must be verging on insanity.

Lawrie told me, in particular, about Graham's performance on the touchline against Holland in Rotterdam in October 1993, suffering a 2–0 defeat which effectively ended his FA career. They had set up cameras near the manager's bench, to film his reaction to events. As they were not allowed to approach too close, they were effectively outwith hearing distance of the bench. But Graham obliged. He took up a position favourable to the cameras. The famous sequences of him walking up and down the touchline berating all and sundry, swearing, fulminating, becoming a man in a state of rapidly accelerating disintegration, was, Lawrie alleges, because he needed to be within camera and sound range. Had he not strayed from his designated area, none of that would have been filmed. Armed with that sort of information about him I could hardly be blamed for believing that I was going to deal with a man who might have been covered by Euripides' assertion, 'Those whom the gods wish to destroy, they first make mad.'

He turned out, in fact, to be immensely sane, and one of the best I ever worked with. Intelligent analysis, subtle wit, totally coherent, called it candidly, didn't need to shout, talked with an authority that clearly demonstrated that he had not been terminally scarred by his traumatic reign as England team manager. After Bryan Robson, it was like having aromatherapy. We did several games together and he talked, in the evenings, almost good-humouredly about how the press had hounded him and his family, and how even after he retired he wondered if he could qualify for the witness protection scheme. He also summed it up in a way which was uncannily similar to an incident which had happened to Craig Brown once, who, like Graham, had been hounded by the press in his day. Apparently the former England manager had bumped into one of his severest critics one day, a man who had savaged him in a column, left him without a name almost, but on seeing Graham said, 'I didn't mean anything personal by it, Graham!'

So I was the beneficiary of a long line of co-commentators who made life that bit more interesting for me. I needed it for that World Cup in France, as a little Englishman, Gary Lovejoy, had come into Eurosport as the new chief executive, and buzzed around the place as if he had a mop in his hand, like Mary Poppins. But he was now running the entire show, and, I am sure, was determined not to let the Scotsman dominate football coverage. He was also plainly annoyed when Wilf Buckley, the journalist and novelist, now of the *Observer*, came across to write about my trials and tribulations as a Eurosport commentator, for no less than *Maxim* magazine. Having entered the pages of *Playboy* in the past, I felt it was my duty to balance things out and stand beside alternative acres of flesh. Anybody who knows Wilf's writing will know that he rarely writes poorly, and he did my endeavours in Paris more than justice. But a headline in the piece seemed to suggest that I was personally duelling with Sky in the battle for viewers, in a kind of David and Goliath battle. I could tell this grated on Simon Reed and the new chief executive. It was not the kind of personal publicity they seemed to appreciate. When the World Cup drew to an end I had an offer to return to Scotland to work for Scottish Television, which I accepted. I found that the simplicity of that acceptance was counter-balanced by discovering that after six years in Paris I had a developed a real affection for this crazy place called Eurosport.

I would even have fond memories of the frequent mishaps which you had to grapple with and which after the relatively cushy, and safe, environment of the BBC, re-educated you in self-reliance. I would recall the feeling of emerging from a booth after a two-hour session almost with a sense of triumph and then discovering that a researcher had got the facts wrong again and had gone into hiding. I would never again listen to a Frenchman telling me so much as the time of day, without checking with the NIST calcium clock, using its clouds of millions of calcium atoms for accuracy, to determine if he was telling the truth or not. I would remember La Coupole on Boulevard du Montparnasse for making eating out seem a theatrical event. And the countless bistros and the gallons of drinkable red wine, especially discovering the nectar called Gigondas. And cheap Metro travel, even though on one occasion, years later, our complacency about such travel late at night ended up with my wife being assaulted by a young mugger and in taking retribution I had to punch, and then, with admitted relish, kick him down the Metro stairs before the police, who had been tracking him all the while, grabbed me to prevent further mayhem.

And curiously, above all, I would recall the early morning of 2 May 1997, when all the broadcasters of the English language and some other Europeans gathered round the various television sets to hear the results coming in from the General Election, with the mood rising to a climax when the result came in, on hearing that Michael Portillo had lost Enfield Southgate. By that time we were standing on the tables, carousing, all of us, with the exception of that lovely man, the tennis commentator David Mercer, a lone Welsh Conservative sympathiser who was taking it badly. The euphoria exceeded anything we had ever experienced after any sports event. For me, who had tramped the streets for the Labour Party and had suffered defeat after defeat through the years, this was like being reborn. We celebrated for hours, like the night they invented champagne. Oh, how foolish that reaction in Paris all now seems.

22

HOMESTRETCH

It is a safe assumption to make that Sir David Murray, the owner of Glasgow Rangers, almost certainly did not relish that night in 1997 as much as I did. But he was not to do too badly out of Blairite Britain, considering his scarcely concealed respect for Mrs Thatcher. By 2006, the Murray Group had a reported turnover of £550 million – a five-fold increase on the previous five-year figure. So whilst the rest of us might have been cursing the day we had ever given support to the Labour leader, he must have been blessing Blair for turning out to be more the heir of the Iron Lady than Keir Hardie. I had been invited by the Scottish Labour Party, the year before he became Prime Minister, to do a warm-up speech for him at a fund-raising dinner in a large Glasgow hotel, in front of many Scottish dignitaries and business people. He thanked me profusely for that at the start of his speech, in the midst of which he used a phrase which struck me as odd, even at the time, and which I actually brought up with my wife on the way home that night. He referred to the business audience as 'you, the creators of wealth'. Now, without wishing to debate the pros and cons of that phrase with anybody, I did find it strange for a Labour leader to attribute such a special, basic quality to businessmen, coming, as I thought he and I did, from a tradition which honoured the 'hewers of wood, the drawers of water' who, we assumed, were the real wealth creators. It was odd, but nothing more than that, but in retrospect revealed much of what would lead to Labour's Peter Mandelson's utterance, 'We are intensely relaxed about people getting filthy rich,' a sentiment that would not have got him a free fish supper in old Shettleston.

Sir David you could describe as being filthy rich, although I doubt if he felt inspired by Blair's original victory. By the time I returned to take up a new contract with Scottish Television, again through the intercession of Sandy Ross, who eventually would move away from his sporting brief and take on a post selling the company's output overseas, Murray was in the process of spurring on yet another Rangers resurgence, through the squat form of the little Dutchman, Dick Advocaat. That Celtic had prevented Rangers from achieving ten title wins in a row must have wounded the billionaire industrialist. Although he was not originally from a football, or Rangers, tradition, there is little doubt that having adopted this identity, like any apostate, he became even more of a traditionalist than the traditionalists themselves, and one afternoon in his office in the Gyle in the western outskirts of Edinburgh he made it clear to me that Rangers would not be hounded into buying players simply to appease those offended by an obvious sectarian policy. To say he was adamant would be an understatement. He used the kind of forceful language that would have gone down well on the Shankill in Belfast. However, his later conversion, which provoked a taunting chant I heard at Tynecastle one day, directed to the Rangers support from the Gorgie faithful, 'You've got more Tims than Celtic' to the appropriately revolutionary tune of Guantanamera, was not of a Damascene nature. He was merely responding, as any successful businessman would have, to rapidly evolving social conditions, and realising that if signing one-legged albino Hottentots meant continuing success then so be it, considering at one stage in their very recent history a one-legged albino Hottentot would have had a better chance of signing for the club than Pelé or Maradona. It was not any moral fervour which swept away the absurdity of that. It was simply the growing awareness that to keep up with the best, you couldn't keep putting up no-trespassing notices.

When you were with him you were aware of the urgency with which he went about his business. Perhaps his verbal animation, and the sharp and abrupt way he could control conversations, stemmed from the need to demonstrate that his abilities were undiminished, despite the dreadful handicap of having lost both legs in a car crash. He was powerfully persuasive. The first time I talked to him was not in a football stadium, but at the side of a basketball court in Livingston. Graeme Souness had asked me to take part in a charity shoot-out during a break in one of Livingston MIM's matches (for the record, Souness potted four out of six baskets to my three). After that I was introduced to this man, sitting at the court-side, who took over the command of the conversation between us, enthusing about some of the American stars he had imported to boost the standing of his side. At that time I knew nothing of his horrendous accident, nor of any accumulating interest in football, but you could easily have been swept away on the back of his enthusiasm and been convinced that basketball had a golden future here. At that time I was looking at a refreshingly apolitical figure, simply somebody who wanted an association with sport, as a by-product of his entrepreneurial zeal. But then he went into the murky world of Old Firm football and a different man emerged. Perhaps the kind of man he really wanted to be, with access to a new kind of populist power and the publicity that accrued from that.

Even so, I was not prepared for his reaction to me, when we first met up after my return to the domestic scene as commentator for Scottish Television. In his first acerbic remarks, I could deduce, from the outset, that he regarded the company I now worked for as a cesspool of anti-Rangers plotters. Yes, there were a few people around me in the Cowcaddens studios who would have felt no pain had Rangers gone into demise, including the little man who effectively ran the sports output, Dennis Mooney, who had been recruited by Gus Macdonald, now of the ermine gown – the Govan socialist who had run Scottish Television with Thatcherite conviction. Dennis was no Thatcherite, but a man of the left, like myself, so we got on well together. But, at the conclusion of a fairly straightforward production meeting of the sports department, to prepare for a Rangers Champions League game, Mooney could contain himself no longer and, stepping out of his executive position, suddenly became a punter, with the explosive utterance, 'And I hope Rangers are fucking gubbed!' Mooney's idea of a sophisticated ending to the meeting was at least original. At best, it was bracingly tactless. I had never heard the likes at that level before. But, in the final analysis, so what?

They could have brought out Murray's effigy, stuck pins in it, muttered incantations over it, and covered it with the blood of a beheaded chicken as an added extra, for all that it mattered in the great scheme of things. Only the team playing Rangers could alter events, not Mooney and his sympathisers. But even though it might have added a certain credence to what the Rangers chairman thought about Scottish Television, what Murray was doing with me, at the tail end of the century and on the verge of the new millennium, was opening up a window to the past, not the future; taking me back to the days of the early 1970s when, for example, a Celtic director and experienced lawyer, James Farrell, invited me into the Celtic boardroom after a game once and, despite knowing of my strenuous efforts to improve relationships with his club, attempted to lecture me on the sensitive use of names. 'We have noted,' he said rather pompously, 'that you refer to the Rangers players more by their Christian names than the Celtic players.' That a lawyer who at that time was a member of the Race Relations Commission could have had a Christian name trip-counter by his armchair almost beggared belief. When I recounted that to Stein he just burst out laughing, as he had no great love for the man. Murray was, consequently, maintaining that robust Old Firm tradition that does not exclude even the Gulf Stream Drift from the possibilities of bias.

In a saner environment it would mean nothing at all. But, lest we think this was all so parochial, where is that saner world in sport? Pay heed to the words of Scott Willborough, spokesman for the USA's national media watchdog group Fairness and Accuracy in Reporting, in his 2004 report: 'In our extensive study of the nation's sports sections and broadcasts we documented countless examples of shamelessly one-sided reporting, obvious speculation, and bald editorialising, masquerading as journalism.' So, it is a truth universally recognised that a single man in possession of a laptop or a mic, anywhere near a sports arena, is potentially a saboteur – with Glasgow, inarguably, as the global epicentre of mistrust. All this would be of great sociological significance in its sectarian context, did it not sound at times like infants squabbling over playdough. Into this quagmire stepped the man they called the Little General, to take over from Walter Smith as manager.

Dick Advocaat's first interview with me was dominated by his head. It became a distraction for me. I had known a good friend of his in Eurosport, a former manager of PSV, Hans Kraay, who had told me that Advocaat had once had a hair transplant. I didn't know at the time whether he was pulling my leg or not, but if somebody tells you that and you are close to the man for the first time, you are not going to be checking if his eyes are emerald green or blue, are you? It is not that I did not appreciate his feeling of vulnerability in losing his top cover, as I shared his problem but favoured the thatching solution, simulating the roof-covering style of a Cotswold cottage. So, there we were inside the stadium just where it opens out into the players' tunnel. (If you wish a more accurate positioning, go into YouTube and search for Chic Young, and there you will find a famous blasphemous interview with Walter Smith. Advocaat and I were on that very spot.) As he is a man who tends to look you straight in the eye when he speaks to you, it was not easy to ask questions and try to examine, at the same time, whether the transplant had taken root effectively. I should have been more focused on this historic moment of talking to Rangers' first foreign manager. But what on earth was this man going to tell me at this juncture, anyway? Celtic had taken the title from them. Rangers wanted it back, and for as many years after that as they could. End of story. In his brisk and not unpleasant, but sort of neutral manner, he conveyed nothing that I could not have put in his mouth in the first place. Had I asked him whether he had bother with his hair in the wind, I might have received a more positive response, if, perhaps, less pleasant. He marched in, he marched out, like he meant business and his hair, immaculately, quivered not once.

It was a new era for all of us, not just Rangers. In the good old days before PR was invented you could reach out and touch a manager. Now, protected by PR people, they were largely untouchable. John Greig, in that role at Rangers, commanded the media brusquely like a sergeant-major. Nobody messed with him. Paul Cooney, of Radio Clyde, had a spell at Celtic in that capacity, but it clearly was too confining a job for somebody like that, and he didn't last long. Billy McNeill ought to have been introduced into that area in some capacity, but strangely, nay scandalously, never was. Then less prominent individuals, but certainly competent, came into the business, and the net result was that the relaxed informal manner of the past had disappeared. Press conferences were formal and with few exceptions, unremarkable.

One of the most stimulating was given some years before by Graeme Souness, when, contractually, he was forced to say something to the press, who at that stage he regarded as carriers of the ebola virus. After a game at Ibrox he opened the door, stepped into the room, said 'Good afternoon', stepped out again and slammed the door behind him. He had fulfilled his obligation, and, at the same time, had offered fuel to those who could write or broadcast even more expansively about his arrogance. Then there was Kenny Dalglish. One of the most famous Scottish players of all time had become Celtic's Director of Football, in 1999, with John Barnes as Head Coach, just after I had returned to the scene. I had never witnessed Kenny in anything other than a triumphant environment before. There had been setbacks in his career, of course, and it is sometimes forgotten that he was ignored for a Scotland cap for a long period when he was at Liverpool. I recall a message being passed on to me when I went to the opening of his pub in Shettleston Road in the late 1970s, by his father-in-law, Pat Harkins, to thank me for reminding the Scottish public so often of Kenny's qualities. I had traced his career from the moment in that crowded airport at Malpensa in 1970, with the rain lashing down outside and the multitudes crowded around in mourning for Celtic's defeat by Feyenoord in the European Cup Final, as we waited for delayed flights, when Stein took the trouble to point this young unknown lad out to me with the four simple words, 'He'll be some player.' He was. Since then, we had coincidentally gone to Minorca on holiday at the same time, and he made friends with my two sons, who played around with him in the pool like he was their uncle. He also developed a lasting friendship with my wife, by playfully pushing her into the pool, during one of those anarchic moments on holiday, ruining her new perm which she had just had done, but more importantly, not realising that she could not swim a stroke. Of such are strong bonds made, especially when I convinced her, as we pulled her splutteringly out, that not too many women had the privilege of being pushed into a pool by King Kenny. He gracefully apologised, and I promised not to reveal, until now, that despite his great athletic prowess in all kinds of sports, he swam rather like a cast-iron railing, even at the shallow end. But these days of jollity seemed like a fantasy world when I witnessed his slow and painful downfall at Celtic Park in this new position.

At his press conferences, Kenny, who could be dour, had developed a screen for himself of sarcasm and ambiguous replies, as the world began to collapse about his ears. You didn't need to be taking sides, for or against him, to find this almost unbearable to watch, with the thought pulsing through it all, why in the name of God did he take this task on in the first place? He failed. The next time I met him after that was when he came to be a studio guest at the Celtic–Barcelona Champions League game of September 2004. He looked and sounded refreshed, with the nightmare of that last period with Celtic apparently out of his system. But during the first half I happened to mention in commentary that I felt Ronaldinho, with his flicks and feints, more or less all of which happened in midfield, was having little influence on the game, and was more a circus act than an influential footballer. At half-time Kenny waded into that comment and praised Ronaldinho to the highest. Halfway through the second half Barcelona subbed the Brazilian and brought on Henrik Larsson, who promptly scored the third and decisive goal in their 3–1 victory, which would never have gone that way had that substitution not taken place. I let the facts speak for themselves. We've never discussed Ronaldinho since.

If all this imprisonment of managers, put out on day release to the media, seemed at odds with everything I had grown up with in broadcasting, which allowed flexible and personal contacts, so were the conditions at Scottish Television. Two months after they had hired me, they had neither produced a contract for me to sign, nor had they paid me. As Samuel Goldwyn once said, 'A verbal contract is not worth the paper it's written on,' but I relied on the good word of Sandy Ross that all would be settled. I still have not discovered (largely because I did not pursue the matter all that resolutely) what was at the root of that. Incompetence? Given what I had heard about STV's internal dynamic, or lack of it, that could have been it. Or, they were arguing amongst themselves about what terms to offer, or that someone simply was opposed to them signing me up. Two months without a cheque didn't exactly put us on the breadline, but from the very outset it meant that whatever faith I had in Sandy Ross was tempered by the caution of not wishing to put too much faith in the company as a whole. I was certainly becoming aware that all was not right with them. They were continuing to shed labour. Each time you bumped into somebody in the corridor, you wondered if you would ever bump into them again. They had become joined at the hip with the *Herald* and the *Evening Times*, thus conveying the outward look of a progressive multi-media company, which was now referred to as SMG. Frankly, after I had my feet inside the door and got my first payment I became less interested in the finances of SMG than of other institutions, like Glasgow Rangers FC.

When, for instance, a tall lanky player who looked more like a college kid from a basketball team came into the Ibrox press room in November 2000 and it was announced that he was transferring to Rangers for £12 million from Chelsea, it was not the sum of money which really set the jaws dropping – after all we simply assumed that Rangers could afford to fork out that sum of money then and still have enough left to take their entire staff to Vegas for a weekend. It was the sum of money in relation to the man they had bought, Tore André Flo, a not entirely successful Chelsea player, that caused astonishment. Dick Advocaat, though, sat with his jaw, and his hair, set firm that day and talked about how this would fit into the Ibrox jigsaw perfectly. For Advocaat, unfortunately, it was like getting a jigsaw of Buckingham Palace but with a piece definitely belonging to the Statue of Liberty. It was one of the most expensive misfits in Rangers history. But the point that day was to witness the utter strength of conviction of the Dutchman. You could feel the power of his personality triumphing over anybody's doubts. We simply did not know just how much sway he held over Murray. But one episode was to say a lot.

When we travelled to Manchester to cover Rangers' Champions League game against United when Alex McLeish was manager, we stayed in a hotel which was also housing some of the club's sponsors. When Andy Walker, my excellent co-commentator, and I were having drinks, measured in a miserly fashion, I may say, considering the commentating task we faced the following day, one of the sponsors joined us for a chat. While he was there he told us of a day of turmoil he had experienced at Ibrox. He was a civil engineer, working for a company making exploratory drillings for a massive project at the Copland Road end of the stadium. The plans were for an extension of the seating capacity, and for a new hotel to adjoin the stadium there. The existence of the drilling itself indicated the advanced nature of the plans. The engineer said that the drilling was causing considerable noise, so that when John Greig advanced across the pitch with the words, 'Would you stop the drilling, please!', he was not at that stage surprised. When he asked him when it could recommence Greig added, chillingly for the man, 'It's to stop for good. We're not carrying on with the project.' He followed Greig across the pitch but kept getting the same blunt request to stop, so when he persisted in demanding a reason for ending a project which had already cost significant sums of money, Greig suddenly turned on him and spelled it out. 'Don't tell the press anything about this, but we've just had a board meeting and wee Dick warned the board that he would resign as manager if we didn't stop this project, right now, this day. He wants the money spent on a new training ground and academy.' So stop it did. Murray could be dictated to, obviously.

The Dutchman at that time was speaking from a position of strength, and he had muscled in on it. But in retrospect when it became apparent that Rangers' debt was mounting and the lavish scale of the training ground had exacerbated the situation, you wonder, on top of the Tore André Flo cost, if Dick Advocaat had been as useful to Rangers as a flamenco dancer in a condemned building. Balance his record, between 1998 and 2000, of two league titles, two Scottish Cups and one League Cup trophy, which you could argue any Rangers manager would have won anyway at that time, given Murray's purse, and with Celtic hosting the Dalglish–Barnes farrago, and it might seem less of an achievement. He was certainly an innovator but with no real competition. He plundered Rangers, in fact, then left unscathed, like the Vikings used to do.

And there could only have been one man who allowed it. I bumped into him at a dinner in the Hilton Hotel in Glasgow, two years later, on the eve of Rangers' Scottish Cup win against Celtic in 2002. Murray saw me walking past his table and hailed me for another salvo of waspish comments about television, and then in the abrupt chat which followed, as he sought to inform me of Rangers' financial worthiness, given the talk about their huge debt, added, 'It's that damned training ground that's round our necks at the moment. We'll sort it out.' The man who had seemed so impregnable through the years was hurting. And hurting because of the tradition of largesse which he had himself established with his players and managers, which on the one hand might have made him look like a soft touch, but on the other brought, for so long, uncritical acceptance by the Rangers multitudes.

But he and others were about to disappear from my ken again, in the rapidly changing contractual television world. Just when I felt I was in it for the long haul, in that summer of 2002 we went to Spain on holiday. It was when we were in Caceres in northern Spain, just before the French border, that I took a call on my mobile from Sandy Ross. We happened to be in the Salvador Dali museum at the time and the surrealist surround-ings could not have been more appropriate. He was to tell me that Scottish Television had been outbid for coverage of foot-ball and that the BBC had won the exclusive contractual rights. Even more bizarrely, we were buying a print of Dali's famous melting watch at the time, and I did feel that perhaps time was indeed running out on me and that the end was nigh. What I had not bargained for, nor had the Scottish Premier League, was how successful the BBC coverage would be, as they drummed out the message that Scottish football could now be seen, every week, live and free.

It proved an irresistible combination to the armchair viewer. But as I listened to my good friend and former colleague Chic Young, whom I had once employed to help me with the produc-tion of *Sportscene* at the BBC, it could hardly escape notice that behind him, on too many occasions, there were tiers of empty seats. The BBC were winning, but was Scottish football? The BBC, however excellent their coverage, were being hoist by their own petard. With the exception of the Old Firm, stadiums were being emptied. It could not last, and I wondered if there would be an alternative, and that perhaps *Scotsport* could return. It did. But some of us suspected it was also on its last legs.

23

SKINT

Towards the end of 2007, a message was posted on STV's website, from Henry Eagles, who is described in it as Head of Sport. It referred to a gathering of many of the people who had been associated with *Scotsport* in its fifty years of existence, which inspired the boast that it was 'the longest running sports magazine programme in the world'. It said, 'Turning 50 is a fantastic achievement for us and we're thrilled that so many of our presenters could join us to help celebrate. Fifty years on, *Scotsport* pulls in around a quarter of a million viewers each week, always winning its slot, which is testament to the brilliant sports team we have here at STV. We've always worked hard at keeping the programme fresh but the most important thing is that Scots are a nation of football lovers and as long as they love it, we'll continue to make the show.'

That could arguably go down as an even more delusional statement than that issued by Comical Ali, Mohammed Saeed al-Sahhaf, who even as American tanks were parading around the streets of Baghdad, like part of Fifth Avenue's Easter Parade, was pronouncing, 'There is no presence of American infidels in the city of Baghdad. There is no presence of the American columns in the city of Baghdad at all. We besieged them and we killed most of them. Today the tide has turned. We are destroying them.' For only months after transmitting an hour-long Hogmanay 2007 programme of that year, specially dedicated to *Scotsport's* fifty-year longevity, in praise of its resilience, its incalculable but indisputable effect on the public's taste for football, its creation of colourful characters, who themselves spawned controversy and debate, its popular touch, the stupendous Montford jackets, the weekly programme was killed off. The Scots were still in love with football (when would they never be?), but STV had been hiring divorce lawyers, even as that phrase 'Scots are a nation of football lovers and as long as they love it, we'll continue to make the show' was being penned. It did not surprise veterans like myself, who do not need to be qualified pathologists to sniff out death by a thousand cuts. It was all presaged by an eeriness you felt when you went into the Cowcaddens building, which housed an operation once described by its original owner as 'a licence to print money'. In truth, when I was a rigorous competitor from the other side of the city, with the BBC, I would nevertheless have some meetings with Arthur Montford in there, and you could never fail to sense the bustling industry and creativity of the place, bulging with ideas and initiatives. But by the time I was halfway through my last phase with this company, by about 2004, when you went into STV you were feeling something akin to how the boarding party must have felt when they climbed aboard the *Marie Celeste*. It was as if some mysterious force had sucked the vitality from the place. Everybody was concerned about their future. Nobody was immune from concern about where they were heading other than, inevitably, out the door. There seemed to be a plethora of empty corridors around the place.

This was simply evidence of a core value of the channel disappearing. Paradoxically, they were becoming anorexic to survive. For although STV had been a cash cow for its pioneers like Lord Thomson, central to its commercial dynamic was the importance of public service broadcasting, of providing the public with programmes that were valued for their own sake and not necessarily for commercial gain. That had been part of its original remit. Their own recklessness, and the downturn in advertising revenue, meant that the public service ethic would have to be ditched, as Labour did with their Clause 4. And in witnessing this chilling spectacle, it hardened my view that if society wished to maintain quality broadcasting, which broadly served the public needs, then, despite its occasional follies and the vociferous squeals of its commercial enemies, we should all fight to the last man standing to protect the integrity of the BBC.

It is not as if there were no facets of Scottish football to inspire anyone working on *Scotsport* during the first decade of the new millennium. For starters, a new exciting figure had entered Scottish football – Martin O'Neill was now Celtic manager. At last Dick Advocaat had a real adversary, not a synthetic one, and in not being able to meet the new challenge from Parkhead would give way eventually to Alex McLeish as manager. O'Neill and McLeish were polarised as personalities. The Irishman seemed profound, cerebral, and although some of his critics would claim that he indulged in too much psycho-babble, I found him refreshing. There might have been some cliché in his statements, but they seemed camouflaged by the embroidering of long sinuous sentences which he delivered like a guru to the uninitiated. When he arrived with due fanfare, the notion was spread that he had been a lifelong Celtic supporter and had travelled regularly with family to see Celtic through the years. In fact, the first time he stepped inside Celtic Park was the day he arrived to sign his contract as the new manager.

This lifelong Sunderland supporter energised the club, though. As he bounced up and down on the touchline like a Mexican bean, you felt that, although he had deep feelings for the English club, the Celtic culture of his home area in Derry had lent him the right identity and the necessary motivation. I had first met him in Madrid, when I had gone there to cover a European game between Leicester City and Atletico Madrid. His club were beaten that night, but two aspects would not be forgotten. He was easy to interview, and fluently spelled out the reasons for the defeat, moaning a little, it has to be said. Then there was the nature of his team. Clearly he liked big men at the back, and big men up front, as he had that night for Leicester in the shape of the behemoth-like Matt Elliott. Hence, Bobo Balde and Chris Sutton joining Celtic later, not without success. But there was one category where he was perfectly orthodox as a manager – his recurring suspicion of elements of the media.

There are plenty of people around to guide new Old Firm managers through the credentials of partiality for one club or the other. When Andy Walker and I commentated on Celtic's Champions League game against AC Milan in 2004, O'Neill made a substitution late on in the game, after which the Italian side scored a couple of goals. Walker criticised the substitution. When O'Neill arrived at the press conference after the game, he launched an attack on the points made in commentary. He could not possibly have heard what had been said, but there are enough wriggly-crawlies in the media for one of them to have sneaked this information to him as he made his way up to the press room. So he was not only decidedly touchy about media criticism, he was prepared to use those who like to be seen to be loyal to his club, for snooping. What separated him from others, though, was his reaction to defeat. In Milan on that occasion, and in Turin in 2001, when Celtic, admittedly, were cheated out of the game against Juventus by a dodgy referee, he sat in the room with us, looking and sounding utterly crushed. I had never seen such mortification in a manager before.

Plenty of anger, yes, but nothing like this morose demeanour. You felt like phoning the Samaritans on his behalf, to come and get him out of there.

Alex McLeish was the opposite. It is not that he giggled and joked his way through a defeat, but he did take some cruel ones on the chin without looking as if life was not worth living. He also restrained himself successfully, after some of the critical abuse he took, and never gave any indication of wishing to be vindictive in return. I always felt that was a flaw in his make-up. If he had one-tenth of the bile of his great mentor Sir Alex, it would have served him better with the media. Scaring the media out of their wits does not win football matches, but it sure makes them think twice about what they will write or say next, and very often the press are the conductors of public opinion, which can either make or break someone in a crisis.

There was only one occasion I recall when McLeish decided to take it out on the press, by simply not appearing in front of them. It was at Falkirk in a match to be played before Rangers set off to play an important game in Europe against Porto. It was crisis time and the press were simply waiting to write the obsequies for a manager who looked as if he was on his last legs, with David Murray having refused to lend him a ringing vote of confidence at that time. He had to come to our camera, by virtue of the Premier League contract. I thought he might give me some rough treatment for some of the lacerating criticism I had heaped on his team. Instead, he looked at me and said calmly, 'Big yin, don't ask me too many questions. I'm under pressure.' Braced for a confrontation, his calm words took the wind out of my sails and I referred to the game I had just watched, not his precarious future. Had that been a Stein, or a Ferguson, or a Jim McLean, I would have been cursed off the pitch. And even after describing his Rangers team as probably the worst I had seen in the past twenty years, he greeted me some weeks later as though we were blood brothers. He wasn't nasty enough to us.

So the battles between these two opposites, culminating in two remarkable last game championship climaxes in 2003 and 2005, we tried to reflect on *Scotsport*, but now in unequal competition with the newcomer on the scene, Setanta Television, who were about to rule the roost and take over all live television coverage. But only for a short period as, unknown to them, the people within Setanta were suffering the same terminal disease as other institutions, of being the serfs of venture capitalists who, although clearly identified at the outset by the Old Firm as being about as transparent and as reliable as a Tommy Cooper attempt at a magic trick, beguiled the Scottish Premier League into thinking they had found Eldorado. It was they who would now bring the curtain up and down on these dramas. STV were left the crumbs.

STV therefore decided on a programme structure which the Brothers Grimm might have devised. They did so with the kind of unabounded, undisguised enthusiasm of those who feel they have struck a format which would sweep the world. This took the form of a highlights programme late on a Monday night, well past the bedtime of bairns, although the new format of *Scotsport* would really have been appreciated more by those who thrill to *Jackanory*. The first programme was stunning, but perhaps for all the wrong reasons. It ended with what you might call a Liberace tone, with a journalist playing Elton John on the piano, demonstrating only that some journalists can tickle the ivories, some cannot. Thankfully, they desisted from the candelabra.

I received a call from Ray Hepburn, a journalist friend whose colourful expressions of incredulity at what he had watched sent shivers up the spine, even though I had anticipated much of what was to come. So, how had it all come about that I found myself, after that first week, sneaking round from doorway to doorway, trying to appear elusive, and avoid folk, like Harry Lime in *The Third Man*? A show had been devised that made a mockery of all that *Scotsport* had represented in the past, as a solid orthodox base for those who wanted to see only football, and then football, and even more football. On the large studio floor they had separated the set into divisions. To one side there was the so-called 'executive' area, which was purportedly for brief interviewing of guests, or residents, with a supposed view on controversial issues. On the opposite side of the studio, they had fabricated what was meant to be a small terracing for fans to stand, to reflect punterdom, I suppose. The fact that terracings no longer existed in mainstream Scottish football, and that if you stood at certain grounds you could be evicted or arrested, had apparently not occurred to them. In the main area was a mock football pitch, indicated by Toytown goalposts, to which the two presenters would walk, opening the programme, as if approaching a penalty-shoot out, or as if they were about to perform the Dashing White Sergeant.

Into this synthetic concoction they had introduced a new co-presenter, Sarah O'Flaherty, a charming buxom Irish lass, with a breeziness which contrasted with her knowledge of football, which seemed to me to be less than that of a llama chewing the cud on a Peruvian slope. She simpered alongside Jim Delahunt, the main presenter, whose marvellous acceptance of this imposition was a triumph of restraint. They had also hired an Orcadian lad with an accent which, through no fault of his, unfortunately grated on people, and who was there to be the joker in the pack, with comical vignettes of little purpose, other than to underline the fact that this programme was trivialising the very sport which had helped *Scotsport* gain its status in the first place. It simply reeked of insincerity. How come?

The two men responsible for this froth were well schooled

in broadcasting. Henry Eagles is an amiable, experienced man with many successful programmes to his credit. Bobby Haines, STV's effective Head of Programmes, came from Radio Clyde where his forte was in light entertainment. There was no gain-saying their broadcasting abilities and their intellect. Both were personable, approachable and articulate. But I am reminded of what the Speaker of the USA House of Representatives, Sam Rayburn, once said, when someone tried to impress him with the sheer intellectual brilliance of the President Kennedy cabinet: 'I'd feel a whole lot better about them, if just one of them had run for sheriff once.' Neither of these two men had ever run for sheriff, in the sense that they had never suffered the bruises of surviving in the world of football; never had to knock on an irate manager's door; never heard abuse being thrown from a stand towards you (although they were soon to learn a thing or two about abuse); never gloried in the transcendental experience of the Archie Gemmill goal in Mendoza; never argued into the boozy nights with fellow journalists seeking words to outdo one another on the subject of the game we loved; never stood shivering on the slopes of a terracing, week after week, as a boy; never got bloodied knees on red blaes playing 30-a-side tussles on a winter's day; never battled trying to find words to describe a damned awful game on a miserable wet day at Firhill. Simply put, they just didn't get it. They were interlopers. Talented though they may have been in their own right, they were as appropriate to the vital task of maintaining a credible profile for *Scotsport* as Rudolf Nureyev would have been coaching the All Blacks. Yet, in a way that I still feel very uneasy about, they were kindly disposed to me and treated my venerability with respect and were instrumental in producing the BAFTA Scotland Award for services to broadcasting for myself, Bill McLaren and Arthur Montford.

It was difficult to reconcile my feelings of despair at their policy with my gratitude for the personal kindnesses they showed me. But, professionally, I simply couldn't accept what they had done to football coverage, for all that. I honestly thought Arthur Montford, on the telephone to me once, during that period, was weeping at the other end of the line when he bemoaned what had happened to the show he had created. It is not that I hid my opinions from management. I had made it clear after only a month of the new format that it would alienate us from a football audience. My views were dismissed, ever so politely, as always, by Eagles, on the ground that television had to evolve, and that by late on a Monday evening, the Scottish football public would be fed up with seeing football highlights. There is a time when you have to leave people to stew in their own juice, and then was that time.

What the Scottish public, in fact, did, was to respond to this farrago by heaping on the programme a torrent of the most heated abuse I had ever experienced in over four decades of sports broadcasting. Scottish Premier League representatives sent messages of distress to STV regarding the format in which the game was being reflected. Viewers in their thousands mounted an internet campaign to show their contempt. The management certainly became aware of that and tried to justify their format by pointing to the size of audiences they were pulling in. They certainly were, for that time of night, but to watch the much too meagre diet of football on offer as there was no other terrestrial station with the rights to show them. That is why they watched – not to find out who had the longest throw-in in Scottish football. This seemed to be escaping their notice.

And to further consolidate their position, an evening was held under the auspices of the Royal Television Society in which the future of televised football was to be discussed with most of the participants present. Why was one of the producers and a writer from the BBC Comedy Unit, which produced the satirical programme *Only An Excuse*, present as well? Apart from trying to chum up to a company which lampooned the programme and perhaps lessen their blows, it was to lend credence to their notion that football on television had to be seen more as a form of light entertainment, and that the orthodox programmes were too leaden and predictable. That evening, for all the stout defence of their ideas, came to nothing. Two years after they had set out to change the ethos of viewing football on the box, they scrapped the format, and cruelly sacked the blonde and the boy with the accent, neither of whom should have been there in the first place, but pointedly, the man who had dreamed it up, Henry Eagles, kept his job. That's the ebb and flow of television for you, when presenters are the flotsam and jetsam of the business and, at the same time, a producer can be prince of the tides.

The harm had been done, though. There was a legacy of ridicule left to cope with, which around football grounds we had to face up to, and from which management were wholly insulated. Although they resorted to the more orthodox approach of the original, *Scotsport* never recovered from two years of mockery. In the next couple of years, before its demise, many people worked hard to restore its battered reputation, especially when it came to coverage of the Champions League, which was an existing ITV contract. Young, enthusiastic people around me, all hoping to have long careers in broadcasting, slaved away on short-term contracts, in the hope of both establishing themselves and securing more respect for the programme. I looked on, as though I was watching people on a lifeboat frantically trying to bail out water rising inexorably upwards. I felt genuinely sorry for them, because throughout the last year they were becoming increasingly aware that the future looked bleak. For SMG, the parent company, was skint.

Now that is an expression I grew up with in Shettleston, but it was not always one of disdain. If you were skint it meant, in most instances, that life had dealt you a bad hand, and that circumstances beyond your control had emptied your pockets. Within the hardship that certainly existed then, being skint was like an appeal to the extended family to bail you out in some way. Rarely did it seem dishonourable. Yes, there were those who would spend the 'broo' money on booze, but generally speaking, being skint did not make you leprous. SMG's plight was different. They had become skint in the worst sense of the word. For although there was editorial folly associated with *Scotsport* in its latter days, it was not that which killed the programme off; it was corporate greed.

Although it was well above all of our heads, we were aware, in general, of the follies which had gone on. SMG, the parent company, bought Virgin Radio in 2000 for £225 million and had to sell it seven years later for £53.2 million. Their shares peaked at 350p in 2000 and, just before the programme's demise in 2008, were about 5p, and in that whole fraught process they accumulated huge bank debt. Sometimes I would walk along an STV corridor and notice the chief executive at the time, Andrew Flanagan, sitting in his office, toying with the keys of his computer like a kid summoning up an internet game from a website, and found myself wondering how many millions of pounds he was playing with at the end of his fingertips. As the company sank, he departed, with compensation of £831,024 to stave off penury, even though the new chairman of SMG, Richard Findlay, fired grapeshot after him, with the statement, 'The group in the past has had a strategy which was fatally flawed and badly executed.'

So *Scotsport* went down the tubes a few months before the 'Credit Crunch' did for Lehman Brothers. A fifty-year venerability couldn't save it. Essentially it was the same lunacy of free-market over-indulgence and lack of transparency which brought it about, as it was also to do to Setanta, whose venture capitalists overpaid for Scottish football and led good professionals into unemployment. Football had become unaffordable. Or put another way, there did not seem to be an inventive, creative mind within Scottish Television, with sufficient guts, to speak up in its support and at least go down with colours flying. There was simply meek acceptance. *Scotsport* would, debatably, still have been around had a different economic environment prevailed; the kind of environment which encouraged us to believe a new order would prevail after the Blair ascendancy of 1997 but which, ultimately, offered nothing of the kind. Some might even have been glad to see *Scotsport* off the air, especially after the travesty they tried to peddle in its name. In our own parochial world, football broadcasting was to carry the can, in the cost-cutting sense, because of being skint. A half-century of regular sports broadcasting ended with not even a whisper of regret from those who had bragged about its existence, but who in the same breath were engineering its demise.

They had shown the insensitively reckless side of being skint. And as we followed Rangers, in particular, down that last season towards their UEFA Cup Final in Manchester, we witnessed the other aspect of institutions battling the financial elements. For the Old Firm were skint as well, in the sense that they could no longer compete with others in the European money markets. When Walter Smith told me quietly in a tiny corner of the Olympique Lyonnais stadium in October 2007, after their amazing 3–0 victory in the Champions League, that his side were, 'punching above their weight', he put it better than any accountant predicting what the Old Firm's future would be. One of the two might be better off than the other, at any given time, but both of them were now relative paupers compared to the billionaires' playthings in the south. Having grown up in the surrounds of their recurring, alternating triumphalism, and boasts of the world markets within their grasps, we were now witnessing the biggest humbling process in the history of the Scottish game.

Some truths are self-evident. One such is that the skint Old Firm will never be the same again. An impenetrable border guarding the riches of the south, the intransigence of football's governing bodies, and the increasingly remote possibility of such as the Sultan of Brunei investing in a market only made dynamic by the culture of mutual hostility amongst their fans, is how we, inevitably, had to appraise the environment of the Old Firm, as *Scotsport* stuttered to its final ending.

24

THE MOTHER OF ALL GAMES

There was only one game left. We all knew it. At least this last live game was going to be special. It was a European Cup Final after all. Manchester in May. We travelled down, on the day before the game, on motorways black with Rangers traffic. Rangers against Zenit St Petersburg was a final hardly anybody had expected. But, eventually, even on a day of cloudless skies and blistering sunshine we nevertheless could ultimately have applied to the outcome that old Mancunian mantra, 'It never rains but it pours.'

As a group of broadcasters we ought to have been brimming over with the confidence of a pub's tug-o-war team about to take on a selection from a postnatal class. One tug and we would be congratulating ourselves on our sense of unity and purpose. In fact, it was beginning to feel, on the eve of the game, that we were part of Captain Bligh's mutinous crew about to set sail down the Manchester Ship Canal. After all, virtually everybody in the *Scotsport* team knew they were about to be sacked. That was just the start of the feeling of dysfunction.

Other factors were heaped on top of that. Our presenter and a studio football analyst were involved in a bitter personal dispute. Most of our group around the dinner table in an Italian restaurant on the eve of the game, astonishingly, wanted this Scottish team beaten by the Russians. A texted message to the editor from a producer back at home left nobody in any doubt that she hoped the Zenit manager Dick Advocaat would triumph. Most of the football chat was about what effect the result would have on the league title race with Celtic, not the European final itself, thus proving that there is no escape from parochial, tribal thinking. And we had with us an executive producer, Henry Eagles, who, while keeping mum about the inevitable and imminent axings which would make the word 'prospects' seem like a sick joke to the young people in the *Scotsport* team who were shortly to hit the street looking for employment, did voice an executive reminder at the coffee stage that our expedition to Manchester was being funded by the dumbed-down quiz competitions run by the station.

Unprecedented thousands had phoned in to win tickets for the final, and ready cash had poured into STV from the cost of the calls which are increasingly used as a means of easing the savage downturn in advertising. As everybody knew that this travel fund was not going to maintain their employment much longer, Eagles' loyal servant-of-the-company reminder was greeted with something like the gratitude of those Parisian poor who had to listen to the classic blandishment of Marie Antoinette, 'Let them eat cake.' A spontaneous burst of 'For He's a Jolly Good Fellow' was as unlikely to erupt as being served borscht in an Italian restaurant. All in all, STV misfits had come to town.

In a personal sense I was worried about the dispute between Andy Walker, our studio presenter, and John Colquhoun, our studio analyst, both of them ex-Celtic players. They were angry men. It had started two nights before on *Scotsport*. In that programme they had been reflecting on a highly controversial Rangers–Dundee United game, after which Craig Levein, the

United manager, complained bitterly that the referee had denied them a legitimate victory, and repeated the age-old belief that there was something of a conspiracy in Scottish football to favour the Old Firm, especially Rangers. This was discussed in the programme, where Walker pursued the matter very frankly with Colquhoun, the former Celtic and Hearts player, who, as Craig Levein's agent, made it clear that something was rotten at the heart of Scottish football.

Colquhoun had turned out to be an excellently pugnacious analyst on television, but in this case took umbrage to persistent questioning when being asked if he believed such a conspiracy to aid Rangers in Scottish football existed. In the programme, he left that recurring theory largely dangling in the air. But after it had ended, he verbally attacked Walker and accused him of trying to put words into his mouth (worried perhaps that he had made public allegations which could not be proved) and that Walker was, in any case, an integral part of such a conspiracy. Anybody who knows Walker would simply agree that such a charge against him would be as absurd as accusing Bambi of matricide. He happens to be as untainted by any kind of prejudice as any ex-Old Firm player I have known. Would this feud raise its head again during a European Cup Final discussion?

Terry Butcher, another guest, had made it clear that he felt that the Scottish Premier League had done the dirty on Rangers with their complex league fixtures arrangements for the title run-in and had made it impossible for them to be fit and ready for a final such as this. Yet another one with an axe to grind. But the show had to go on, despite the feeling that disintegration was in the air. The last time I had experienced such a public masquerade of togetherness was when a teenage uncle of mine had a 'huvtae' or shotgun wedding in Shettleston and we all sat around, cramped into the 'single-end' room, trying to appear happily connubial, but underneath simmering with the hope that the family of the lady in question would all be had up for resetting.

Instead, all we had to deal with in Manchester on the evening of 14 May 2008 was a major anti-climax. The UEFA Cup Final was so bland, so predictable, so drab, that warring parties would have signed a peace treaty to avoid having to comment on it. Rangers had done remarkably well. But at that footballing altitude they lacked oxygen and surprisingly appeared to be a team that had come to accept their own failings. Unquestionably, outpacing their own mediocrity had been an inspiring achievement. But, now, they had been truly found out. Andy Walker and I jumped in a car straight after the game and headed back to Glasgow, listening on the radio all the way back about the disturbances in Manchester, none of which we had observed amongst the multitudes in the afternoon before kick-off. It overshadowed our own post-mortem. Not that there was much to discuss as things had gone smoothly during the programme, with Walker and Colquhoun sounding distinctly formal with each other, with fangs discreetly at a distance. We were both relieved that it was all over. By that, I mean our relationship with STV, as we had known it. Certainly, for me, there was no way back. The impoverished company was to turn to Setanta for their coverage of European football, and in a strange way I felt a sense of relief that the whole agonisingly inevitable rundown process of sport coverage within the weekly *Scotsport* tradition had reached closure.

Part of that relief came from the arduous last season. The programme of 2007/8 had incorporated the aggravatingly tiresome task of not just coping with both European and domestic football but also trying achieve a balance of reporting on the increasingly competitive and bitter fight for the league title, whist at the same time realising that the programme was doomed. Walter Smith lost the Scottish league title that night in Manchester as well, just as surely as *Scotsport* had now finally lost its bearings. After that last live game for us, you could see in Smith's eyes, as you talked to him, the realisation that events were getting beyond him. To his credit, his main asset was self-restraint.

Interviewing managers, in any case, was a form of bondage. It was a ritual, part of the business, without which most sports editors would feel the sky would fall in. It is not that it was always negative, and sometimes it was good fun, although not often enough. Sometimes you felt you would rather sit down cosily with an income tax self-assessment form. Hardly anybody would dare essay a startling revelation, especially in the last decade, surrounded by PR people as they were.

There were exceptions over the years. Stein, smouldering like a rumbling volcano could brilliantly use the chat with me to promote one of his causes. Jim McLean at Tannadice, mono-tone of voice but always provocative, would send you away thinking you had just heard a harbinger of the end of the world. Sir Alex Ferguson shouted abuse into the camera just after winning the Scottish Cup Final for Aberdeen in 1983, aston-ishingly against his own side's performance, which provoked a lifelong rift between himself and one of his players, Gordon Strachan, who refused to attend the after-match dinner because of that. Eddie Turnbull, manager of Hibernian, having the micro-phone pinned on his lapel after winning the Drybrough Cup Final against Celtic in 1972, simply tore it off and walked up the tunnel before the camera could turn, because I couldn't tell him how much he was to be paid for the interview. His impetuous decision did not deny civilisation shafts of enlight-enment. By and large, a thumbscrew, or electrodes attached to the genitals ought to have been part of the apparatus of the interview to get anything remarkable out of them. The fault lay in the system which assumed that these largely bland affairs were necessary to allow the public to know that the manager was still alive and kicking. And then along came Gordon Strachan.

Even in a standing position in front of camera, you felt not even a marksman with a telephoto lens would be able to pin him down. He bobbed from side to side, his heading wagging continuously away from the camera, like one of those little mechanical nodding dogs you used to see in the rear windows of cars. A lengthy interview with him, with the eye trying to focus on the movement in front of you, could induce symptoms rather similar to seasickness. The way I interpreted his body language is as follows: 'I don't really want to be doing this. I suspect neither do you. You are going to ask me questions which I am not really going to answer frankly, and indeed I'll try to foil you with a put-down. Indeed if you don't watch I may even try to make you look like a hick. So let's get this bloody thing over and done with as quickly as possible so I can get back to the things that really matter in a manager's life.' He didn't seem to mind that this was all public, and probably knew that even amongst his own support he was being perceived as simply an irascible character without any due diligence to the image of the club. Indeed, Willie Haughey, a prominent Glasgow businessman and former Celtic director who came to the SFA's rescue with sponsorship of the Scottish Cup, told me on the phone after a Celtic defeat at Ibrox, and after watching a Strachan interview, that the manager ought to be sacked. For his tactics going wrong? No. 'A Celtic manager shouldn't be chewing gum throughout a television interview,' I was told.

Does all of this matter to a man when his prime responsibility is putting a winning team on the park? That's the rub. When you are winning you could thumb your nose at your detractors, but when the going gets tough then there are people queuing to put the boot in. The most stable of all the interviews I had with him was at Celtic Park on a Saturday in April 2008, when a ten-man Motherwell side beat Celtic at Parkhead 1–0. From my commentary position, high above the pitch, I could plainly hear a chorus of dissent rising from the Jock Stein Stand end of the ground, in the form of a choral obscenity directed towards Strachan, which even for this page remains unrepeat-able, but which in essence was telling him to pack his bags and go. On my way down to interview him, I was accosted by a group of supporters, still standing in the lower enclosure, and assumed I was going to get an earful from them about their manager. In fact, these perfectly civilised people asked me to convey to the manager their apologies for the abuse he had just received from a sizeable element in the stands. In the space of a few minutes I had witnessed the sharp divide amongst his public, which, incredibly, must have perplexed Strachan, despite his apparent, gritty indifference to it all.

I certainly met a very chastened man that day. He admitted to me before the cameras started rolling that the league title was probably now beyond their grasp. During his actual inter-view he was not as pointed in his remarks, but was soberly negative. None of the head-bobbing side-to-side chirpiness to which we had become accustomed. Several weeks later he had won the title for the third successive season. That did not silence his detractors, who gave the impression that they were simply lying in wait to revolt. But that gave an insight into the image problem Strachan faced. Firstly, he had not emerged from the Celtic tradition, and the green blood in his veins was for his childhood favourites, Hibernian. There are those, of the mytho-logical persuasion, who, although largely inarticulate on the subject when you press them on the man's origins, do believe in having the right kind of DNA for that job. Both sides of the divide have them, although Rangers are predominantly associated with such fans. Perhaps that is the reason Celtic, quite needlessly in my view, cultivated the myth that Martin O'Neill was a regular supporter of the club from his childhood. Strachan clearly did not believe his reputation would be enhanced by appearing to be a dispenser of charm.

The week before he resigned from the club, on Monday 25 May 2009, I had to interview him at a Celtic dinner to announce their Player of the Year in the Hilton Hotel. It was a difficult evening for everyone associated with the club, since they had failed to beat Hibernian at Easter Road, and with Rangers two points in front, needing a victory at Tannadice against Dundee United to clinch the title for the first time in four years, the mood was subdued, with occasional outbursts of defiance from the supporters in the hotel, refusing to concede anything to their great rivals. These are occasions when your role is simply to give a manager the opportunity to say something nice about his players and the supporters. When he came on to the stage he didn't acknowledge me, and stared around as if I wasn't there. He simply evaded eye contact and made it clear in his curt, snapped replies to two innocuous, banal questions that I represented some source of contamination. He then walked off the stage to a decidedly lukewarm reception. I found it astonishing that he could put on a display like that, especially to someone who had known him for years and had enjoyed much of his company. I was angered by it and told a Celtic official at my table that I would never interview him again under any circumstances.

There had been an occasion when he had acted like that before with me but it was never seen in public. We were in the normal interviewing position in the dressing room at Celtic Park and he was on the verge of signing the German defender Andreas Hinkel. The cameras rolled and I asked him simply if the signing was imminent. He replied, as follows, 'I am surprised you, with all your experience, should ask me a question like that. You should have been professional enough to warn me in advance what you were going to ask.' Only royalty, as I have already written, try to get away with pre-programmed questions. The reply seemed so fatuous that somebody who edited the programme decided it did not show him in a good light, and it was never broadcast. So it was not good enough to say that it was simply red-top journalism that provoked and jaundiced him, although, to be sure, it could not have brightened his life.

Fundamentally, I think the 'wee man' syndrome operates within him. He virtually always has to look up, literally, at the figures around him, particularly in the world of football, and that might suggest it is nature that he is resentful of, and is up for the fight to show that he has, after all, stature. The need for respect becomes overpowering. And he knew he wasn't getting it from a significant element of the Celtic support who did not believe he 'belonged' at Celtic Park and was one of them. And when you watched him at ease in a London studio, perky and bright and responsive, you had to conclude that after his long spells in English football and returning to Scotland he felt the Scottish media, as a whole, were not fit for purpose. If ever a Scot looked like an exile in his own country, it was he. And then there was his other problem, Walter Smith.

To talk of Smith's personal qualities might seem like another assault on Strachan's personality. For Smith embodies the measured, self-controlled, cooler, more often than not, dignified soul, even amidst a buffeting by the 'slings and arrows of outrageous fortune'. I used to field telephone calls from the public asking why the media treated Smith apparently with kid gloves, even when he looked to have made howling mistakes in tactics and suffered humiliating defeats, like losing to Kaunus and being knocked out of European football in 2008. Simple. He knew what he was doing with the media. Can you call common sense manipulative? If so, he was manipulative. His low-key, carefully considered reactions took the sting out of any potential attack on him. Even the Celtic-inclined members of the media would rather approach Smith than Strachan to make some point. Of course, it could be put down to a fawning acquiescence by some. Smith's longevity in the game, unquestionably, generated some of that. And when he did have to rebuke somebody, it was prefaced by a long silence, staring at the questioner as if Smith had been asked what colour of underpants he was wearing at the time; then he would reply with a tone and words, well short of ridicule, but whose very blandness was almost murderously effective. In losing in Manchester, in the UEFA Cup Final; in being knocked out of Europe before the season had begun, just some weeks after; in losing the League Cup Final to Celtic in 2009; but in winning the Scottish league title and three cups since rejoining the club, you could barely tell the difference between the failed manager and the successful one. That was the difference between the pair. It is not that one was a better person than the other. It was that one was clearly more level-headed and more aware of the importance of image.

That last season of *Scotsport* heightened my appreciation of their two clubs and my indebtedness to them for helping mould me as a commentator. With no disrespect to others, nothing else influenced me in Scottish football as much as their encounters. The awareness of the political sensibilities of both clubs, which no commentator in the south had to cope with, sharpened my focus on steering the hopelessly uncharted path of neutrality, with wildly varying results. It was the only game in which you had to admit to yourself that you were ending up mentally preparing a case for the defence. At one stage of broadcasting life I was accused of wearing a badge on a suit lapel which looked like the Red Hand of Ulster, or alternatively, as others put it, the Sacred Heart. It was in fact a Fiorentina badge, presented to me when Celtic played that club in the quarter-final of the European Cup in March 1970. The Old Firm sharpened my instinct for survival, and how to tough out accusations of bias one way or the other.

I had survived longer than I had believed I would. After all, in the week of my very first sports broadcast, in 1962, a short radio piece about a Hamilton Accies game, Khrushchev and Kennedy were contemplating the game to end all games, over Cuba. Anything and everything seemed like a bonus after that. Sitting watching football throughout that time placed me in a kind of time-warp, because as society has evolved dramatically in that period, this sport remains resolutely rooted to some ill-defined ethic which seems to command it to resist the changes adopted by others. As we watch cricket played in what look like pyjamas, under floodlights; see the product of tiny cameras installed in cricket-bails; rugby matches held up, in suspense, as we await judgements from the second referee at a monitor in the stand; Andy Murray appealing to Hawkeye on a tennis court – football holds modern technology askance. There is some consolation to be found in this. The lack of change is testament to the game's continuing popularity. Intrusive, investigative cameras, after all, would perhaps dilute controversy, the very substance which stokes our passions, and without which the game would be like returning to the days of silent cinema. I was privileged to observe and feel that passion, which at times was like being caught up in a rip-tide. Some affected me more than others. Which were they? Which the best? Which the MOTHER OF ALL GAMES?

When Danny Boyle received his Oscar in 2009 for Best Director for the film *Slumdog Millionaire*, I could not help recalling how I had met him in strange circumstances, as he was in the throes of making the film which helped shoot him to stardom. I was in Paris at the time, when his producer called me at my hotel to ask if I would come to London to put a voice to a sequence in a film he was making. They would pay the expenses and a fee. Fine. That's just what you want to hear when the French are driving you up the wall. I took myself off and ended up in a studio in Soho, where Danny sat me down and explained in his perky, irresistible manner that he wanted me to hit top C in a commentary for the film, even though I had already done it in 1978 in a stadium in Argentina. I was curious. He explained that he had made a film set in Edinburgh, from a book by a man called Irvine Welsh. I had never heard of either the author or the book, which was called *Trainspotting*. I did assume though, that since they had gone to the trouble of making it into a film, it was not about nerds taking notes on Waverley Station platform. He then talked about the theme, which was about the drug and, let us say, libertine culture in Edinburgh, where once I had been Rector of the University and had come across nothing more alarming than attending a rugby club dinner where students formed a human pyramid on top of a table, and one bared an arse. That, I had naively assumed, was Edinburgh at its grossest. It wasn't, of course, as my conversation with Danny revealed.

He told me that my assistance would be greatly valued, as I suppose all directors do when they want something from you. I was to re-do one sequence of my commentary on Holland against Scotland in Mendoza in 1978. I found that puzzling, since they already had the soundtrack from the original. But no, he wanted 'more pizzazz, more oomph' in the sound as he put it. So there I was in the darkness of a commentating booth, in the middle of London, trying to sound as if the Andes mountain range, which had loomed above the stadium in Mendoza, was reverberating with the echoes of an ecstatic, soaring Scottish voice, describing Archie Gemmill's famous goal in Scotland's completely surprising 3–2 victory over the eventual finalists

Holland. Except, Danny didn't like the first take, or the second take, or the third take. Pernickety bugger, I thought. But now, after years of obsession with the silver screen, here I was experiencing the painstaking reality of the other side of major film-making.

I cannot recall how long it took, but it was some while before I left the studios, blinking into the sunlight of the London streets. I had no idea how it had gone, except that Danny gave me a thumbs up and a broad smile before I left. It wasn't until over a year later that I saw that film in one of the grandest of cinemas on the Champs Elyseés in Paris. My background commentary to the pictures from the game in Mendoza added piquancy to a bedroom scene in which Ewan McGregor is mounted by his girlfriend, and in keeping with the excitement in my voice, his obvious delight in reaching orgasm is articulated in his words, 'I've never felt like that since Archie Gemmill scored against Holland in 1978!'

That goal, and that game, have now been immortalised by a piece of film shown around the world and this suggests, to some people, that it must have been the MOTHER OF ALL GAMES, for me and for many a Scot. Let us just say, it was a contender for the title. You wouldn't get that belief from a Celtic supporter who had Lisbon in 1967 to savour, or from Rangers people who witnessed Barcelona in 1972, or from the hordes of the north who went with Aberdeen to Gothenburg in 1983. Having commentated on all three obviously makes them major career landmarks. And when I am asked for the most memorable of all in commentating, they keep cropping up in contention with Mendoza. Lisbon in 1967 offered a transformation of European football, burnished indelibly by the Portuguese sun. Barcelona in 1972 was a mix of dark drama and livid excitement that affected the gut. Gothenburg in 1983 demonstrated to the continent that a new dimension to Scottish football existed beyond the Glasgow boundary line, at a time when Fergie seemed, then, like a mate.

Then there was the whole range of Old Firm games, every single one of which took me back to my roots and the blatant sectarian excitements which enveloped the fixtures. There was the 1980 Scottish Cup Final between them, which ended in a wholesale pitch invasion. The game itself was a doleful effort at a final, largely devoid of skill, but after the final whistle it was, from a commentating point of view, superb. What more could a commentator wish for after ninety minutes of mediocrity than a riot on the field? As the hordes invaded, the bottles flew, the white police horses rode in, and disgust was being expressed all around, I was actually relishing the spectacle as it lent me the opportunity to launch into a mode that is largely absent from football commentating: moral indignation and a critique of sectarianism. I wasn't supposed to be enjoying it, but I was. Some of my words were mentioned in editorial columns on the following Monday morning, and there I had been, that Saturday morning, wakening up to what I thought would be another run-of-the-mill final. So that one keeps edging into the memory as well. As does the moment at the end of Celtic's game with Vojvodina in the European Cup in 1967, when sitting above the old Celtic 'Jungle' you could sense the frustration of the masses underneath you, until that eruption of sound, in the last seconds, as McNeill's head wrote history.

But outside the Old Firm, certain games still cling to the mind. There I was, in the early days, in 1965, when you had to peek round the infamous pillars of the enclosure at Tynecastle to do the commentary, to observe Willie Waddell, as Kilmarnock manager, rush out of the dug-out wearing his Harold Wilson-like Gannex coat, to hug his captain Frank Beattie after his side had just beaten Hearts 2–0 to win the league title for the first time ever. Then there was the game at Easter Road, in 1980, after which Sir Alex ran, like Forrest Gump, towards his supporters, or Arthur's Seat, because it didn't look like he wanted to stop, after he had heard Aberdeen had just won the league title as Celtic had drawn against St Mirren that same afternoon.

In the final days of *Scotsport*, one face stood out to illustrate a memorable game in the city of the Renaissance – Nacho Novo, running towards the camera, just after scoring the penalty in the shoot-out against Fiorentina which took Rangers to the UEFA Cup Final in Manchester.

Then there was Cardiff on 10 September 1985, the night Jock Stein died. It comes back repeatedly. I recall that Wales–Scotland game, in association with the sight of men and women in tartan, slumped around the streets of that city, in the middle of the night, distraught and bewildered, after hearing the shocking news. There were others which bubble up to the surface from time to time; many of them. But in the hierarchy of memory which exists, one remains to be identified, at the top.

It was at Wembley. 4 June 1977. Sunny Wembley. Wembley as we used to know it. Barely an Englishman in sight. It was the best of times. It was the worst of times. The Scottish supporters had made central London a zone where anarchy seemed to reign. The night before the game a group of them, spying myself and my English producer approaching our favourite Italian restaurant in one of the seamier streets in Soho, where strip-clubs abounded, surrounded us, and with a chant of 'Ey-ay-addio' suggested that I was seeking more than Penne Amatriciana in that street. The following day, on the pitch, the two goals by Gordon McQueen and Kenny Dalglish, and the one from the penalty-spot by England's Mick Channon, sparked off a pitch invasion which ended with supporters ripping up bits of the Wembley pitch and sitting on top of a crossbar until it snapped. You could laugh. You could cry. You could even wish you could leave the commentary position and join them cavorting in victory, to get away from the rather prudish English BBC colleagues immersed in indignation at what they were seeing. It mattered because I felt, then and there, that this fixture would never be the same again. It wasn't.

There were three Wembleys after that in the Home Championship series but they were more sober, regulated affairs and they let more Englishmen into the ground as well. That day when I exulted in the victory, fended off the over-stern English criticism of my exuberant countrymen, kept a level head as I described the capitulation of the crossbar, linked the horticultural activities on the sacred pitch to the harmless digging in the National Stadium in Lisbon in 1967, and enjoyed conceding the fact that the English players took defeat rather well since they were of the minority nationality in that stadium, I was on a high, and guessed at the same time that this would herald the end of a tradition.

In over four decades of commentating, that was THE MOTHER OF ALL GAMES for me. It linked me to the childhood days of standing around the Wembley-bound bus in Shettleston Road, wishing well to the supporters in their neat tartan tammies, off to usurp our oppressors, as we saw it. We would wave them off as if to the trenches, filling our guts with the air-bubble of anxiety for all the days leading up to kick-off and learning, eventually, how to live with the emotions of suicidal depression when the result was the wrong one, or, very occasionally, the delirium of success. The unique test of it all, that day of the broken crossbar at Wembley, had also been like being challenged to teeter along that high dyke in childhood, and when reaching the end of it, looking down contentedly at the faces who had dared to call me 'Feartie!'